Family Counseling in the Schools

Effective Strategies and Interventions for Counselors, Psychologists and Therapists

J. Scott Hinkle, Ph.D., NCC, CCMHC
University of North Carolina
Greensboro, North Carolina

Michael E. Wells, Ph.D., NCC
Surry Community College
Dobson, North Carolina

ERIC/CASS Publications
School of Education
University of North Carolina at Greensboro
Greensboro, NC 27412
1-800-414-9769

ISBN 1-56109-064-6

This publication was funded by the U.S. Department of
Education, Office of Educational Research and Improvement,
Contract No. RR93002004. Opinions expressed in this
publication do not necessarily reflect the positions of the
U.S. Department of Education, OERI, or ERIC/CASS.

This publication was funded by the U.S. Department of
Education, Office of Educational Research and Improvement.
Contract No. RR93002004. Opinions expressed in this
publication do not neessarily reflect the positions of the
U.S. Department of Education, OERI, or ERIC/CASS.

Introduction

At a time when school reform is focusing attention on what are and are not essential school programs and services, it is highly appropriate to have a publication which explores in depth the role of family counseling in schools and offers a broad array of viable strategies and interventions which can be employed in the school setting. A massive body of research and experience has put into bold relief the crucial role that the family plays in the overall development of students including achievement in school basics. Clearly families play an extremely crucial role in how students view school, their motivation towards and in school, how they respond to and interact with other students, how well they achieve and, ultimately, how long they stay in school and respond to other educational opportunities. For all of its importance, it is surprising that assistance to families, particularly as family systems, has typically been thought of as a service which is provided outside the school by agencies in the community. Never mind that such service is not only difficult to obtain but, divorced from the school setting, may lose much of the potential it has to enhance student school performance and enrich family life. Moreover, there has long been an accepted dogma that school helping specialists could and should not provide family counseling on a regular basis.

There is today a large body of literature on family counseling butvery little of it focuses on strategies and interventions which can be used by counselors, psychologists and therapists whose major work setting is in school. This volume by Hinkle and Wells fills a long neglected void to provide those who work within the school a clear strategy for making family counseling a major priority. Admirably, they have not stopped at identifying the need but have gone on to provide specific assistance in what interventions to use, what techniques are well suited to the school setting, and how a helping specialist or teacher can prepare themselves for this new role.

To those who would say that doing family counseling in the schools is just another field that the school should leave to

Family Counseling in the Schools:

"outside agencies", the authors of this volume offer eloquent testimony that, by focusing on the family, school personnel rather than diluting the focus on student learning, enhance it by assisting students and parents to function together in ways that are both more harmonious and supportive of improved student school performance.

It is easy to predict that this unique volume will usher in an awareness of the new role that school helping specialists can perform and lead to school student services programs providing family counseling in fact and not just in name. I strongly recommend this volume to all persons who are interested in the family and what can be done to make families contribute to student development and greater student achievement in and out of school.

Garry R. Walz
Director and Editor-in-Chief
Eric Clearinghouse on Counseling and Student Services

About the Author

J. Scott Hinkle received his Ph.D. in Counseling Psychology from Florida State University. He is an Associate Professor at the University of North Carolina at Greensboro where he teaches family counseling, mental health counseling, and clinical assessment.

Dr. Hinkle maintains an independent practice in marriage and family counseling and consults with and provides training for several agencies concerning systems interventions. He has served on the American Counseling Association Governing Council and has held national board appointments in mental health and family counseling.

Dr. Hinkle is married to Shari Funkhouser-Hinkle and they have one son, Jordan Scott. His family enjoys the out-of-doors where they can be found camping, backpacking, kayaking, rock climbing, motorcycling, gardening and playing in the sandbox.

About the Author

Michael E. Wells received his Ph.D. in Counseling and Development from the University of North Carolina at Greensboro. He has worked at state residential facilities for developmentally disabled adults and psychiatric patients, at a local mental health clinic, and a maximum security juvenile detention facility. In eleven years of private practice he has consulted with school systems and private and public agencies as well as providing counseling to children, adolescents and their families.

He has always been involved in community interests, having served on the NC Psychology Licensing Board and local mental health boards. Dr. Wells is now serving his second term as chair of a board established to build and operate a shelter for abused and dependent children.

As a single parent, Dr. Wells adopted four teenaged young men over the course of a decade; Joe, who is currently 31 years old, John, 28, Donny, 27, and Bart, 23. He is currently married to Dianne and has added daughters-in-law Patricia and Peggy and grand children Corey, 5, Travis, 3 and Megan, 2, to his family. He lives with his wife and a black lab, Maggie, in a log house in the historic village of Rockford in Surry County, North Carolina.

Acknowledgements

The authors would like to acknowledge the following persons: Kathy Glenn, Deanne Hyers, Pam Sides, and Eric Shinault for assistance in researching materials for portions of the book; Thomas A. Burgess, Holly Cravens, Susan S. Crawford, Michael Kahn, Helen Hoggatt Price, and Kenneth Simington for case contributions; and Brooke Paulson and Susan Wilmoth for helpful editorial comments.

This book is dedicated to Jordan, Shari, Joe, John, Peggy, Megan, Donny, Patricia, Corey, Travis, Bart, and Dianne— our families.

Preface

A recent analysis by the National Board of Certified Counselors (1993) revealed four fundamental work behaviors performed by counselors. These behaviors included fundamental counseling practice, career development, group counseling, and counseling families. Extrapolating from this report, this book espouses the utilization of "counseling families" in the schools - not by clinicians from outside the confines of the school, but by school counselors. Kaslow (1991) has indicated that the school—second only to the family—is the largest system to affect the lives of children. She has stated that "schools are the only major social institutions that come in contact with all children" and that "school personnel are on the front line to see children who are abused, neglected, or ill, or who are the casualties of divorce" (p. 624). Profound changes have occurred in schools over the past 30 years, however, conventional counselor-based programs serve too many students and employ too few counselors to be truly effective (Arnold, 1991). Arnold's emphasis on the "revolution" in school organization is timely, but a greater focus is needed in school guidance and counseling. Moreover, Ford (1986) has indicated that there is an ever increasing need for parent and family involvement in the education of children. Ford's perspective reflects the fact that family counseling is the necessary next step in the professional development of teachers, administrators, and school counselors. Shore and Vieland (1989) found that 75 percent of the children participating in family counseling improved their behavior according to teachers and parents.

Similarly, the American Counseling Association's (ACA, 1993) report, *The Crisis in School Counseling,* indicated that school counselors need to understand family systems and the impact such systems wield on children's education. This ACA report also stipulated that school counselors are not recognized as providers connected to the mental health and academic performance of the child. At a time when school counseling programs are receiving less attention, or being abandoned altogether, it is important to acknowledge the role of the school counselor and the potential influence the counselor has on a child's, school's, and family's functioning.

Although Braden and Sherrard (1987) have focused on referrals to agencies outside the school, their list of reasons for referral for family counseling is no less meaningful. These reasons include abrupt fluctuations in the child's behavior, simultaneous behavioral and family changes, the family's support of misbehavior, and denial of the child's problems by the family. Essentially, there is a relationship between a family's behavioral patterns and a child's school performance (Friedman, 1973).

School counselors can help families make changes, including establishing behavioral norms, setting family goals, assisting with understanding family roles, and developing family conflict resolutionstrategies. The school counselor can also assist families facing divorce or special clinical problems (e.g., substance abuse). Multiple family counseling techniques, including strategic, structural, multigenerational, and behavioral approaches, are all within the repertoire of the school counselor (Carlson, 1987; Hinkle, 1994).

Family counseling has been utilized in various modalities for over four decades. The seminal work of Gregory Bateson, *Steps to an Ecology of Mind* (1972), Murray Bowen, *Family Therapy in Clinical Practice* (1978), Paul Watzlawick, John Weakland, and Richard Fisch, *Change: Principles of Problem Behavior* (1974), Salvadore Minuchin *Families and Family Therapy* (1974), Jay Haley *Problem Solving Therapy* (1976), and Cloé Madanes *Strategic Family Therapy* (1981), paved the way for family counseling. Following these influential works, insightful visionaries applied family counseling to school issues. Walsh & Giblin, *Family Counseling in School Settings* (1988), Amatea, *Brief Strategic Intervention for School Behavior Problems* (1989), and Fine and Carlson, *The Handbook of Family-School Intervention*

(1992), incorporated family counseling and mental health into the school environment. Although they opened schooldoors to family counseling, these books focused on "outsiders" providing family interventions for school children within, as well as outside, of the school. Fish and Jain (1992) have reported that much of the literature on family-school interventions has emphasized the consultant as external to the school. This viewpoint is exemplified by Fines' (1992) contribution to the literature regarding systems theory and school problems. Although significant, Fine does not focus on school counselors who provide family counseling services. In contrast, family counseling has been considered necessary for interventions with children in the schools (Palmo, Lowry, Weldon, & Scioscia, 1984) and it is time more school counselors were providing this much needed service.

As we approach the millennium, the complexities of life are making it necessary for schools not only to focus on education, but also on school-based counseling services, including family counseling. Difficulties with such assistance include coping with child rearing, relationships in the family, home management, and even neighborhood living (Blatt & Starr, 1988). Therefore, it is imperative that family and school come together in an interchangeable systemic ecology because of their mutual interest in the education of the child (Merrill, Clark, Varvil, Van Sickle, & McCall, 1992).

Aliotti (1992) has reflected that students not coping successfully within the school system will also find it difficult to cope within their family system. Children become relationship-oriented rather than task-oriented when over involved with parental anxieties (Beal & Chertkov, 1992). For example, parent-child conflict, school performance, and oppositional behavior were the three presenting problems of largest magnitude in the Topeka Public Schools program (Merrill et al., 1992).

There exists a controversy about the degree school professionals should be involved in family counseling. Yet, even with limited resources, family counseling is beginning to take place within schools and school systems. Gerler (1993) has suggested that school counselors will need to develop innovative approaches to assist children, parents, and families. He has stated that "Counselors must assume a more proactive stance by collaborating with parents, teachers, and school administrators to develop and implement family programs aimed at preventing some of the difficulties experienced in today's families" (Gerler, p. 243). Such a transition within the school setting appears to create a nice adaptation (Fine, 1992; Fine & Holt, 1983; Hinkle, 1993; Peeks, 1993a, 1993b; Plas, 1986).

This book is about turning a good idea into reality. When family counseling is based at the school, parents will show up. Likewise, the inclusion of teachers in the counseling process will enhance both the lives of school children and their school performance, as well as increase the effectiveness of teachers in the classroom. It is argued here that the reformation in counseling and the revolution in public education befocused on parents, students, and school professionals, especially school counselors. Students will be best helped by parents and schools working cooperatively as a problem-solving team. Furthermore, children learn at their maximum level when they are free of problems, which, in turn, improves the level of achievement in the school.

While referrals and collaboration outside the confines of the school are often necessary, the literature offers school counselors no guidance in the provision of family counseling services. This book emphasizes school counselors, themselves, working with families in the schools. Although this has not been the traditional course of counseling in schools, society's rapid changes, and the revolution within education, demand that school counselors enter this new and exciting territory.

Table of Contents

Chapter One

A Systems Perspective in the Schools

Recent extensions of systems theory and family counseling into school interventions have indicated "a greater awareness of the 'power' of the family in creating or maintaining school-related problems of children and a greater appreciation of the interfacing of the family and school system in treatment" (Fine & Carlson, 1992, p. xi). Problem behaviors within the school are thus not considered to have a foundation in the individual child, but, instead, exist contextually in the relationships the child sustains. Indeed, Becvar and Becvar (1982) insist that "the systems perspective is a universal view. It does not interpret events in isolation from other events" (p. 3).

Bloch (1976) has stated,

Children are the same as everybody else, only more so. Their involvement in family consultations may be as primary patients; or their involvement may be secondary to disorders elsewhere in the family system. Whatever the apparent reason for therapeutic involvement, there is always significant expression at the family level. One may pick up the ball of twine at any point and follow the thread back to the same configuration. Child therapists (have) observed that changes in the psychosocial functioning could not be achieved or maintained unless associated changes were achieved in the family system (p. 168).

Due to the continuous changes in the educational system and the expanded role of counseling services, education and counseling need to come closer together within the context of the school (Peeks, 1993). Moreover, Cetron (1985) has

Family Counseling in the Schools:

predicted that schools of the future will become family centers. The establishment of family-centered programs will "necessitate family involvement in the context of the school by school counselors who understand the powerful systemic connection between the student and the family" (Peeks, 1993, p. 249).

School counselors are ideally situated to assume the leadership in promoting such a restructuring process in our public schools (Hinkle, 1993; Peeks, 1993). School counselors can assist families with a host of problems. For example, as the divorce rate continues at about 50 percent, school counselors can be instrumental in establishing innovative family programs within the schools for those facing divorce transitions (Peeks).

Additionally, it is the school counselor who must decide what to do with a referred case. The person that makes the referral initially defines the problem, however, there may be many competing hypotheses to explain the problem and what needs to be done about it. Amatea (1989) has indicated that when selecting a hypothesis, "the practitioner must consider how much the terms implied in such a perspective limit her (or his) ability to resolve the problem effectively and make (their) own decision concerning whom to work with" (p. 58). One of the important aspects of deciding with whom to work, is to consider who has the most *power*, who is in the most *distress*, and who is to gain from *positive change*.

Parent teacher conferences are fertile ground for new information regarding the student and can help change the system in which the child exists (Fine, 1992). Educational decisions based solely on psychoeducational information, without consideration of family circumstances, may in fact be harmful to the student (Power & Bartholomew, 1987). Although there appears to be much interest in family counseling in the schools, many school personnel stubbornly continue to conceptualize children's problems as idiosyncratic (Fish & Jain, 1992).

Nicoll's (1992) review has revealed significant correlations between academic achievement and parent-child relationships. Good and Brophy (1986) and others have indicated that a variety of *family-related factors* affect school achievement more than school-related factors. Although a substantial amount of empirical data has documented the crucial relationship between family functioning and school academic and behavioral success, Nicoll has stated that "schools typically pay insufficient attention to this area when assessing and intervening in cases of student adjustment difficulties" (p. 352). Nicoll elaborates that, by and large, the learning disability model dominates public education's approaches to assisting children with learning problems while family models are mostly ignored. For example, power struggles between adolescents, parents, and the school are often intensified when parent conferences result in the school demanding more coercive approaches be implemented in order to compel the family to comply with school performance demands. In another example, Nicoll reflected that "a child's self-doubts regarding his or her ability may be a reflection of family dynamic factors such as overprotectiveness, discouragingly high expectations, or constant self-comparisons by the child to a more successful sibling" (p. 352).

It is likely that today's schools will play a larger role in health care as a result of political and economic realities. Already in place are programs on sex education, drug abuse prevention, and AIDS education. However, some schools continue to resist including parents in mental health programs. In fact, Woody and Woody (1994) have indicated that some school systems work fervently to minimize parental access and involvement in the schools. In contrast, children will receive more mental health services if they are delivered in the schools because the school system is often perceived more favorably than mental health clinics and hospitals. This essentially means that monies would be more readily and efficiently spent if the schools were the recipients. As all mental health disciplines are re-examining their roles, children's mental health services should focus on the school and family and utilize school resources to this end.

Correspondingly, Woody and Woody (1994) have asserted that family systems counseling is the treatment of choice for many problems and "virtually every school counseling program can reasonably be expected to adhere to the tenets of family/social systems interventions" (p. 20). They refer to this as the "fourth revolution" in mental health, which is identified as the use of family/social systems in school-based services.

Woody and Woody (1994) have reported that Public Law 99-

3

Family Counseling in the Schools:

457, the Education of the Handicapped Act Amendments of 1986, has mandated family and community involvement in school programs. Infants and toddlers with handicaps are to receive family counseling, training, and home visits. In order to accomplish this, the law decrees that the involvement of parents is necessary for individual educational planning and that there must be an Individualized Family Service Plan (IFSP) developed by a multidisciplinary team. Whereas Individual Education Plans (IEPs) (School & Cooper, 1981), encourage individualized approaches tailored for the student to promote achievement and personal independence, the IFSP will improve the services to children in the schools by including their parents in educational planning. It is hoped that this process will improve difficult family circumstances.

The two most influential and powerful entities in a child's life are the family and the school. It would be incredible for a school system of today not to be organized, as well as administered, with meaningful family involvement in educational programming and decision making. Schools should be responsible both for the child's academic learning and for the child's universal welfare (Woody & Woody, 1994). An *ecostructural* approach to school problems, described by Aponte in 1976, recommended meetings which included the student, the family, and school personnel.

A child's school behavior problems are part of a larger system that interfaces between home and school (Power & Bartholomew, 1987). However, almost half of all adults have had some contact with mental health services and these adults tend to feel highly ambivalent about such contacts (Blatt & Starr, 1988). Since parents who are agitated with the school may actually be frustrated with their children (Blatt & Starr) it is important to include parents in school meetings. These authors have asserted that working without the family can encourage dysfunctional family patterns.

Palmo et al. (1984) have indicated that current problems (e.g., geographic mobility, discipline, and school absenteeism) have an impact on the family as well as the school. As a result, today's challenges also influence the services provided by school counselors. Difficulties presented by a child in school may not be just the child's problem; it may be the manner in which the parents are dealing with the child, stresses on the family, marriage problems of the parents, or pathology in one of the parents. In any of these cases, working solely with the child will be much like "spitting in the wind" (p. 274).

Rather than work exclusively with the surface symptoms presented by the child in the classroom, Palmo et al. (1984) have suggested that the school counselor should explore family dynamics. Symptoms may be serving the purpose of maintaining equilibrium in the family (Stark & Brookman, 1992). For example, refusal to attend school usually elicits the involvement of other subsystems in the child's community (Aliotti, 1992). Awareness of the symptom's purpose, therefore, results in school counselors becoming more efficient in their delivery of services. Furthermore, family counseling services can be provided in the school without having to utilize mandated referrals to outside agencies. With the time constraints put on the school counselor, it seems that effective and economical counseling approaches, such as family counseling, need to be developed and implemented within the school counseling clinical program. Such an approach also eliminates the potentially burdensome cost of private or agency counseling for the family (Nicoll, 1984a, 1984b).

Nicoll (1984a) has reflected that a student's behavioral and learning challenges must be understood and dealt with within the framework of the family. He has recommended that school counselors combine their existing skills and knowledge of the field of education with the skills of family counseling.

Only about 30 percent of families referred for family counseling make any contact with an outside agency and only 8 percent continue after 2 sessions (Conti, 1971). Nicoll has indicated that parents will be more likely to follow through with family counseling recommendations when the counseling takes place at school. This approach will be less threatening to the family and it decreases the chances that the parents will infer pathology for their family.

Family Counseling: A Paradigm Shift

The mental health profession's paradigm shift to a systems perspective currently has a major impact on the way counselors work with their clients (Capra, 1982; Fine, 1992; Hinkle, 1993; Peeks, 1993a, 1993b). Exclusively analytical thought processes

5

Family Counseling in the Schools:

have proven to be inadequate for understanding family dynamics. Plas (1992) affirms "the mechanistic perspective dominated the world view of European and American lay persons and scientists from the seventeenth century until just yesterday" (p. 46).

A systems-ecological approach recognizes that families and other subsystems continually seek stability and may resist change in order to maintain a homeostatic balance (Fine, 1992).

Family problems result in significant emotional distress for children which in turn is reflected in school performance (Carlson, 1992). From a systemic perspective, providing counseling for a child's problematic behavior is pointless unless the context of the problem is considered (Carlson; Haley, 1987). Systemic interventions determine which system or subsystem is maintaining the problem (Carlson; Haley). In contrast to behavior modification approaches to change, Fine has indicated that there are no hard and fast rules or "standard operating procedures" for a systems perspective (p. 9). Systemic hypotheses about family functioning should always consider the family's *hierarchy, boundaries, alliances and coalitions,* ability to make *adaptive changes,* and the *meaning of the symptom* (Carlson, 1992; Haley, 1987; Minuchin, 1974).

When taking a solution-focused perspective, systemic counselors identify and understand the problem well before they intervene. They focus on what can be changed and believe that rapid change is possible (O'Hanlon & Weiner-Davis, 1989). Systemic counselors also trust that focusing on relationships is more useful than studying related objects. Psychological and emotional problems are conceptualized as relationship problems (Haley, 1970). Individual behavior is not meaningful unless it is connected to the context in which it exists. Reasoning through analogy, therefore, is more beneficial than inductive and deductive reasoning.

Conclusion

The school child should be perceived as part of a large ecological system in which all aspects of the child's life are interrelated (Hobbs, 1966). This means that when school problems are being addressed, the child's family relationships cannot be ignored. Implementing family counseling in the schools is not simple, but it is attainable and necessary (Palmo et al., 1984). Palmo et al. have indicated that family counseling in the school, performed by school counselors, will necessitate professional growth; and school counseling, as a profession, can only grow "when each individual counselor attempts to grow professionally" (p. 278).

Lack of family counseling training among school counselors in graduate school is partially responsible for the lack of systemic activities in the schools. However, this is beginning to change. For example, the University of Florida has recently provided a family counseling course option for school counselors interested in working with families. In contrast to some writers in this area (e.g., Beal & Chertkov, 1992), we feel that direct involvement with the family-school system by school counselors is needed to deal with school problems effectively and is long overdue. The school and the counselor must accommodate the child and the family (Blatt & Starr, 1988).

There are times when the school counselor can find him or herself in the middle of intense difficulties between the child, family, and school personnel. However, a durable and meaningful change for the student means a complementary change for the family and school system. Family counseling interventions are appropriate for school counselors if counselors have acceptable training. School counselors can offer family counseling services in much the same way as school nurses and rehabilitation counselors (Wilcoxin & Comas, 1987). Wilcoxin and Comas have stated, "School counselors should increase their understanding of the principles of family systems theory and family counseling intervention strategies, because students in schools are influenced significantly by their family units" (p. 223). Furthermore, they indicate that, "School counselors becoming involved in these exciting and innovative developments may greatly enhance their effectiveness in professional services in their school settings" (p. 224).

Nearly 25 percent of America's children are on an educational path leading nowhere (Gandara, 1989). The school a child attends makes less difference in academic achievement than the family from which the child comes (Gandara). If students are not doing well within their family they cannot be expected to master school. Teachers can identify high-risk students through family circumstances. However, a dividing line continues to exist between school and family. Gandara believes "if schools are to meet the real needs of children, they must meet the needs of the whole child" (p. 42).

Ten years ago, Nicoll's (1984a, 1984b) reviews revealed that the interrelationship between academic and behavioral school problems and family relationships was becoming increasingly evident. Our book attempts to expand upon the sparse literature regarding family counseling in the schools. Unfortunately, the application of systems theory to school interventions does not have a history of investigation, either in quantity or quality. Therefore, what is presented in this book is largely the result of clinical and supervisor experience rather than the result of empirical research.

Chapter Two

Systems Theory and School Counseling

Family counseling is one of the rapidly growing specialties within the field of counseling (Cowger, Hinkle, DeRidder, & Erk, 1991; Hinkle, 1993). This growth has been related to a change of focus from individual psychology to a *social context* (Fritjof, 1984). Moreover, family dynamics have been identified by research studies as important factors in the behavioral, as well as academic adjustment, of school children. School performance also has been shown to be affected *more* by family variables than school variables (Blechman, Taylor, & Schrader, 1981; Hinkle, 1993). For example, Worden (1981) has reported that the mother is usually the family system's representative and handles school-related issues. However, if the student's problem has come to the attention of the school counselor, it is a good idea to include the father. His participation can be revealing and he may assist the counselor with a treatment plan. If the father comes in willingly and participates in the family counseling, this may suggest the system's willingness for open communication and problem-solving. On the contrary, Worden has indicated that if the father does not come to school, it may indicate that he is operating separately from the family system. However, this may not necessarily be the case. From a systemic perspective, the mother may have her own agenda for the father not to participate in family counseling (e.g., avoiding a couples conflict) and she may therefore keep the counselor in the dark regarding family functioning (Worden).

As alluded to in Chapter 1, family counseling as a therapeutic modality departs radically from individual counseling models. Generally, education professionals have seldom had the impetus, or luxury, of working with parents in a family systems context. Specifically, school counselors have typically not been

Family Counseling in the Schools:

exposed to this approach to handling school-related problems.

School counselors are becoming more aware of family and systemic interventions as validated both by the 1984 special issue of *Elementary School Guidance and Counseling* (Rotter), and by this journal's recent special edition (Peeks, 1993a) concerning family counseling in the schools. Counselors in the public schools are beginning to educate parents, as well as teachers and principals, about the family's relationship to the child's school successes and school failures.

Systems Theory: An Overview

Family counseling is essentially based on systems theory (Bertalanffy, 1968). This theory characterizes the human condition in an interrelated manner within a social context. The problems of children and their families are thought of as relationship problems (Haley, 1970). Behavior is not meaningful unless it is connected to the context in which it exists (Stark & Brookman, 1992). A family systems philosophy suggests that family characteristics, interactions, communication, functions, and life cycle are important to positive change (Turnbull & Turnbull, 1990; Wells & Hinkle, 1990). Nicoll (1992) has indicated that one systems theory principle, *circular causality,* maintains that problems are not the result of a linear, cause-and-effect process brought about by some primary factor. Rather, problematic behavior results from mistaken or dysfunctional interaction patterns that develop between people in a mutually reinforcing manner and, thereby, serve to maintain the problem rather than change it (p. 355).

An analysis of the social context in which a school problem exists is imperative. The school counselor considers information regarding the student, the school (including all personnel such as teachers, principles, etc.), the family, and the larger social system. Thus, the solution to a school problem may exist in any one or all of these entities (Amatea, 1989). Although some family practitioners utilize a one-person focus, an individual's difficulty always includes a social context. For example, if a female student were to indicate that her problem with shyness is that she simply is not attractive, it may seem, on the surface, that idiosyncratic self-esteem counseling would be the treatment of choice. However, upon further exploration it may be found that the student's parents have repeatedly indicated that she is not "as pretty as her older sister." In this case, an individual focus may help by providing attention to the student, but her parents may indirectly sabotage any real individual progress.

Amatea has reported that people maintain problem behavior for two reasons. "First, they may not realize that what they are doing is actually contributing to keeping the problem going. Second, even when they are aware of this, they often feel that it is still the only right way they can respond" (p. 28).

Problems that school children encounter may be maintained by *triangulated* relationships. In such relationships, two people experiencing stress in their interactions will engage a third person (Bowen, 1978).

Since counselors develop within the context of their society and profession, this context affects their views of their clients (Hinkle, 1994). Unfortunately, such acculturation often includes an idiosyncratic approach to people that focuses on cause-effect relationships. Hinkle has offered an analogy by comparing psychiatry to physics. Physicists discontinued much of their adherence to linear thought for explaining physical phenomena with the splitting of the first atom over 50 years ago (Capra, 1982). This occurred contemporaneously to the development of systems theory. Today, many psychiatrists continue to reflect the individualistic thought of Sigmund Freud and they fail to utilize the extensive literature available over the past 40 years concerning social and contextual theory. Psychological scientists have known for years that predicting human behavior is difficult. Unfortunately, the historic recourse to this difficulty has been for professionals' to attempt to become better predictors of human behavior. Instead, it would be wise to develop models that explain the challenges with behavior prediction.

Systems have many properties. For example, movement in one component of a system has an effect on all other components of the system. Similarly, systems have *subsystems* or *microsystems* that are affected by the larger system and vice versa. *Subsystems* refer to groupings of people who are within the system yet who have relational boundaries that set them apart. To illustrate, refusal to attend school usually elicits the involvement of other subsystems in the child's community, such

Family Counseling in the Schools:

as the police and the courts (Aliotti, 1992). An element of a system may be affected, or changed, by beginning with any component of the system. This means that individual problems have various pathways along which a solution may be sought (Stark & Brookman, 1992). This process is often referred to as *equifinality.*

The boundaries within systems and subsystems are either *enmeshed* or *disengaged. Boundaries* determine who participates and how, and where the authority lies. Enmeshment and disengagement are not healthy or dysfunctional in and of themselves, but are merely relationship styles. For example, a couple with no children are perceived as enmeshed, and rightfully so. After the birth of a child, the mother and child's relationship becomes enmeshed and the father is disengaged. Later, the father and mother may be enmeshed and disengaged from the adolescent (Minuchin, 1974).

Multigenerational family systems are *dynamic* or *process* oriented. Such systems are constantly moving through developmental stages of change. Carter and McGoldrick (1980) have described six stages of family life development and transition:

1. the unattached young adult between families
2. the newly married couple joins two families
3. the family with young children
4. the family with adolescents
5. children leave home
6. the family in later life

Similarly, Minuchin (1974) has suggested a family life cycle that includes the following transitions:

1. newborn into the family
2. child to adolescent
3. adolescent leaves home

Theoretically, systems theory deviates markedly from the traditional idiosyncratic cause-effect philosophy typically taught to school counselors and education professionals. Goldenberg and Goldenberg (1980) have indicated that individual counseling focuses on uncovering intrapsychic conflicts, whereas family counseling emphasizes the family system itself. Thus, analogical thinking is more clinically productive than inductive and deductive thinking (Bertalanffy, 1968). The counselor is part of the context of the counseling process whereby the counselor's active participation affects family change. Family members are encouraged to talk to one another rather than through the counselor.

Bowen (1978) believed that changes in the family system impact the individual, and that changes in the individual influence the family. A major concept integral to Bowen's depiction of family systems is *differentiation of self*. The focus herein is on the way people deal with the intermix between emotional and intellectual functioning. At the highest level are those individuals with the most differentiation between emotional and intellectual functioning. They generally live full emotional lives and make life decisions based on intellect and reasoning. Those people at the lower levels of differentiation have fused emotional and intellectual functioning. Intellectual functioning becomes dictated by emotional functioning. When stressed, less differentiated individuals regress to an emotional state. Bowen's *multigeneration transmission process* refers to the transmission of the family emotional process from one generation to the next. To illustrate, in each generation, the most emotionally involved child moves toward a lower level of differentiation of self while the least emotionally involved child strives toward a higher level of differentiation.

Hoopes (1987) has indicated that people are influenced by, and also influence, the three-plus generational system in which they are born, live, and die. The multigenerational system's patterns and influences are stored, transmitted, transformed, and manifested within the family's multigenerational system. Sometimes, this dynamic process is covert and earlier dysfunctional family patterns and behavior may suddenly surface in a nuclear family. These past patterns are presented to a school counselor as new problems the family is not able to solve. These transmissions can govern functional and dysfunctional beliefs, attitudes, behaviors, self-esteem, and interactional patterns within the system (Hoopes). Therefore, a person develops on at least three levels: 1) as an individual, 2) as part of the nuclear family, and 3) as part of the extended

Family Counseling in the Schools:

family (Holman, 1983).

Although people create families that are different from their parent's family, in many ways these families remain quite similar. This familiarity has the power to stimulate the replication of patterns, attitudes, and parent-child interactions which may be like those of the families-of-origin. Functional as well as dysfunctional patterns influence multigenerational family systems. Family members also bring their experiences from outside the family (society) back to the family for integration into the family system (Hoopes, 1987).

Multigenerational systems have hierarchical boundaries in that one person in a system or subsystem has more power and responsibility to determine what will happen than another. In healthy nuclear families this hierarchy is most often observed in parent-child relationships with the parents in the position of power (Hoopes, 1987). From a structural perspective, the closeness and boundaries within families depicts family members' ability to make needed adjustments in day to day living.

From a family systems viewpoint, the *nuclear family* represents a two generation system consisting of the marital couple (i.e., the parental subsystem) and their children (i.e., the sibling subsystem). The *extended family* is an extended system which includes other generations extended in at least two directions, upward or downward in the "family tree." Nuclear families are influenced by their extended families. Adults bring into a marriage the heritage from their family-of-origin, just as each of their parents did. This *process* cannot be avoided; no matter if the parents are living or dead, or if adoption or foster care is involved (Hoopes, 1987). The extended family includes relatives such as aunts, uncles, cousins, great-aunts, and second cousins. A *blended,* or *reconstituted* family, is one in which two different family systems join to form a new family system. For example, a divorced parent re-marries a spouse with children (Hoopes).

It is important to note that not all school children in today's society live in a traditional family with two parents and siblings, grow up, then marry, have children, and remain married. Today it is common to find married-couple only systems, single-person systems, parent-child systems, step-sibling systems, half-siblings systems, step-parent-child systems, and foster children and adoption systems (Hoopes, 1987).

Defining the Healthy Family

The *family roles* played by each member in a well functioning family are known to all in the family and may change over the course of time. There is a degree of elasticity and adaptability in all healthy family roles. One member picks up the duties or expected behaviors of a member who is absent, ill, or otherwise unable to play his or her part. When the changes that are a part of usual family development occur, such as the increased separation from the family by a teenager, or the marriage of an older child, the healthy family adjusts and adapts. This adaptation especially applies to families facing a crisis. As already noted, a crisis, whether from within or outside the family, puts stress on the entire system. As a well-functioning family absorbs this stress, the members adapt their roles to accommodate the situation and following a transition period, the family continues to operate. There will be times when the family feels this stress more than others and times when the family does not function optimally. But, a well-functioning family will either return to normal patterns or will make the necessary transitions and then settle into their new, adaptive behavior patterns.

Virginia Satir (1967) perceived healthy families as those that are mature. Green and Kolevzon's (1984) review has indicated that, according to Satir, the *mature* individual possesses a sense of being in charge and makes decisions based on his or her perceptions of others in a social context. In healthy families, the parents are mature and communication is clear, specific, direct, and honest. Satir also favored the concept of *family rules* which govern family behavior (Satir, 1967, 1972). Healthy families develop flexible rules that are subject to change; whereas, less healthy families embrace rules that are nonnegotiable and rigid. Satir's family counseling process focused on rule making and the consequences for rule violations (Green & Kolevzon, 1984).

Haley, Madanes, and Minuchin also developed models of the healthy family. These models exhibit similarities in that family health reflects the relationship characteristics within the family and its subsystems. High-level functioning is dependent on

15

context, timing, and the changing family life cycle (Haley, 1980; Minuchin, 1974).

Within the structural-strategic model of family counseling, boundaries are essential to family health. Boundaries "are intrafamily rules that define both the participants in subsystems and how they are expected to participate" (Green & Kolvezon, 1984, p. 15). These rules help to protect both the individual and the various subsystems. Rules govern the power and status among family members, emphasizing the power of the marital or parental position in the family hierarchy. The hierarchy in healthy families is well defined. Rules regulate the healthy family's operations and are understood by all subsystems within that family (Green & Kolevzon). Confusion within the hierarchy results in unhealthy families and is often first noticed in the *symptoms* of children.

Haley and Minuchin also focus on strong and satisfying marriages in healthy family functioning (Green & Kolevzon, 1984).

The strategic-structural models contend that healthy families are capable of adaptation and change during crucial phases of the family life cycle. For example, when a new child comes in to the family, when a child leaves home, or when a family member becomes ill, the family reorganizes its boundaries and rules, and practices accommodating behaviors (Green & Kolevzon). Unhealthy families lack such flexibility, as evidenced by their repeated attempts to apply the same, ineffective strategies to solving family problems.

Likewise, multigenerational issues can affect family health. Such issues may remain hidden to family members, being transmitted at unconscious levels until the appropriate context is presented for these issues to manifest themselves. For example, some of these concerns may not surface until children leave home, become adults, and create a similar context (Hoopes, 1987).

Similarly, language and its meaning is necessary for the shift from thinking about individuals to thinking systemically. For example, Madanes (1981) has defined *metaphors* (see Chapter 5) associated with family interventions as the problem behavior which needs to be abandoned in order to end its abuse in the system. Therefore, the school counselor using a systemic approach needs to listen carefully to similarities in language associated with the child and parents' fears, failures, and behavior (Madanes, 1981). Aliotti (1992) has indicated that in the beginning stages of working with a family, more *thinking* about the case is needed by the school counselor than *action*. In essence, the counselor must think about the family in terms of its language and metaphors as well as generate hypotheses about the related behaviors. For example, in a case involving brothers who soiled their pants, an hypothesis reflected that problematic components of the family system, namely the parental subsystem, were contributing to the encopresis (Wells & Hinkle, 1990, see Chapter 11). Following a family assessment that utilizes systemic concepts and the establishment of hypotheses regarding a school problem, a series of interventions can be planned and strategically sequenced. Counselors interested in further information regarding systems theory should consult the suggested reading list in Appendix A.

Strategic Family Counseling

Strategic family counseling is a major school of intervention within the discipline of systemic family counseling. Although components of other types of family counseling are alluded to in this volume, *strategic family counseling* and *structural family counseling* constitute the foundation of the school interventions depicted in this book. (Other major family counseling approaches that are particularly useful in school settings are briefly presented in Chapter 4). Strategic counselors, employing the major propositions of systems theory, introduce new behaviors into the existing set of transactions manifested by a family (Burgess & Hinkle, 1993; Haley, 1976). The strategic model suggests that family structure can be "observed in the repeated transactional patterns of communication that occur between family members and between the family and other systems" (Stark & Brookman, 1992, p. 260).

Family systems theory focuses on the structure, hierarchical relationships, and rules within the family. As with other family counseling approaches, strategic family counselors contend that problem behaviors result from problematic family interactions rather than from individual psychopathology. These interactions represent complex sets of interlocking behavioral

Family Counseling in the Schools:

patterns, cognitions, and affects which define family functioning as well as individual behavior (Anderson & Hinkle, 1994).

Dysfunctional family behaviors develop when unexpected crises unbalance the system beyond its natural ability to recover (Haley, 1973, 1976; Kerr, 1981; Pittman, 1987). Rather than explore individual personality dynamics, the objective of strategic counseling is to restore functional family equilibrium. Strategic family counseling typically utilizes a brief counseling approach and therapeutic techniques such as re-establishing family hierarchies and readjusting family interactions.

Family counseling in general, and strategic approaches in particular, are not appropriate for all school problems. Amatea (1989) has suggested that strategic approaches to solving school problems are useful when simplistic, direct, and common sense methods have been proven ineffective. In strategic family counseling, the school professional initiates the change process (Amatea, 1989; Hinkle, 1994).

School personnel expect particular behaviors from various school employees. For example, principles administer educational goals; teachers teach school children about their respective disciplines; and, school counselors counsel children and serve as consultants within a specified human services format. Many strategic counseling interventions, however, appear to be unconventional to mainstream school counseling procedures. Amatea (1989) has indicated that many strategic family counseling tactics are "based on working against common sense and in unexpected ways" and "such tactics may appear incomprehensible to other school staff members and to parents" (p.76). She elaborates by indicating that a support base is often necessary in order to have the freedom to practice in a manner that is effective as well as efficient, even though it may be uncommon at times and not in line with typical school counseling activities.

Amatea (1989) has illustrated a planning process for attempting strategic interventions which includes information gathering concerning what solutions have been tried in the past, establishing who has the problem, analyzing commitment to change and client beliefs, identifying small outcome behaviors, developing specific solution strategies, and monitoring and sustaining change. However, this model must be modified and expanded to meet the specific needs of school counselors. Case conceptualization and hypothesis development are strongly encouraged, especially for school counselors who are in the early stages of applying systemic interventions in the schools.

In conjunction with an emphasis on past events to effect change, concern with historical or intellectual insight based on past events is limited. Interpretations, if used at all, are not aimed so much at producing a deeper awareness in the client as they are to reframe a situation for useful strategic intervention. Moreover, Haley (1972) argues that insight and self-understanding have not been proven to produce behavioral change, particularly in children.

Additionally, the strategic approach is pragmatic, emphasizing what works in the here and now. Strategic counseling's strength lies in its use of innovative *directives* and other strategies designed for particular family needs. Strategic family therapists are distinguished by the commonly held assumption that if the individual is to change, the context in which he or she lives must change. The unit of treatment is no longer the individual, even if a single person is interviewed; it is the set of relationships in which the person is embedded (Haley & Hoffman, 1967). According to Thomas' review (1992), Haley believes that problems do not emanate from the individual, but from the social situation in which the individual interacts. Haley (1972) has suggested that the ills of the client are not really separable from the ills of the social context the client creates and inhabits. The school counselor cannot pull the student from the "cultural milieu" and use such labels as "sick" or "well." Madanes (1984) reiterates that even though there is increased agreement that the social situation rather than the person is the problem focus for counseling, there is no collective agreement concerning how to approach the problem.

Haley (1972) has defined strategic family counseling as a type of family intervention in which the counselor takes an active role initiating what occurs in counseling. The school counselor must identify problems, set goals, select interventions that are tailored to the particular needs of the student, analyze responses to the interventions, assist in developing future strategies, and measure outcomes in terms of goal accomplishment and problem resolution (Thomas, 1992). In addition, Haley believes that not only should a counselor initiate strategic interventions, he or she should also take responsibility for what happens during

Family Counseling in the Schools:

counseling (Stanton, 1981).

Haley also espouses other theoretical concepts important in strategic family counseling. He explores power in the family, the importance of *family life cycle transitions,* and how two people on different levels of a hierarchy establish a coalition against a third person. As family members struggle for power to make rules in the family, the strategic family counselor assesses the interactional sequences around the problem linking the family members to the coalitions, triangles, and hierarchies in the family. These struggles for power become more apparent as the family goes through different lifecycles or as members enter or leave the family system. If a family tries to maintain the same structure at these transition points, symptoms will result and a family can become *stuck* in their efforts to adapt to change (Anderson & Hinkle, 1994; Thomas, 1992).

Regardless of the strategic intervention implemented, Haley proceeds systematically through stages as he negotiates to discover the kinds of programs that exist and to formulate plans of intervention and action. Haley (1987) proceeds through four stages in working with families: a) a *social stage* which involves observation of family interaction with everyone participating, b) a *problem stage* which establishes why the family has come to counseling and how committed the members are to change, c) an *interaction stage* during which the family discusses the problem as the counselor observes communication sequences, coalitions, and power hierarchies, and d) a *goal setting stage* in which the counselor and family determine the presenting problem they wish to solve, resulting in a contract which clearly defines goals and directives for change. In this process, the strategic counselor assumes the role of "family change maker" and intervenes by becoming temporary leader of the family. Haley (1972) posits that the therapist must continually make decisions in response to what is occurring both in and around treatment while maintaining control at all times. However, Haley cautions that rather than demanding clients to behave in a certain way, the counselor should always permit the client to behave in a manner that results in the achievement of positive goals.

During the therapeutic process, strategic family counselors do not probe heavily into the past of the family. Madanes (1981) asserts that "current situations" are causal to the presenting problem and, therefore, the past is irrelevant. Therapeutic strategies and concepts include shifting hierarchies, setting appropriate boundaries, identifying triangles, alliances, and coalitions, understanding symptoms, reframing behavior, and implementing directives (e.g., encouraging adaptive changes, prescribing the symptom paradox), and making a problem behavior an ordeal (Aliotti, 1992; Carlson, 1992; Haley, 1984, 1987; Minuchin, 1974; Weeks, 1991). Clinical cases in Chapter 11 illustrate many of these strategic family counseling concepts.

Family Hierarchy and Boundaries

In strategic family counseling, hierarchies represent the manner in which a family is organized. Hierarchies within social contexts are inevitable, although they do not have to be in any particular order (Haley, 1976). Haley has written that "...every family must deal with the issue of organizing within a hierarchy and rules must be worked out about who is primary in status and power and who is secondary" (p. 103). Nevertheless, families often have confusing hierarchies that result in family problems (Haley, 1987). Madanes (1984) has indicated that all organizations have a sense that one person has more power and responsibility, for a particular situation or context, than another person. For example, in one case a father was assisted in regaining family power he had relinquished to his mother, and he and his wife were subsequently empowered as the joint voice of authority in their family. In the same case, a younger brother was instructed to tell his older brother when he had soiled his pants. The older brother would then help his younger brother clean himself, wash the soiled clothing, and help his brother dress. This process established one brother in the "hierarchical role of older brother" (Wells & Hinkle, 1990, pp. 522-523) (see case in Chapter 11). The family and the school exist to socialize children and to provide nurturance, education, and assistance in learning appropriate behaviors. Families and schools are similar in that they are organized hierarchically with different members having various roles (Carlson, 1992).

Power is associated with hierarchies. Although this term may seem "hard to swallow" for some school counselors, power is an important component in family relations, just as it is in the classroom. When families organize themselves, issues of power

Family Counseling in the Schools:

become a major concern (Madanes, 1981). It is important that this concept be properly defined within the context of family counseling. Madanes has indicated that if power is perceived as a negative concept associated with hostility, aggression, and exploitation, then the concept is not helpful to the practice of family counseling. However, if it is associated with the kind, helpful, and benevolent potential of people within families, then it is a positive concept.

The concepts of power and hierarchy are critical to the strategic therapeutic process. Haley (1972) sees the immediate issue between the counselor and client as who will control behavior. The resolution of this issue is the source of therapeutic change. However, Haley cautions that the struggle for control should not center on controlling the client in a negative sense, but rather the struggle should address the definition of the relationship from a systemic stance. This process is one in which the client insists that the counselor be one-up while desperately trying to place the counselor one-down, and the counselor insists that the client remain one-down in order to help him or her become one-up, with the goal being the separation of counselor and client (Haley, 1972). Madanes (1981) reiterates Haley's position when she notes that strategic family counseling addresses the power in the relationship between counselor and client as well as members of the family system. Strategies of counseling are designed to utilize this power to effect behavioral change (Anderson & Hinkle, 1994). Counselors must ensure that parents do not shift their power to the counselor. For example, parents who are overwhelmed with their child may have a tendency to "put the ball in the counselor's court."

As reflected by the strategic school of thought, family boundaries are generational in nature. From a *structural* family counseling perspective, the closeness, or boundaries, within families depicts the families' rules, roles, and their ability to make needed adjustments in day-to-day living. Such adjustments are a function of the rules and regulations within the family system (Minuchin, 1974). Regardless of the strategic or structural family counseling perspective (as well as the difficulty in separating them), boundaries remain important concepts in family counseling. To illustrate, parents may disengage from one another resulting in marital dysfunction;

grandparents may become enmeshed with their children's families, and children may develop confused roles within the family (Andolfi, 1978; Haley, 1976; Madanes, 1984; Minuchin, 1974; Wells & Hinkle, 1990). Implicit and explicit rules, or boundaries, dictate how family members may interact. The boundaries between parents and grandparents, older and younger siblings, and other smaller family groups form subsystems. The boundaries between these family subsystems determine who sets the rules and the amount of privacy and independence accorded each family member. When a member violates a family rule, or external stressors affect the system, negative communicative feedback loops are activated in order to re-balance the family. These loops re-establish accepted, yet sometimes dysfunctional, family roles, behaviors, and patterns, including triangles (Aponte & Van Deusen, 1981; Haley, 1976; Minuchin, 1974).

Triangles

A triangle describes the predictable emotional forces between any three people (Bowen, 1978). This has been referred to by Bowen as the *molecule of emotional systems*. Emotional systems remain in flux since the most uncomfortable person in a triangle continually seeks a more comfortable state of closeness or distance. When the uncomfortable person achieves equilibrium, he or she typically disturbs the balance between the other two people involved in the triangle and the activity of achieving equilibrium switches to the more uncomfortable of the pair. This process repeats itself in a precise and predictable manner allowing a counselor who understands triangles to predict the next move (Bowen). *Triangulation* may occur when two people, who are uneasy with their dyadic interaction, attempt to defuse the tension in the relationship by focusing on a third party. The undifferentiated person then carries this pattern of interaction into other people-oriented organizations such as marriage, sibling relationships, or school or work relationships.

Family Counseling in the Schools:

Coalitions

One of the more apparent concepts in systemic relationships are coalitions. Haley (1976) has indicated that information and coalition are synonymous: "the act of giving and holding information across a boundary is an act of forming and dissolving coalitions. To conceal from parents what their child has said is to form a coalition with the child on that issue" (pp. 217-218).

Similarly, counselors must be constantly aware of the formulation of covert coalitions and the family symptoms such unions represent (Haley).

Understanding Symptoms

Symptoms in families serve the purpose of maintaining homeostasis (Stark & Brookman, 1992). For example, brothers may begin soiling their pants in an attempt to relieve the tension of their parents' stressful, disengaged marital relationship (Wells & Hinkle, 1990). Another illustration includes an adolescent avoiding school in order to stay home and keep her family intact (Burgess & Hinkle, 1993).

Aliotti (1992) has reflected that students not coping successfully within the school system will find it difficult to cope with their family system as well. Systems theorists assume that an individual system component, for example, a family member, may express a family symptom in an attempt to change the family. Moreover, school children belong to a larger unit that includes the family; from a systemic perspective, they react to changes and distress within this unit. Children become relationship-oriented rather than task-oriented when over involved with parental anxieties (Beal & Chertov, 1992). For instance, it is common for children to become symptomatic at school when a crisis occurs at home. Symptoms may then serve a systems function by obtaining help for the troubled family.

In strategic family counseling, a symptom is considered a *communicative act* with message qualities that define a relationship between two or more people. Communicative acts function within the interpersonal network of a social organization (Anderson & Hinkle, 1994). According to Madanes

(1984), a symptom is a message which can have a second referent (i.e., a second meaning or *metamessage*) which may refer to someone other than the person expressing the message. This could affect a sequence of interaction between two people and could represent a metaphor for, or take the place of, a different sequence of interaction between two other people.

In another communicative context, Haley (1972) defines a symptom in terms of the client's behavior. This behavior must be extreme in its influence and the client must indicate in some way that he or she cannot help or stop the undesirable behavior. Madanes (1984) has indicated that a counselor should generally think of all symptoms (except for organic illnesses) as voluntary and under the control of the client. She believes that at times the first step in resolving a presenting problem is to redefine the student's or family member's behavior as voluntary rather than involuntary. This redefining may be the only intervention necessary in some cases because the client may solve the problem once it is accepted that the problem is under personal control. In addition, Haley argues that symptoms are perpetuated by the influence of other people. He reflects that "psychotherapeutic tactics" should be designed to persuade the client to change behavior and/or persuade "intimates" to change their behavior in relation to the client.

Reframing

The concept of reframing facilitates the understanding of symptoms. Reframing behavior from negative to positive is a helpful and necessary strategic family counseling technique. Such reframing, or relabeling, provides the opportunity for a family to redefine a child's, or other family member's, difficulty as having a different purpose. For example, an elementary school student may initiate fights that result in a parent/teacher/principal conference. However, this negative behavior can alternately be perceived as protective and helpful if it deflects the family's focus from a parental or marital relationship problem and results in the family's engagement in counseling. A school counselor involved in such a case could reframe negative behavior in a manner that puts the parents in the position of looking differently at their own relationship.

Essentially, reframing changes the meaning of an event and

Family Counseling in the Schools:

places it in an entirely different frame of reference (Watzlavick, Weakland, & Fisch, 1974). Reframing challenges family members to alter accepted perceptions of events; subsequently, the family behaves differently (Burgess & Hinkle, 1993). To illustrate, Wells & Hinkle (1990) reframed encopresis (involuntary passage of feces) as a metaphoric message representing a family problem with a family solution (see Chapter 11). Another example reflects parents not making their teen-age daughter attend school. The reframe included the "new" perception that refusal was an indication that the parents would be relieved of their burden if their daughter were removed from their home and placed in an alternate living situation (Burgess & Hinkle, 1993, see Chapter 11). Such a change in perspective resulted in increased school attendance. Metaphors and relabeling (discussed in Chapter 5) are often used in reframing problem behavior and in formulating directives.

Directives in Strategic Family Counseling

In order to persuade a family system to change, strategic family counselors rely heavily on directives (Anderson & Hinkle, 1994). Stanton (1981) has noted that just as psychodynamic therapy relies heavily on interpretation, the essential tools of strategic counseling are directives. Goldenberg and Goldenberg (1991) have indicated that directives, or the assignment of tasks, are often completed outside of the therapeutic session and are given for several reasons: a) to motivate individuals to behave differently so as to have more positive subjective experiences; b) to intensify the therapeutic relationship by involving the counselor in the family's actions during the time between sessions; and c) to gather information through reactions of family members in order to design future strategies. What makes a counselor choose a particular directive is based on how the problem, as well as the characteristics of the problem, are conceptualized by the counselor. However, it is important for the school counselor not to attempt to use directives until the case is conceptualized and hypotheses about the case have been established. Premature directives given without thorough forethought often end in failure because the counselor's notions about the problem are either inadequate or wrong. Once conceptualization is completed, be it in one session or three, the counselor can competently address directives for change. For example, the unhappy parents of a student could be asked to go on a date in order to take a break from parenting responsibilities. This activity also indirectly relieves tension in the marital subsystem and fosters change (Wells & Hinkle, 1990).

Encouraging Adaptive Change

Paradoxical intention. Prescribing the symptom, or utilizing paradox, delivers a subtle message to the family concerning the interactions they use to maintain or support the problematic symptom (Burgess & Hinkle, 1993; Fisher, Anderson, & Jones, 1981; West & Zarski, 1983). Symptoms are conceptualized as being under the individual's control. The therapeutic *double bind* places the family member in the position of freeing him or herself from the symptom by consciously producing the symptom. Therefore, if the individual does not lose the symptom, but enacts it, "it becomes within the realm of conscious control" (Burgess & Hinkle, 1993, p. 135). Burgess and Hinkle have provided the example of prescribing the symptom to an anxious adolescent female. She was instructed to become as anxious as possible each morning before school so that she and her family may better "understand the source of her problems" (p. 136). This ultimately resulted in a reduction in anxiety for the student.

Watzlavick, Weakland, and Fisch (1974) have reported that people attempt to resolve dilemmas by applying first or second order change. *First order change* is characterized by applying more of the opposite, or desired behavior. This application may lead to exacerbation of the symptom, which often results in even more of the opposite behavior. An example of first order change is phobic avoidance. Here, an anxiety arousing situation is encountered. The student expects that when the situation occurs again it will provoke a paralyzing fear or awkward reaction. Subsequently, a dysfunctional cycle develops where the fear of being fearful amplifies the symptom, and the phobic situation is avoided (Anderson & Hinkle, 1994; Dowd & Milne, 1986; Frankl, 1975; Gerz, 1966).

Second order change introduces a new set of rules and behaviors into the existing behavioral repertoire and results in

Family Counseling in the Schools:

a metachange, or *change of change.* This metachange occurs in paradoxical interventions, or a therapeutic double bind (Watzlavick, Beavin, & Jackson, 1967; Watzlavick, Weakland, & Fisch, 1974). For example, the avoidant student is told to be free of a symptom by consciously producing it (symptoms by nature are beyond the client's control). If the student resists the symptom prescription and loses the symptom, it is no longer a problem. Conversely, if the symptom is not lost, but enacted, it becomes within the realm of conscious control. In addition to symptom prescription, paradoxical techniques include *reframing* and *predicting a relapse* (Anderson & Hinkle, 1994; Haley, 1976). Predicting a relapse is frequently used following significant symptom improvement. For example, the school counselor may construe the positive change as a fluke and predicts that it will not continue. This prediction challenges the student to prove the counselor wrong (Anderson & Hinkle, 1994). If there is a relapse, its occurrence shows that it was expected and under the counselor's control (Weeks & L'Abate, 1979, 1982), at which time the counselor will alleviate the symptom via a directive agreed upon by the family. In summary, relabeling and prescribing the symptom are useful techniques in family counseling and are often utilized by strategic family counselors.

Ordeal Therapy

Ordeals can help individuals, couples, and families solve a wide range of problems. Theoretically, an ordeal is defined as a symptom being made more difficult to keep than to retain. The counselor imposes an ordeal appropriate for the problem the person wants to change. The ordeal is more severe than the problem itself, but should not harm the person or anyone else in any way. For example, insisting that parents repeatedly discuss the consequences of having a *normal* child can be perceived as an ordeal. Discussing over and over again the various consequences of improvement (e.g., spending more time together, investing in family activities, facing extended family issues, spending more time at home in the evenings) is a great ordeal and puts the parents in a position to change (Haley, 1984). In another case, an acting-out child may be forced to remain in his room after the parents agree that time-out is appropriate. The power of the parents' agreement, as well as their consistent follow-through, creates an ordeal for the child that is worse than having the symptom. Subsequently, the child gives the symptom up.

Structural Family Counseling

The structural, as well as the strategic approaches to family counseling, emphasize the behaviors of family members (Green & Kolevzon, 1984; Haley, 1976; Minuchin, 1974). One of Minuchin's (1974) major concepts is that family *structure* is sociocultural. It integrates both the demands of society and the internal family system in configuring the individual. Structural modifications are accomplished through *boundary negotiation.*

Minuchin's model of family development includes couples communication. It portrays couples as engaged in a complex process of negotiation that involves three areas. One area is *patterned transactions.* For example, who will shop, cook, clean, and care for children. A second area includes separating from families of origin by developing new *boundaries.* Finally, reorganizing and regulating the world of work must be negotiated.

When a couple has children, they must redefine their functions to meet the demands of children. This includes renegotiating boundaries with extended families who now have different roles (e.g., grandparents). Siblings also must learn boundaries by negotiating with the family and with their peers.

Furthermore, Minuchin believes that there are two major constraints on family development. First, there are universal rules governing family organization. For example, any family with children will have a *power hierarchy.* Families also have idiosyncratic *rules.* These include the unique, individual expectations and intentions of each family member. These rules are explicit and they sometimes persist even after their need is no longer present.

Boundaries

For Minuchin (1974), subsystem boundaries are the rules that define who participates and how. Minuchin's concepts of enmeshment and disengagement refer to relationship styles; extremes in these styles reflect the possibility of symptom formation. *Enmeshed* families respond to situations quickly, whereas *disengaged* families respond slowly.

Transition points such as a newborn into the family, a child becoming an adolescent, and the adolescent leaving home result in stress on the family. If the family is unable to adapt to stress by renegotiating its boundaries and engaging its structure, regardless of whether its relationships are too enmeshed or too disengaged, the family becomes problematic. In applying Minuchin's (1974) structural counseling to family counseling in the school, the school counselor must be aware of three major therapeutic tasks. These include joining the family as a leader, assessing the underlying family structure, and creating circumstances that will allow for change in the family. This approach to family counseling places responsibility on the counselor for modifications in the family. Similar to Haley's approach (1976), the counselor effects change by hypothesizing about the family and its social context, which includes the school subsystem.

The school counselor forms a therapeutic system by decreasing the distance between him or herself and the family. This is often referred to as *accommodating* the dysfunctional system since restructuring requires the initial support of the structures that eventually must be changed. This process aids the school counselor's formulation of a working diagnosis. At this juncture, the school counselor considers the family structure in terms of its subsystems, the system's capacity for change and its sensitivity to individual members, sources of stress, the family's developmental stage, and the ways in which the student's symptoms maintain the family's behavioral patterns.

The school counselor challenges the family's interactional patterns by encouraging family members to behave in the session as they would at home. Boundaries are defined by assigning agreed upon tasks. Systemic theory dictates that stress induces family members to change their behavior. Stress is, therefore, escalated by the counselor from time to time to facilitate change. Prescribing the symptom, or utilizing paradox, can exaggerate the symptom, allowing it to be redefined and altered.

If the counselor has some family counseling experience, it is sometimes helpful to manipulate the mood or atmosphere of a family session. For example, one family member can be put in a position to assist or recognize another member. The counselor also can attempt to relabel the way family members feel.

Finally, structural family counselors are prepared to utilize psychoeducation, particularly in parent training.

Structural theory emphasizes organization and boundaries, whereas strategic theory focuses on hierarchical organization and the patterns of behavior (Haley, 1987; Minuchin, 1974). Structural family counseling is based on the concept that context influences change and that change in the context will produce a change in the child (Woody & Woody, 1994).

The literature seems to indicate that although structural and strategic family counseling have their differences, there appears to be considerable overlap (Fine, 1992). While structural and strategic approaches to family counseling both focus on identifying and modifying patterns of communication that maintain behavior, they do so from different standpoints. Haley's notions of power and flexibility within the system augment the structural model (Stark & Brookman, 1992). Moreover, structural and strategic principles are often used in combination (Stanton, 1981). By now, members of the helping professions, including school counselors, are aware that a child or adolescent's problematic behavior is supported and maintained by the family (Goldenberg & Goldenberg, 1988).

Integrating School and Family Counseling

School counseling and educational professionals are ideally situated to make family interventions in the schools. Counselors can begin this process by *conceptualizing* a child's problem within a systems format which will help solve the difficulty (Hinkle, 1993). To be successful at family counseling in the school setting, concise guidelines for appropriate referrals are necessary. Presenting problems need to be addressed in a manner that will logically and clearly produce a solution for the problems. The conceptualization of a student's presenting problem requires that the school counselor, who uses this method of problem-solving, have a step-by-step thought process that can be employed with most problems involving students

Family Counseling in the Schools:

at school (Goodman &Kjonaas, 1988).

When a student's difficulty persists, it is typically connected systemically to the family. Therefore, it is best to solve the problem by including the school and family in formulating a solution. School counselors who engage in family counseling stop many school problems before they become difficult to manage (Hinkle, 1993) making costly special placements unnecessary.

Furthermore, a student's problem is viewed within a context of how the parents and other family members respond when the behavior occurs. It is important for the counselor to ask: *How is the problem maintained in the system?* Individual approaches to school problems have at times required inordinate amounts of time resulting in only minimal improvement (Hinkle, 1993). In summary, the child should be perceived as part of a large ecological system in which all aspects of the child's life are interrelated (Hobbs, 1966).

Conclusion

School counselors exploring a family systems approach in their work with children and adolescents will lead the reformation in education. Nicoll (1984a, 1984b) has reported that failing to address family dynamic factors may result in schools running the risk of making intervention recommendations that are either ineffective, or worse yet, counterproductive, serving only to make existing problems potentially more difficult. It is important for the school counselor working with families in the school environment to focus on the school problem. If the school difficulty is not emphasized, the family and particularly the parents may lose interest in counseling or sabotage its effectiveness. Counselor education programs are beginning to broaden the scope of their training of school counselors to include family counseling. Practicing school counselors need training opportunities and an avenue in which to develop confidence in themselves as family counselors. It is important for school counselors to be given permission to learn about and to apply family counseling concepts without feeling that they have crossed a professional boundary (Hinkle, 1993). We believe that the "new frontier" of the family-school system is ready to be pioneered in earnest by school counselors.

The school counselor can engage a variety of relationships to solve children's and adolescents' problems (Amatea & Sherrard, 1991). This includes the child-teacher-family relationship. School counselors must involve parents, and even other family members, to be successful in helping since the family has such a commanding influence on school behavior. Often two or three sessions will be enough to cause positive changes in parent-child and teacher-child interactions and relationships (Nicoll, 1992).

Even when the school counselor cannot work with the family as a whole, the system in which the child functions must be remembered (Goldenberg & Goldenberg, 1988; Haley, 1976).

Whenever possible, the school counselor should counsel the family as a group. Parents' relationships and the quality of the marriage can have a bearing on the child's functioning. Furthermore, the stability of the marital relationship plays a central role in structural as well as strategic counseling (Stark & Brookman, 1992). A core problem may be the underlying marital difficulties and retraining may be needed by the parents. Although it has been suggested that counselors develop a broad view of the family counseling field so as to fit in with differing communities, we are encouraging a more circumscribed approach: namely, strategic and structural and family counseling.

Family Counseling in the Schools:

Chapter Three

Training in Family Counseling for School Counselors

Over the past thirty years a paradigm shift has evolved in counseling (Hinkle, 1993). This shift has been associated with a change of focus from the individual to social networks (Amatea, 1989; Bernstein & Burge, 1988; Nevels & Marr, 1985; Wilcoxin, 1986). The problems of today, typified by increases in divorce and dual-career families are not only affecting school children, they also alter the entire family (Palmo at al., 1984). As a result, family counseling is becoming a major specialty area in the field of counseling (Gladding, Burggraff, & Fenell, 1987; Hinkle).

Family counseling departs radically from the individual models to which most school counselors have been exposed. School counselors, however, are beginning to focus on larger units of intervention which include the family (Amatea & Fabrick, 1981; Gladding, 1984; Hinkle, 1993; McComb, 1981a; Meadows & Hetrick, 1982; Wilcoxin, 1986). Wilcoxin has stated that "this trend reinforces the convictions of many professionals regarding the importance of intervention for the client-within-the-family" (p. 272).

Family counseling has been practiced in a variety of clinical disciplines, including psychiatry, psychology, social work, and counseling. School counselors are finding family counseling an effective and needed skill for resolving persistent problems in the schools (Amatea, 1989). However, the school counselor who uses family counseling interventions must be "willing to commit time to gathering information about the problem/ solution cycle, thinking through a solution shift, and motivating those involved to act differently" (Amatea, 1989, p. 191).

McComb (1981a) has indicated that family counseling by school counselors can arrest many school problems before they escalate. Peeks (1990) and colleagues (e.g., Hinkle & Peeks, 1992; Stone & Peeks, 1986) have demonstrated that family interventions by school counselors can address a child's misbehavior effectively. Conversely, individual approaches to school problems have at times required inordinate amounts of time and resulted in little substantial improvement. On the contrary, Stone and Peeks have reported a successful family counseling intervention needing only five hours compared to 30 hours previously spent in individual counseling. Comparable brief family counseling successes also have been reported (e.g., Wells & Hinkle, 1990; Burgess & Hinkle, 1991). Essentially, school counselors occupy a unique position to appreciate the effectiveness of family counseling approaches with children (Goldenberg & Goldenberg, 1988; Hinkle, 1993; Hinkle & Peeks).

School children belong to, as well as react to, distress within a significantly large unit that includes the family (Peeks, 1991). For example, some children become symptomatic at school when a crisis occurs at home. The symptoms they display serve the systems function of getting help for the troubled family. Using a systemic approach, school counselors can use family counseling to solve a child's problems and assist the family in finding solutions to problems within a social context (Haley, 1987; Hinkle, 1993; Madanes, 1984; Minuchin, 1974; Peeks, 1989, 1991). Consequently, from a systemic perspective, cause-and-effect logic becomes meaningless when dealing with children in school (McDaniel, 1981).

Peeks (1991) has suggested that after eliminating intra-school causes for presenting problems, school counselors should consider causes that are *out-of-school*. According to the aforementioned systems theory, a child's problem is usually connected to the extended social unit or family. The student's negative behavior is viewed within a context of how the parents and other family members respond when the behavior occurs (Hinkle, 1993; Peeks, 1990).

There are many approaches to family counseling, including

experiential (e.g., Satir; Whitaker), psychoanalytic (e.g., Ackerman; Adler), intergenerational (e.g., Bowen; Framo; Boszormenyi), behavioral (e.g., Patterson; Stuart), and systemic (e.g., Palazzoli). However, brief formats (e.g., Haley; Madanes; de Shazer; Watalzwick, Weakland, & Fisch, 1974) appear to fit the school counseling environment the best. Amatea (1989) has indicated that a "brief, problem-oriented intervention has begun to find its way into school practice" (p. xii). Moreover, brief counseling utilizes a short-term focus making it particularly appealing to school counselors.

If a problem can be solved in short-term family counseling, the trained school counselor can render the necessary service (Golden, 1983). However, if the predicament is more complicated, or requires long-term counseling, family interviews conducted by school counselors can subsequently aid in an appropriate referral to an outside community agency (Palmo et al., 1984; Whiteside, 1993). If the family is referred outside the school, the school counselor may even attend the first session (Hinkle, 1993; McComb, 1981a).

Family Counseling Competencies for School Counselors

Counselor educators have recognized the overlap between the training competencies in traditional counseling and family counseling (Meadows & Hetrick, 1982). As a result, there has been an increase in family counseling courses in community counseling programs (Cowger, Hinkle, DeRidder, & Erk, 1991), as well as the establishment of a marriage and family counseling specialty by the Council for Accreditation of Counseling and Related Educational Programs (CACREP) (Stevens-Smith, Hinkle, & Stahmann, 1993). On the other hand, the limited family counseling training in graduate school counseling programs has caused school counselors not to include family counseling as part of their intervention plan (Hinkle, 1993).

Family counseling training has a brief history. Likewise, family counseling training opportunities for school counselors have been limited. The competencies presented in this book are by no means exhaustive. However, they will minimally provide counselors in service with direction for beginning family counseling in the schools. In the future, counselor education

Family Counseling in the Schools:

programs will need to broaden the scope of their training of school counselors to include family counseling. Practicing school counselors will need re-training opportunities and an avenue in which to develop confidence in themselves as family counselors (Palmo et al., 1984).

Historically, there has been limited family counseling training in school counseling programs. This lack of family counseling training among school counselors is partially responsible for the lack of systemic activities in the schools. However, this situation is beginning to change (Hinkle, 1993). For example, the University of Florida has recently recommended that school counseling graduate students elect to take an introductory course in family counseling (Joe Wittmer, personal communication, October 23, 1993). Similarly, family counseling classes at the University of North Carolina at Greensboro have had as much as 50 percent enrollment by school counseling majors.

There are two nationally recognized bodies associated with accrediting training programs in marriage and family counseling on a national level. They are CACREP and the Commission on Accreditation for Marriage and Family Therapy Education (COAMFTE) (Stevens-Smith et al., 1993). The former is affiliated with the American Counseling Association (ACA) and the latter with the American Association of Marriage and Family Therapy (AAMFT). The philosophical viewpoint of AAMFT is that marriage and family counseling is a distinct profession or discipline, similar to psychology, social work, or counseling. However, the ACA holds that marriage and family counseling is a disciplinary specialty (Remley, 1992). Stevens-Smith et al. have indicated that clinicians are "initially trained in counseling, and subsequently complete training and skill building in working with couples and families as marriage and family counselors..." (p.118). Stevens-Smith et al. also have stated that graduate preparation "programs accredited by CACREP reflect the philosophy of comprehensive counselor training prior to or concurrent with training" in marriage and family counseling (p. 118). CACREP-accredited programs train students in individual counseling and technique and then allow them to "specialize" in marriage and family counseling.

Educational institutions need to make immediate changes in the way they train school counselors. This change could include courses in family counseling theory and technique and practicums involving families (Woody & Woody, 1994). After support from administrators is established, family counseling training will ultimately require some alterations for those counselors previously trained in one-to-one counseling. To utilize the family systems approach, the school counselor will need to become more directive, less passive and neutral, and expand upon skills developed during individual counselor training (Goldenberg & Goldenberg, 1991; Hinkle, 1993). Effectively dealing with the transition from the role of helper to change agent will also be a necessary aspect of re-training (Cleghorn & Levin, 1973).

Fenell and Hovestadt (1986) have discussed a three-level training format for family counseling. Level-1 training is described as a specialty degree graduate program where a degree in family counseling is offered. Level-2 training entails family studies as a subset of another graduate mental health specialty. Level-3 training is described as elective study in family counseling which may include additional graduate courses, continuing education, and/or in-service training. Level-3 training, which includes short courses and in-service training, would be appropriate for most school counselors already in the work force and is consistent with preparation suggested by Palmo et al. (1984) and Amatea and Fabrick (1981).

Level-3 training prepares a counselor to work with families. This family work, however, may depend upon the amount and level of family training. Level-3 training includes introductory graduate courses in family counseling, supervised practice, and workshop attendance. A disadvantage to this training format is the limited preparation it provides in dealing with complex systems problems. However, among its advantages is the exposure it offers to family counseling without extended training.

Nicoll (1984b) has suggested three training approaches: 1) one counselor from the school systems is sent to be trained in a recognized graduate program and returns to train other school counseling personnel, 2) utilization of a consultant for in-service training, and 3) employment of a new school counselor already trained in family counseling in order to train existing staff. Counselors who are able to do so, may select to obtain further training from a family counseling/therapy institute.

Family Counseling in the Schools:

Knowledge of the literature in family counseling is essential to re-training. Readings should begin with family counseling theory (Goldenberg & Goldenberg, 1988) and should include specific information concerning special groups such as single-parent and dual-career families (Palmo et al., 1984). Training should also include a focus on family counseling skills and technique. School counselors wanting to counsel families will find this study rewarding since these counselors typically have not been exposed sufficiently to family counseling techniques (Bernstein & Burge, 1988; McComb, 1981a). General reference materials have been cited in Carlson (1981), Goldenberg and Goldenberg (1991), Gurman and Kniskern, (1981, 1991), and Walsh and Giblin (1988). Wilcoxin (1986) has suggested a reading guide specifically for school counselors engaging in family counseling. A list of resources is included in Appendix A. However, this list of books is not exhaustive. Numerous, good references in the professional literature, as well as new, innovative texts, make significant contributions to family counseling. For example, Moshe Talmon's (1990) *Single-Session Therapy* offers intriguing ideas both for the neophyte and for the more experienced family counselor. These books address such issues as convening family counseling sessions, using paradox, brief family counseling, utilizing symptoms, innovative programming, and suggestions for making the most from a single family counseling session.

It is important to note that while theory and technique are teachable, style and charisma are not (Kaslow, 1991). Therefore, each school counselor engaged in family counseling training needs to develop his or her own style of interacting with families and his or her own orientation to a family counseling model (Hinkle, 1993).

It is advantageous for school counselors training in family counseling to form study groups and affiliate with professionals who specialize in family counseling. Study group members can learn by sharing their family counseling experiences and by studying the video tapes of master counselors (Hinkle, 1993). Role playing and consulting with each other regarding cases also will be helpful (Goldenberg &Goldenberg, 1988). In addition, school counselors can seek out local family counselors willing to provide consultation and/or supervision. Co-counseling with experienced family counselors and participation

40

in supervision/consultation groups should be sought in order to develop specific family counseling competencies (Overton & Hennies, 1988; Palmo et al., 1984). Networking with counselors with similar family intervention interests also is a helpful way to train. Additionally, studying popular films for family content and analysis can be a helpful way to supplement understanding in family dynamics (e.g., *Ordinary People, The Great Santini, Prince of Tides, Prizzi's Honor*).

Two primary skills for school counselors conducting brief family counseling are assessing the family's capacity to change, and defining the key concepts of the problem within a social context (Hinkle, 1993). The brevity of this book does not allow for an extended analysis of family assessment (see Chapter 6 regarding family assessment). However, assessment should minimally include the gathering of new information which leads to hypothesis generation. Identifying family hierarchy and knowing how and where family information flows also is important (Peeks, 1992). Assessment should include the family's understanding of the problem, the family's strengths in relation to the problem, and the family's action thus far in solving the problem (McDaniel, 1981). Knowledge of family assessment is important in order to conceptualize the case. Discovering the level of flexibility and cohesion, as well as the chaotic patterns in the family and generational background, facilitates family assessment (Hinkle, 1993).

Family interventions should include the development of a plan, a prescription which reframes problem behavior, and homework tasks (Bernstein & Burge, 1988; Hinkle, 1993; Peeks, 1991). School counselors must establish rapport with the family, show care and concern, and should share positive characteristics of the *problem* child with the family (Peeks, 1991) (see Chapter 5 concerning family counseling technique).

Consulting with parents about their child and assisting with their understanding of child and adolescent behavior are desirable family counseling skills (Hinkle, 1993; Meadows & Hetrick, 1982). Many parents need assistance with re-establishing their executive position as primary decision-makers within their family. In many cases, relationships between parents and grandparents, as well as other extended family members, must be defined (Hinkle; McDaniel, 1981; Wells & Hinkle, 1990). Parents frequently need help in establishing

Family Counseling in the Schools:

behavioral expectations and discipline for their children (Peeks, 1991). In addition, child behavioral problems that are a function of marital discord should be identified and an appropriate intervention or referral be made. From a systems perspective, child behavioral problems identified as a function of marital discord should not be avoided. Parents may hesitate to accept the responsibility for their child's problems. Yet, when the parents are engaged appropriately (i.e., in a sensitive, respectful, manner) by the counselor, they can be extremely helpful with their child's school difficulty. The parents may also enhance their marriage (see Chapter 8 regarding marriage and divorce issues).

Once rapport with the family is established, assessment completed, and an intervention planned, the school counselor should organize a meeting among school professionals. This meeting is beneficial because every component of the system will help his or her efforts (Hinkle, 1993).

One of the major contributions of marriage and family counseling is its espousal of systemic thought. However, the Western educational system has been entrenched in linear cause/effect thinking. This idea is epitomized by thinking like: *"if A, then B."* Individualism in America is valued, as is science, and, thus, the strong adherence to linear thought. This method of organizing knowledge has served science well. In fact, it has been so ingrained in our culture that early psychologists adopted this traditional, linear approach in order to attain credibility with the world of science (Becvar & Becvar, 1993).

Unfortunately, time limitations and lack of administrative tolerance and support have interfered with systems orientations within the schools (Carlson & Sincavage, 1987). School systems obviously vary in the amounts of time, money, and support they are willing to make available for school counselors interested in family counseling. It is imperative that school counselors' training in family counseling be supported by school administrators. Administrative changes, such as the institution of flexible hours in scheduling, will be needed. Late afternoon and evening hours are necessary for families to maintain their school and employment responsibilities (Hinkle, 1993).

Collaborating with School Administrators

The organizational pattern in schools places the principal at the top of the hierarchy. However, Carlson (1992) has indicated that the degree to which power at this position is shared with counselors depends on individual personalities and competencies. An example of administrative support is found in the Topeka Public Schools described by Merrill et al. (1992). Administrators need to "...sanction and support staff time, money for equipment, and training/learning materials. The school district where the program is to be placed must have a belief in the role of clinical services in the schools" (Merrill et al., p. 411).

As noted earlier, school counselors working with families will need flexible schedules so that they can work after typical school hours and possibly on week-ends if necessary. Most family sessions will require about one hour; however, an hour and fifteen minutes is more realistic in many cases due to the number of people who may need to speak. As a result, school counselors will need to adjust their schedules accordingly. Likewise, Merrill et al. (1992) have indicated that flexible work schedules are helpful in providing family counseling services in the schools. In addition, the school counselor should begin with a limited number of cases. He or she should use video tape for educational and training purposes and should also use a one-way mirror. Participants in the Topeka Public Schools program rated the following training methods in order of preference: viewing tapes, discussions, reading, attending lectures, and role playing.

School systems vary in the amounts of time, money, and support available for school counselors wanting to do family counseling (McDaniel, 1981). School counselors who desire re-training in family counseling will need to obtain support from school administrators. "Money talks" is how Woody and Woody (1994) have described the rationale for school administrators potential support for family assessment and intervention in the schools. In the long run, money can be saved if early family/school interventions are utilized.

Various types of interactions surface when families and schools come in contact. Power and Bartholomew (1987) have

Family Counseling in the Schools:

described five types of relationships: 1) The avoidant relationship which is inflexible and lacks communication and planning; 2) The competitive relationship characterized by each system believing it is superior to the other; 3) Merged relationships which have common goals, but lack separation between the school and family; 4) The one-way relationship in which one system attempts to communicate while the other system does not reciprocate; and 5) Collaborative relationships which are reciprocal in communication and result in positive decision-making for the child, family, and school.

Today's school counselor is responsible for more than career guidance. Comprehensive interventions within an educational realm involving human development are paramount. Base support from teachers, parents, students, and administrators is essential for such interventions. A community support system also is needed. This service may include consultation and advice from community mental health, social service, and other agencies. An advisory committee can assist with direction and can provide a foundation for understanding the counseling program. Determining the make-up of the advisory committee should be a joint venture between administrators, teachers, and counselors. Interested parent groups, youth groups, business and industry, and civic and county government personnel would be good candidates for the advisory committee (Rye & Sparks, 1991). When new programs are developed and implemented, counselors and administrators need to have regular meetings to share information and concerns. Communication must be often, open, and honest. Counselors must get a sense of support from administrators that will foster the confidence to fulfill program needs. They need the administrators' respect for their skills and competence in family counseling as well as allocation of time and resources to make the family counseling program work effectively. Counselors must have planned discussions with principals for leadership support (Tindall & Sklare-Lancaster, 1981).

Moreover, school counselors need to articulate to their administrators their duties to the school and its students. Counselors must engage in anticipatory management that will positively influence their problem-solving and decision-making. Counselors need input and feedback from administrators when serving the critical needs of students, while, at the same time, counselors should understand that not everyone values their work in relation to school children. Interpersonal skills are vital in building rapport with school administrators. "Administrators have to be persuaded to see what counselors do, as a prerequisite to their knowing how to identify the critical skills school counselors exercise in dealing with students and others" (Eddy, Richardson, & Allberg, 1982, p. 123).

Conclusion

Training in family counseling should be a long-term commitment. Investing in good supervision and sticking to one training model during the initial training and family program development stage are important considerations. This plan makes effective and efficient learning possible since all counselors are developing the same knowledge and skills at the same time (Merrill et al., 1992).

Palmo et al. (1984) have indicated that to meet the challenge of providing family counseling services in the schools, school counselors will need additional training, new opportunities, and confidence in themselves as family counselors. Training should begin by learning one family counseling approach or model well and then applying it in the school (Overton & Hennies, 1988). (Models that have been proven effective in the schools are included in Chapters 5 and 6).

Family Counseling in the Schools:

Chapter Four

Additional Family Counseling Approaches In the Schools

Knowledge of additional family counseling approaches can be helpful to the school counselor. Although numerous methods may be beneficial, we have included three approaches that can be easily integrated into the school context. They include Milan Systemic Family Therapy, the Interactional View (MRI), and the Adlerian approach.

Milan Systemic Family Therapy

Of the three major approaches to family counseling to grow from the work of Gregory Bateson, the approach of the Milan group comes closest to Bateson's circular model for living systems (McKinnon, 1983). Although the original model continues to develop and change and individuals in the original Milan group have separated into different camps, leading to a number of Milan-based groups now in practice, practitioners continue to be more alike than different. The Milan groups' approach has been called "long brief" therapy (Goldenberg & Goldenberg, 1985) since they advocate few sessions (usually ten), that are four to six weeks apart. This developed out of a practical need to allow families time between visits due to long distances traveled, but this approach has worked well regardless of physical proximity to the place of counseling. The time between sessions allows the family to assimilate the ideas from the sessions and to put them into operation. This schedule is strictly followed. In fact, counselors will resist a family's request for an unscheduled meeting, and generally, such a request is seen as a sign of rapid change. The counselor will not help the family avoid this change by acquiescing to an exceptional meeting. The counselor allows the change to occur and then processes the result with the family at the next scheduled meeting.

Those who practice the Milan approach to family counseling follow a specific, predictable, and team-based method. There is either a single counselor or a male-female co-counseling team in contact with the family. The remainder of the team, which is usually at least two additional individuals, observes the family counseling sessions through a one-way mirror in order to provide input in the overall planning for the intervention with a family. The number of individuals involved, coupled with observation, would be the most difficult aspect of the Milan approach for school counselors to implement. The actual techniques used and the theoretical basis for the techniques are easily translated into a school counseling setting and videotape may be utilized instead of a one-way mirror.

The interview format has five stages: the pre-session, the session, the inter-session, the intervention, and the post-session discussion (Boscolo, Cecchin, Hoffman, & Penn, 1987). The entire counseling team meets prior to the initial visit with the family in a *pre-session,* to develop *hypotheses* about the presenting problem. One or two members of this team then meets with the family for the *session,* as the other team members observe from behind a one-way mirror, in order to validate or modify the hypotheses developed in the pre-session. After spending some time with the family (usually less than an hour), the treating counselor meets separately with other members of the team to develop treatment strategies in the *inter-session* stage. The team "behind the glass" is used in a strategic manner. They offer suggestions, and either confirm or disagree with conclusions made by the treating members of the team. Once developed, the *interventions* are taken back to the family session and delivered to the family. These interventions usually consist of either *positively connoting* the problem situation or the imposition of a *ritual.* The final stage involves the entire counseling team once again meeting for a *post-session discussion,* during which the family's reaction to the day's session is examined and the process of the next session is planned.

Milan Systemic Family Counseling assumes that the symptoms of a family's presenting problem serves a function within the dysfunctional family system. This usually involves the "sacrifice" of one of the family members who is the identified patient. The family member with the problem must continue to have the problem in order for the system to continue to function. Milan-based counseling attempts to change the dysfunctional family by interjecting a second-order change, which is a change at the system level rather than at the individual level. Solving the problem involves changing the interaction patterns within the family system. No specific behavioral goals are negotiated with the family. The change is a result of information being added to the system through the use of positive connotation, circular questioning, and behavior change task assignments (e.g., rituals and behavioral prescriptions) (Griffin, 1993).

A *positive connotation* is a message that the problem is logical and useful in the context of the family. This is similar to the *reframe* in other family counseling approaches. Everyone in the family is assumed to be motivated by the same desire to keep the family together. The family can better accept this information since it is a supportive, approving statement rather than a criticism. The predicament has in fact placed the family in a paradoxical situation. They have come for help for a problem in one of the family members, but they have found that the perceived problem promotes a good thing — *family cohesion.*

The *prescriptive intervention* is designed to bring about a change in a family's *rules* by focusing on changing the family myth that maintains the system. Prescribing a *ritual* directs the family to arrange some specific behavior, often a symptomatic behavior, such that it must occur under designated circumstances (e.g., only on certain days, or at certain times of the day, or at certain places). An example would be to direct a bedwetting child to wet the bed on Monday, Wednesday, and Friday nights.

Circular questioning encourages interaction within the family. It acts as an effective diagnostic tool as well as a therapeutic technique. The counselor asks questions that highlight differences in family members' perceptions. He or she may ask one child to compare the reactions of others in the family to a specific situation, or to rate feelings on a ten point scale. Family members may be asked to speculate about reactions to hypothetical events, such as a child who refuses to eat who suddenly starts to eat again, or parents getting a divorce.

The Milan model is one of the communication models of family counseling that approaches problems by recasting them as difficulties with family interactions. The goal of the Milan approach is to impart information to the family in order for the family to change rules which are repetitive and destructive.

The Interactional View - MRI

The Mental Research Institute (MRI) of Palo Alto, California has been associated with a number of prominent researchers and theorists in family counseling. Many of the current approaches used in family counseling grew from ideas which originated at the MRI. The basis of the MRI approach is that all behavior is communication. It is not possible to avoid communication and every communication has a content and a relationship aspect (Griffin, 1993).

Communications occur in many dimensions, much of which does not include spoken language. Communication can consist of body posture or movement, gestures, tone of voice, or facial expression, in addition to actual spoken words. All communication takes place on at least two levels: the basic content of the message occupies the first level, while information about the first-level message is on the second level. This information about the message is known as *metacommunication* (e.g., see Goldenberg and Goldenberg, 1985). Problems occur when the level-one message is contradicted by the information contained in the metacommunication (e.g., "This is a terrific party" is contradicted by the fact that the speaker is leaving before everyone else). Double-bind messages are perceived as contradictory. With a double-bind message the receiver is given information, while within the metacommunication there is a message to ignore the level one message. Such contradictory and difficult to understand communication patterns are typical of dysfunctional families. For example, a classic double bind is when a parent says, "Disregard what I just said." If the child does disregard what the parent said, the child actually regarded what the parent said.

As noted above, every communication also contains

information about the relationship. While this is certainly true in a family, it also is true in other systems or subsystems. When a teacher says, *"There is too much noise in this classroom,"* the amount of noise is only part of the message. The teacher also is telling the students that he or she is in charge and expects the students to get quiet. The subsequent response of the students tells the teacher whether they accept the teacher's definition of the relationship.

In order to fully understand a student's behavior, school counselors will have to understand both the teacher-student interaction and the interactions within the student's family. The first information available to the school counselor regarding the student's relationships may come from knowing who made the referral. If the referral is not from a parent, the counselor can subsequently gain useful information by knowing how the parent reacts to the referral and also by observing which parent makes first contact with the school. The patterns of communication that exist in a family tell much about the relationship of the sender and receiver of the message.

The MRI approach operates under a number of assumptions. Common to any systems approach is the assumption of *circular causality,* which assumes that behavior is at the same time a cause and a result of other behavior within the system. Counselors utilizing the interactional process of MRI must understand *equifinality* and *equipotentiality* (Watzlawick & Weakland, 1977). Equifinality means that different circumstances can lead to similar results; therefore, the input cannot be inferred from the output. Equipotentiality suggests that similar circumstances can, in fact, result in vastly different outcomes. Therefore, it cannot be assumed that similar events experienced by individuals will have similar effects. Every system is viewed as a whole in and of itself, and cannot be explained as the sum of its parts. Likewise, a family must be understood as a system and not simply as a combination of the members of the family.

According to an interactional model such as MRI, there are behaviors and responses in which healthy, functioning families routinely engage (Gurman & Kniskern, 1991). All of these behaviors may be characterized as effective communication. By contrast, one could expect that dysfunctional families would be unable to complete these tasks or would complete them in a less than satisfactory manner. A dysfunctional family would be unable to:

1. complete transactions, follow-up, and question the communication of others in the family;
2. interpret or recognize hostility
3. perceive themselves through the perspective of others;
4. understand their own self-perceptions;
5. tell one another how they manifest themselves;
6. share their hopes, fears, and expectations of each other with other family members;
7. disagree;
8. make decisions or choices;
9. gain through experience; learn with practice;
10. free themselves from the negative effects associated with past models;
11. give clear, congruent messages with a minimum of hidden messages and a minimum of difference between feelings and communicated message;
12. be direct in criticism, evaluation, fault finding, acknowledgment of observations, and reports of annoyance or puzzlement;
13. use language that clearly acknowledges attributes of the speaker and not those of the listener; and
14. be clear in gaining knowledge of the direction or intention of others by using direct questions.

In applying this model, the presenting problem is a representation of what the client wants to remove and should, therefore, be used by the school counselor as the index of change (Bodin, 1991). All behavior is shaped, maintained, or eliminated by the social interactions within the system in which the behavior occurs. Associated therapeutic tasks are initiated in order to remove the presenting problem. There is not necessarily a right or wrong behavior for a family or any of its members. MRI does not propose interventions in additional areas unless a family member has identified that area as a problem. Proponents of MRI prefer the term "conventional" instead of normal (Jackson, 1977). It is assumed that the presenting problem is a situation that has been mishandled and subsequently made worse; therefore, the family member(s) must do something other than what they have tried before in order to alleviate the problem. The counselor must not only completely understand the presenting problem, he or she must analyze previous efforts to solve it, determine what interactions have been maintaining it, and decide what changes will effectively relieve it.

There are a number of specific techniques that can be employed as agents of change in conducting family counseling when using the MRI model. Most school counselors will at some point use *relabeling* (similar to reframing and discussed previously), as a means of changing a family's interaction patterns. Relabeling puts the family in a bind while the school counselor provides a different perception for a situation that needs to be altered. As family members become more aware of the rules under which they operate, they gain an understanding that previous patterns can be changed. The goal is to modify the structure of the interactions and relationships in the family.

Additional techniques often utilized in MRI family counseling that may prove useful include, prescribing the symptom, replacing the symptom, the Devil's Pact, harnessing the self-fulfilling prophecy, and prescribing other behaviors. As discussed previously, when *prescribing the symptom,* the school counselor creates a double-bind for family members by directing them to continue to behave as they have, or perhaps to even exaggerate their efforts at producing the presenting problem. A girl who "talks back" to adults may be told to do so on a more frequent basis. This is easy to do for the family and undermines resistance by making it unnecessary. If the child, in order to be rebellious refuses to follow the directive, then the presenting problem will be reduced and a positive feedback system will begin for "not talking back." The family rule has now become more obvious and the notion that there was nothing that could be done to change the presenting problem has been challenged. Change is now much more possible for the family.

When change itself is resisted so strongly as to sabotage any therapeutic effort, the school counselor may need to engage a member of the family in what MRI refers to as a *"Devil's Pact."* The Devil's Pact is made when the school counselor has a family member agree beforehand to undertake whatever task the school counselor assigns. Agreeing to do any task sight unseen is the important element of the technique. The school counselor should then choose a task well within the ability of the individual. This may be a good opportunity to *replace the symptom* with a more acceptable behavior. For example, if a teenage boy refuses to get a job or be productive around the house, and instead stays in his room and listens to music, the parents and perhaps teachers are going to focus on this behavior as the problem. The school counselor can break through the resistance by entering into a Devil's Pact with the teen. The counselor can then *harness the self-fulfilling prophecy* that the teen will eventually leave his room by assigning mom or dad the task of noting on an hourly basis the teen's location. This should provide evidence that the teen is in fact out of his room a good bit more than the parents realize. The school counselor may assign a task to the teen which involves *prescribing other behaviors,* such as painting his room. This is likely to be completed, and since it is productive, it counters claims of nonproductiveness made by parents.

As counseling progresses there are likely to be modifications in the school counselor's role. Once the school counselor has explained the counseling process and has gained the trust, or at least the compliance of family members, his or her task then requires continued assessment, information gathering, and conceptualization of the presenting problem. The school counselor must develop and implement the behavior interventions that will eventually lead to changes in family interactional patterns and to the resolution of the presenting problem. It has been suggested that at termination the school counselor should express some pessimism regarding future progress or doubts that current gains can be maintained. This tactic would challenge family members to act on behalf of the changed patterns rather than return to old unproductive patterns of family functioning. The school counselor using MRI approaches must always remain in control and expect to be directive in his or her counseling process.

The Adlerian Approach

School counselors would benefit from knowledge of Adlerian family counseling principles. While Adler did not work with families — he focused on children, teachers, schools, and parents — he believed that behavior has a social meaning and should be understood within a social context. Adler surmised that the major social environment for children was the family. Hence, he was interested in associated social institutions which affected children, namely schools (Thomas, 1992). Adler also focused much of his energy on the practice of parenting. Several followers of Adler's concepts about parenting have developed parenting training systems such as the STEP program (see Dinkmeyer & McKay, 1982, 1983). Thomas (1992) has indicated that, in Adlerian family counseling and parenting groups, parents are taught to study their children's motivation to help their offspring meet their goals in positive ways. "By giving children encouragement, parents can help them to grow, to develop social interest, and to be happy, successful adults" (p. 246). In Adlerian family counseling, the counselor models parenting behavior while being optimistic and encouraging.

The counselor faces many tasks during the initial session. They include establishing rapport, gathering information, focusing on problems, generating hypotheses, recommending changes, encouraging the family, and, finally, summarizing the session. In gathering information, the counselor asks about the family members' birth order, which Adler referred to as the family constellation. Additional information obtained in the first session includes the relationship of the parents and developmental information concerning the children. Early recollections or memories and information about a typical day in family life also are discussed.

Adler believed that all behavior was goal directed and had a social direction. Families were thought of as holistic systems. "Give and take" marked acceptable behavior in families, while misbehavior arose from mistaken beliefs about how to fit into the family (Dinkmeyer & Dinkmeyer, 1991). What takes place between family members is crucial to Adlerian family counseling. Individuals experience problems when personal significance, as determined by a sense of belonging to the family social system, is not achieved. This is reflected in alienation, a lack of self-worth, and non-acceptance from other family members. Power and control comes from the need of individuals, as well as the family, to protect themselves via movements that are in order with their beliefs. Moreover, the family is more concerned with family relationships than individual goals. The family's lifestyle includes beliefs and goals

Family Counseling in the Schools:

which are used by the counselor to help the family understand difficulties (Dinkmeyer & Dinkmeyer). Family roles are assumed through the family constellation, as well as by subjective perceptions.

Adlerian family counselors believe that behavior always makes sense when viewed within the private logic of the family. Although the behavior may seem restrictive and problematic to outsiders, it has purpose and meaning for the family (Dinkmeyer & Dinkmeyer, 1991). Adlerian family counselors also perceive troubled families as facing issues concerning power, having inadequate social interest, or lacking in cooperation. Counselors adhering to an Adlerian framework will ask various questions in order to establish counseling goals. These may include,

> What does each person want to change in the family relationships and what is the major challenge facing the family?
> Is the family ready to change, rather than simply complain?
> What does it feel like to live in this family?
> What does the family believe and think about each of its members?
> What is the family atmosphere (e.g., autocratic, democratic)?
> What is the "lifestyle" of the family?
> What role and position does each family member hold?
> What rules govern the family?
> Where is the family in terms of cohesiveness and cooperation?
> What is the family's level of self-esteem, social intent, and family humor?
> What *boundaries* exist in the family?
> Who is the most resistant to change?
> What is the diagnosis as well as the assets of the family? (Dinkmeyer & Dinkmeyer, 1991).

Following these questions, the family counselor must formulate hypotheses regarding the family problem. Tentative hypotheses involve the purpose of the behavior and often focus on goal-directed misbehavior (Dinkmeyer & Dinkmeyer, 1991).

Sherman & Dinkmeyer (1987) have indicated that the counselor helps the family with change by redirecting power, finding new insight and understanding, refining goals, solving problems, resolving conflicts, enhancing empowerment, increasing social interests, developing new roles, and making a clear commitment to growth and positive change. Family members share their goals for counseling and make a commitment to change the family.

Adlerian family counseling adheres to the concept that all problems are relationship problems. As a result, conflict resolution skills are essential in family counseling. Dinkmeyer and Dinkmeyer (1991) advocate Dreikur's (1971) four-stage model of conflict resolution. This includes teaching family members to not overpower another member of the family, but, at the same time, to not give in. Secondly, real issues must be specified. Next, common ground or areas of agreement must be settled as well as the need to cooperate. Lastly, mutual participation in decision-making is needed.

During the family counseling process, the counselor is perceived as a leader and directs attention to family communication. Understanding how family members communicate with one another is imperative. Such communication may be verbal or nonverbal, from a superior or inferior position, and goal directed (e.g., to gain power, to get even, to please). Many problems within families may be due to a lack of communication skills. Adlerian family counselors teach families to communicate through modeling, identification and expression of feelings, use of "I" messages, and giving appropriate feedback (Dinkmeyer & Dinkmeyer, 1991). Family members learn in Adlerian family counseling how to communicate directly with one another.

Conclusion

Dinkmeyer & Dinkmeyer (1991) have indicated that Adlerian family counselors focus on the "real issues" and encourage the family to change. Encouragement includes *reframing* symptoms positively and identifying family strengths and assets.

Role reversal techniques and *paradoxical intention* also are used in Adlerian family counseling. By "wearing the other person's shoes," family members learn to relate to different

Family Counseling in the Schools:

feelings and beliefs within the family. Whereas, the prescription of a symptom (paradox) changes the symptom's purpose and brings it under conscious control. For example, asking a parent and child to argue for five minutes while the other parent times the argument changes the problem into something that can be controlled (i.e., begins at a specific time, has a definite ending, and lasts a specific amount of time).

To conclude, family meetings are a hallmark of Adlerian family counseling. The counselor asks the family to establish weekly meetings so as to facilitate communication, problem-solving, and, leisure and fun. Family meetings should allow for expressions of feelings, encouragement, and conflict resolution (Dinkmeyer & McKay, 1989; Thomas, 1992).

Chapter Five

Family Counseling Technique in the Schools

Effective family counseling in the schools will require information on family counseling theory and clinical technique. The brevity, as well as the specificity, of this book limits the amount of family counseling technique presented. What is offered, however, is technical information that is helpful in establishing and practicing successful family counseling in the schools. Information on additional techniques is obviously needed and can be achieved by reading the materials suggested in Appendix A as well as by seeking additional professional training. Family counseling that has a favorable ending must start with an equally favorable beginning — the telephone contact.

Initial Telephone Contact

The first telephone contact is crucial in family counseling. The telephone call can provide the counselor with valuable information regarding family functioning and can assist the counselor in preparing for the first family session. Prata (1990) has indicated that the initial telephone call is the foundation of the counseling process because hypotheses regarding the family are first established at this time. Prata has developed a telephone recording chart that is helpful for the counselor. We have modified this chart to facilitate the information gathering process for school counselors (see Table 1).

Family Counseling in the Schools:

Table 1. Telephone Recording Chart for Initial Family Contact

Caller:

Phone No.

Referral Source:___ Teacher ___ Parent ___ Student
___Principal ___Coach
___ Other (_____)

Address:

_____

_____

Family Residents/Age	Position or Role in Family
_____	_____
_____	_____
_____	_____
_____	_____
_____	_____

Caller's definition of the problem:_____

_____

_____

Tentative Diagnosis:_____

Invited to first session:_____

_____

Additional comments: _____

_____

_____

_____

_____

_____

_____

Prata (1990) has indicated that the telephone record is best used when the data is studied *before* the family comes to the first session. During the telephone conversation other cases will come to the counselor's mind and will help direct the line of questioning. Additional important information can be addressed in the comments section of the telephone chart.

It is important to involve as many relevant family members as possible (Merrill et al., 1992). If a family member crucial to the counseling outcome refuses to take part, the family may be told about the limited opportunities for success (Merrill et al.). This information can result in the family seeking out the nonparticipating member and encouraging his or her attendance. One of the most important aspects of the initial telephone contact is to determine who is to attend the first meeting at school. This consideration includes which school personnel as well as which family members will attend. It is typically important to ask the parents to bring to the first session all members of the household. Thus, in addition to nuclear family members, a grandparent or foster child could be asked to attend. After the initial session, the counselor will need to indicate who is to return to the second session and he or she must speculate about the potential attendance patterns for future sessions.

Although Nicoll (1992) has suggested that sessions with multiple school personnel can foster a defensive posture by the parents, this is not always the case. In some instances, a student's teachers, parents, and principal could be asked to attend a family session if such a plan were strategically sound. When first meeting with a family, it is wise to refer to the parents formally, using their surnames (e.g., Mr. Smith, Mrs. Smith, Dr. Smith, etc.). When rapport has been sufficiently established, often during the first meeting, it is reasonable to ask if you may address the parents by their first names. This informality reduces the distance between the counselor and parent (Nicoll, 1992).

Talmon's (1990) guidance in family counseling is quite helpful. When the school counselor asks, "Who can be helpful in assisting the student in solving his or her problem?" - parents and other family members should come to mind. It is critical to include in the counseling process those people who are involved in the student's social and environmental context.

Family Counseling in the Schools:

Including only school personnel neglects the systemic nature of the student's problem and, therefore, may create a vacuum in the helping process. This does not minimize the logic of utilizing the smallest effective systemic unit to manage a problem. The family systems perspective emphasizes the need to include the family, at least temporarily, in the conceptualization of the helping process.

When one parent is not committed to family counseling, it is a good idea for the cooperating parent to ask the resistive parent to attend (Talmon, 1990). Parents having difficulty getting their partner to attend may need assistance from the school counselor. Such assistance may range from providing structured suggestions for communicating to actually placing a telephone call to the resistant parent. "School counseling" and "meeting" are purposefully used instead of "family counseling" and "therapy session" so as to reduce resistance to participation.

Unfortunately, mothers tend to be the cooperating parent and fathers the resistive parent. When mothers need assistance getting their partners to attend the family counseling session, increasing their confidence level and educating them regarding different verbal approaches are very helpful. Mothers can learn to solicit their significant other in an engaging conversation. In addition, it is often helpful to ask the mother to invite the father to school. For example, the counselor may say, "Ms. Southern, would you like to ask Joy's father to come in, or would you like for me to do it?" (Talmon, 1990). If the counselor eventually calls the father to invite him to school, it is important to utilize the same bonding processes on the telephone that are used in personal counseling. For example, the counselor may ask, "I'm sure you would agree with me that you care about and love your son enough to come in for a family meeting." Once the family agrees to attend a family meeting, it is important to be ready to record important aspects of family information and functioning.

After the initial session, a simple format for recording information about the session is helpful. A family conference progress form can facilitate record keeping and counseling progress (see Table 2).

Table 2. Family Conference Progress Form

Counselor: _____
School: _____
Date: _____
Conference #: _____

Name of Student: _____ Grade _____ NOTES:
Reason for Referral: _____
Referred By : _____
Name of parent(s) in home: _____
Name of parent(s) not in home: _____
  (*denotes step-parent; **denotes deceased)
Siblings in same school:
_____ Grade _____
_____ Grade _____
Other siblings:
_____ School _____
_____ School _____
Student's definition or description of the problem:
_____
_____
_____
_____

Parents' definition or description of the problem:
_____
_____
_____

Counselor's/Teacher's conceptualization of the
problem:
  (Hypothesis): _____
_____

  Solution/Directives: _____
_____

Barriers to success (e.g., student, family, school?):
_____

Next Appointment _____ Who is to attend:
_____

Family Counseling in the Schools:

Although use of this progress form is crucial following the initial session, it is beneficial to treatment planning if it is used after every session.

Family counseling sessions may take various routes in resolving the interrelated school and family difficulties. From a systemic perspective, the family experiencing trouble is in need of someone within the family to express its problem. Such action is typically manifested in the first session when the family is stressed and ready for change. However, the counselor will need to keep some focus on uncovering family behavior patterns, structures, and beliefs that maintain problems (Nicoll, 1992).

The initial family counseling process during the first session can be broken down into four stages or phases, namely the *social, problem, interaction,* and *goal-setting* stages (Haley, 1976). During the social stage the counselor joins the family and makes them feel comfortable. Everyone in the session is then asked to share his or her theories about the problem in the problem stage. The family discusses the various aspects of the problem during the interaction stage, while the goal-setting stage focuses on interventions and directives to solve the problems (Haley, 1976).

The Social Stage

The first stage is the social stage (Haley, 1976). This stage is a critically important part of the first session. It is important to socialize with the family by joining or bonding with each family member. Resistive family members will need more attention than those members motivated towards family counseling. It is important that the social stage continue until a feeling of rapport is established. This rapport is crucial for the relationship between the counselor and parents. For example, if a father is disengaged and continues in this manner, the counselor can rightfully hypothesize that the father may directly or indirectly sabotage any potential positive changes to which the family may have initially agreed. Any family member (or school personnel) believed to be the most resistive, will need some additional regard. Moreover, beginning family counseling sessions with the presenting problem may suggest to the parents that the difficulties are their fault (Nicoll, 1992).

The school counselor should avoid this situation. If the family persists in talking about the problem "prematurely," the counselor should take control of the session and ensure that a socialization stage occurs.

Family members should always be treated with respect and rapport. This rapport should invariably be well established, particularly with parents. School counselors need to be aware of the various ways in which they can be *subtly disrespectful.* For example, most parents attending a family session due to the identified behavioral problems of one of their school children will have, on some level, feelings of inadequacy or failure as parents. Therefore, it could be perceived as indirectly disrespectful to bring this inadequacy to their attention, directly and publicly. The authors generally refer to this as "rubbing their noses in it." In fact, it may be strategically sound during the first session to de-emphasize parental responsibility, even when the parents admit inadequacy. This assists the counselor in appearing to be unbiased and supportive of the parental hierarchy. Opening comments to the family may include the following:

> Counselor: I am so pleased that you could all come to school today. It is always a pleasure to meet with a student's family. Mr. (or Mrs.) Smith, how has your day been?
>
> Mr. Smith: Alright I guess. I've been thinking about John's problems here at school. This whole thing has been so upsetting.
>
> Counselor: I'm sure that you have a lot of thoughts about your son and family. I was wondering if I could take some time and get to know each of you a little better.
>
> Mr. Smith: Sure. That would be fine.
>
> Counselor: Okay. Well, Mr. Smith, what do you do for a living?

This initial conversation makes a social process possible and provides the counselor with an opportunity to assess the family's interactions before the problem is addressed. Subtle evaluations can be made by the observant counselor during this process. For example, who sits where and what may these seating arrangements mean? Who speaks readily? Who is taciturn? Who speaks for another family member? It is important not to begin the problem stage before the socialization process is complete. However, the social stage must end at some point so that the problem can be addressed by the family. School counselors who do not eventually introduce the problem stage may be perceived by the family as being incompetent.

The Problem Stage

Notwithstanding the importance of the social stage, it is essential that the social stage not become the major focus of the session; the problem must be addressed. If the problem does not receive adequate attention, a family member may feel that the critical issue has been ignored and this perception could inevitably undermine any therapeutic progress.

Solving school problems should always begin with an analysis of the problem from a systemic perspective. A clear idea of the interactional cycle and context in which the problem exists is crucial (Amatea, 1989; Hinkle, 1994). Since the relationships associated with the problem-bearer often maintain the problem, they will require attention when developing a solution. Case conceptualization is paramount to this change process.

Amatea (1989) has indicated that a systemic point of view emphasizes the "problem-bearer" and those with whom the problem-bearer interacts while he or she searches for solutions. People may make repeated attempts to solve a problem in a particular way because they believe that their solution should work (Amatea, 1989). As a result, Amatea (1989) reports that clients feel that the problem is extremely serious and that they are inadequate, rather than believing that the solution is deficient.

It is the school counselor who must decide what to do with a case. Although the referrer initially defines the problem, there may be many competing hypotheses to explain the situation and what needs to be done about it. Amatea (1989) has indicated that when deciding which hypothesis to use, "the practitioner must consider how much the terms implied in such a perspective limit her ability to resolve the problem effectively and make her own decision concerning whom to work with" (p. 58). Some important aspects in deciding with whom to work, is to consider who has the most *power,* who is in the most distress, and who is to gain from positive change.

The problem stage is the *getting-down-to-business* segment of the initial session (Haley, 1976). The problem should be both addressed by each family member and defined by the counselor in a palatable way for the family. To facilitate this process, the counselor can utilize reframing or relabeling of the presenting problem. A good lead statement may sound like this:

> Counselor: I understand that John has been having some problems in the classroom. Mrs.(or Mr.) Smith, can you tell me some more about him so that I can better understand the situation?

An alternate lead question may include:

> Counselor: Now that I've had an opportunity to meet your family, I'd like to ask you an important question Mr. Smith (or Mrs. Smith). What is your *theory* of the situation here at school?"

Defining the problem should include the student's, the family's, and the school's (including teachers' and principal's) description of the problem, information concerning previous attempts to solve the problem, and what the student, family, and school believe should be done to solve the problem. Problems should be defined within a specific frame or context (Amatea, 1989). The more one tries to solve a problem within a context without changing the context, the more futile the attempts to correct the behavior will appear. In order to ensure that student, teacher, or family member will try a new behavior, the school counselor has to present it in a manner that is attractive as well as acceptable (Amatea, 1989; Hinkle, 1994).

In child school problems, an adult (parent or teacher) often is more bothered by the problem behavior than the child is (Amatea, 1989). Then why work with the child alone? For example, if a teacher describes a student behavior as problematic in the classroom, what may be under the surface is that the teacher feels overwhelmed and frustrated. Parents describing the behavior may be giving the school counselor the message that they believe they are inadequate or incompetent in their parenting skills. However, adults are often the most prepared and the most effective in helping children change (Amatea, 1989).

During the problem stage, the counselor may hypothesize that there is a marital problem between the parents. School counselors with family counseling training will not find this information intimidating, and the chances for a successful outcome are increased when the counselor formulates this hypothesis (Palmo et al., 1984). However, such a theory should not be readily shared with the parents, especially not in the presence of the children. Parents come to family counseling at school because of their child's school problem, not their relationship problem. It is important to respect this fact and maintain the parents' theory about their child's problem (Minuchin, 1974), but, at the same time, develop a plan to improve the relationship. The counselor should resist a marital problem as the cause of the school problem if it is offered as a theory by the parents. For example, if the parents were to say, "We think our marital problems have affected Junior's school performance," the counselor would respond with something like, "I'm not so sure about that. I've worked with hundreds of children and they are rather ingenious at developing some of their own problems, in a creative sort of way." This approach avoids embarrassing the parents, lets them "off the hook" for the first session, and increases the chances that they will return (possibly at some point to address their marriage).

The Interaction Stage

The interaction stage is critical. It is at this time that the counselor encourages the family to discuss the problem among themselves (Haley, 1976). Haley (1976) has indicated that when any two people are talking, the counselor must be ready to introduce a third person into the conversation. Examples may include a father and son disagreeing about a family issue. The counselor could interject by asking the mother or another sibling what they think or feel about the issue. During the interaction stage, the counselor can shift from talking about problems at school to associated problems at home. School problems should be addressed first, however.

The Goal-Setting Stage

The goal-setting stage defines desired changes and includes directives for positive family outcomes (Haley, 1976). Everyone in the family should be allowed an opportunity to share what changes they would like. Haley has indicated that the counselor is essentially making a contract with the family. For this reason, the defined goals should be as clear as possible. Haley has stated that the problem the counselor settles on "must be a problem the family wants changed" and "put in a form that is solvable" (p. 40). This allows the counselor to focus on the family's goal while achieving other goals that will assist the family.

Directives are often used in family counseling. Directives entail family members agreeing to do something that will help them solve their problem. This technique may be difficult for some school counselors since they have not customarily told clients what to do. However, once counselors accept the fact that they typically tell clients what to do (e.g., "Tell me about that problem." "How was your week?"), then they will find that giving directives is not difficult and is quite helpful. Directives may range from giving good advice to changing family patterns.

It is extremely important to motivate families to follow directives. A direct approach would entail the counselor agreeing with the family that their issues are problematic and then joining with them in solving their problems. For an uncooperative family a counselor may take an indirect approach toward a solution. Successful indirect approaches often lead to more direct approaches later. Some of the ways to ensure that families follow agreed upon directives include the counselor exerting his or her power as an expert, using the power among the various family members (particularly parents), or adopting techniques developed to deal with resistance. Haley has a good illustration of dealing with a resistive family: "I'm going to ask you to do something that you will think is silly, but I want you to do it anyway" (p. 57). Debate about the directive is cut off because the family cannot say that the directive is silly since the counselor has already said it.

It is always necessary to check on the progress of the directive task at the next session. If the counselor does not ask about the homework, the family may perceive that the counselor arranges frivolous directives that are not important. If the counselor minimizes noncompliance with homework, the family also may misinterpret the counselor's motives. For example, if a family indicates that they have not completed agreed upon homework, it is not good for the counselor to respond by saying, "That's all right." It would increase the chances that future homework will be completed if the counselor said something to this effect: "I'm sorry you didn't complete your homework. We will never know how much that would have helped you."

Contrary to some viewpoints (see Nicoll, 1992), the authors contend that parents can have an impact on their child's school behavior. However, Nicoll has recommended that parents and teachers be asked to work on different facets of the same problem. Following agreement to this request, a series of interventions, or directives, can be planned and strategically sequenced. Strategies can include, but are certainly not limited to, shifting hierarchies, setting appropriate boundaries at school and home, prescribing the symptom (paradox), making a problem behavior an ordeal, and reframing behavior metaphorically (Aliotti, 1992; Haley, 1984, 1987).

Strategies must be thought out from a sequential perspective. For example, if the intervention does not work, it may be because it was the right directive at the wrong time, the wrong directive and the right time, or most unfortunately, the wrong directive at the wrong time.

Behavioral Metaphors

Aliotti (1992) has indicated that in the beginning stages of working with a family, more thinking about the case is needed than action. In essence, the counselor must think about the family in terms of metaphors and hypotheses generated about the case. Metaphoric language about behavior and its meaning is necessary for thinking about families in systemic terms.

Metaphors of the literary type offer the reader a different understanding regarding a concept, whereas metaphors of the behavioral type offer the observer a different understanding regarding the associated social context. Expanding a metaphor from the literal to the behavioral allows the counselor to understand a child's behavior from a social perspective (Peeks, 1989). Barker (1992) has reported that "When direct communications are ineffective, conveying the same message by means of a metaphor may succeed" (pp. 72-73). Metaphors can be used in various ways. For example, Barker has discussed metaphorical stories, analogies, tasks and rituals, objects, and relationships. For example, one of the authors consulted with a boy experiencing extreme problems at school. His parents were going through a divorce. His mother could never talk about the problem because it was so painful. The boy, as well as his mother, had seen the father being affectionate with another woman. The author successfully helped the boy without discussing the divorce and infidelity. The term "secret" was used throughout the counseling and his grandparents helped him to deal with it in a "secretive" manner.

Peeks (1989) provides another example of behavioral metaphor:

Eleven-year-old Jenny was unable to walk and was hospitalized with painful leg swelling of unknown origin; she was referred to the children's psychiatric unit. Mother and children were separated from Father after moving across country when Mother's father became ill. Grandfather engaged Mother in a death-bed promise to care for his wife, which immobilized Mother. Jenny's psychosomatic inability to take steps without pain was metaphorical of Mother's inability to take steps to resume her life with her husband in another part of the country. It would be painful to leave her mother and break a promise to her dead father.

The professional asked Grandmother to release Jenny's mother from the death-bed promise and directed Mother and Father to make a three-month plan for their lives. This procedure would relieve Jenny of her admitted worry about the possible divorce and permit her to use all her physical and emotional energy for healing. After Mother and Father told Jenny they planned to reunite the family, her leg immediately began to improve... (p. 22).

Similarly, Madanes (1981) defines metaphors associated with intervention as the disturbed behavior which needs to be given up in order to end its use to the system. The counselor needs to be aware of similarities between the child and parents' behavior (Madanes). Relabeling or reframing become quite useful in the metaphoric process (also discussed in Chapter 2).

Family Counseling in the Schools:

Relabeling

Redefining problem behavior is commonly referred to as *relabeling* or *reframing*. By changing the name for the behavior and giving it a different and often positive connotation, the family can perceive behavior in a different light which renders it more in their control and, thus, changeable. This relabeling enables the student to have the freedom to choose other ways of relating. Relabeling also is effective in dealing with resistive families.

Families may label a child as disruptive, disturbed, or crazy in order to stabilize a conflictual family relationship, often between the mother and father (i.e., spousal subsystem) (Power & Bartholomew, 1987). Relabeling or reframing helps family members and school personnel alter their perceptions of the problem (Overton & Hennies, 1988). It is important to do this in a manner that respects both the family's and the school's values. Frames of reference that need altering within the school context include the medical perspective (e.g., specific developmental disorders such as learning disabilities) and the moral outlook (e.g., irresponsibility, lazy, worthless) (Nicoll, 1992). Examples of common relabels are illustrated in Table 3.

Table 3. Examples of Common Relabels Used in Family Counseling in the Schools

Behavior	Relabel
Withdrawn	Taking care of personal needs
Lying	Protecting others from the truth
Tardy	Appreciates flexible scheduling
Anger	Open and expressive
Seductive	Attracted to others
Stealing	Good knowledge of what is needed
Dropping out	Knows exactly what he or she wants
Drug abuse	Likes to take risks
Disrespect to teachers	Values own opinion
Fighting	Taking up for one's self
Need to control others	Appreciates a structured environment

Crying	Sensitive and expressive
Failing Grades	Has other interests
Sexual acting-out	Uninhibited; enjoys freedom
Depression	Sees things very clearly
Cheating	Achievement oriented

Effectively Dealing with Resistance

It is helpful to deal with resistance from different approaches. One approach includes using the skill of one-downmanship (Amatea, 1989; Overton & Hennies, 1988). This technique involves the counselor putting himself down hierarchically in relation to some family member or members. For example, placing oneself lower in a family whose father is perceived as impotent, will allow the father the opportunity to assume a more powerful role without hinderance from the counselor. This can be further illustrated with another brief example. If a student is demonstrating a lack of ownership for a problem, the school counselor could deliberately act confused about the student's description of the problem. Enough confusion for the student may result in the student clearing up the puzzle for the counselor by more accurately depicting the problem. During this process the counselor has assumed a one-down position in relation to the student in terms of who the authority on the problem is — the student!

The development of a personal sense of humor also helps when dealing with resistant families. Many counselors lack this type of atmosphere about their counseling and need to make plans to include some levity in their family counseling approaches (Overton & Hennies, 1988).

Overton and Hennies (1988) and others have suggested that school counselors learn to relate to families on the latter's terms. This approach reduces resistance and puts the family in a position to follow helpful suggestions and directives. The school counselor must realize that families have a unique language that must be addressed and respected.

Lastly, when dealing with families, especially resistive families, it is important to realize that many cases last only one or two sessions (Overton & Hennies, 1988; Talmon, 1990). Counselors must seek approaches to counseling that are sensitive to time

Family Counseling in the Schools:

constraints and are efficient (Downing & Harrison, 1992). The effective counselor should operate on the notion that counseling opportunities are limited and they must be exploited to their fullest (Downing & Harrison). Therefore, it is crucial that appropriate levels of joining occur and that the family is shown the respect they deserve. The authors contend that situations in which the counseling is not going well, the counselor has not put enough emphasis on the joining or bonding process. The following case depicts several family counseling techniques.

An Example of a Family Counseling Intervention in School

Family Counseling Session #1
Mr. And Mrs. East

Dr. W.: Hello. You are Mr. and Mrs. East, right? The principal said that you wanted to talk with me. What did you want to talk to me about?

Mrs. E.: We found out a short time ago that my husband, David (Mr. East), has cancer and someone told us that you would be a good person to talk to. We are seeing the doctor tomorrow and we thought that we could see you before hand. The main thing is that we have a son, named Heath, who is 12 years-old. He is a student here. Heath is a very bright student. He usually makes very good grades, and he plays on the school soccer team. Lately he has seemed distracted, his grades have fallen a bit - but not terribly, and he is talking of quitting soccer.

Mr. E.: He talks about quitting soccer about this time every year, but he never does.

Mrs. E.: I know but I can't help but think that maybe he senses something is going on at home, you know with the doctor's visits and both of us being kind of on edge. We don't exactly know how to go about telling him or when it would be a good time to tell him. His father will probably be receiving some kind of treatment. They are going to determine tomorrow at the appointment in what direction they are going to go.

Dr. W.: So you are not sure about where the course of treatment is going, and you haven't said anything to

Heath about why you have been going to the hospital?

Mrs. E.: Right.

Dr. W.: Before we get into this any further I would like to know a bit more about your family if that's all right.

Mrs. E.: Heath is David's adopted son. He is mine from a previous marriage. We have a two year-old daughter, Mandy. David and I have been married about three years. We have almost no contact with my first husband's family now.

Dr. W.: I see. Can you tell me about your first husband?

Mrs. E.: My first husband passed away when Heath was small. Heath was about five years old. My husband had a heart attack on the job. He was a carpenter. He was in the hospital for a few days and had another heart attack, apparently, and died. Heath never got to see his dad once he was in the hospital. Heath was at the hospital, they just wouldn't let him go back to the room, but he was in the waiting areas and such.

Dr. W.: Mr. East, how did you and your wife meet?

Mr. E.: We were both at a friend's house for a July 4th cookout. Actually, I sort of took up with Heath first. We were kicking a soccer ball around while everyone else was talking or cooking. He invited me to one of his soccer games and I asked Teresa, his mom, if it would be all right for me to go. She said sure and told me to come sit with her during the game. It kinda went from there.

Dr. W.: So your relationship with Heath is a good one?

Mr. E.: Yes.

Mrs. E.: I tell them sometimes they should have gotten married and left me at an orphanage, hah. Seriously, David has been really good for Heath.

Dr. W.: I like soccer myself, Mr. East - May I call you David?

Mr. E.: Sure. . . Mike.

Dr. W. : Mike is fine. And you are Teresa, is that right?

Mrs. E.: Yes, I really like that better than Mrs. East. It sounds like I'm old or something.

Dr. W.: I know what you mean, being called Doctor sometimes makes me feel the same way. I was asking David about soccer. From where does your interest in soccer come?

Family Counseling in the Schools:

Mr. E.: I played a little in school in Chicago where I grew up and I've coached a peewee team or two.

Dr. W.: I wish I had time to do some coaching, I think I would like that. You have to be pretty good with kids though, I would guess.

Mrs. E.: David is really good with kids. It's one of the reasons I was drawn to him initially.

Dr. W.: Kids can be a lot of fun.

Mrs. E.: And the occasional headache, but worth it. I love my kids.

Dr. W.: It's the really good moms who have headaches and worries over their kids, right? Let's get back to your concerns regarding Heath. You said he was five when his father died and he didn't get to see his dad before he died?

Mrs. E.: Right. He was around the hospital but they wouldn't let him go to the room, so it was kind of a bad experience for him because he knows that his dad died at a hospital. And we may be in a situation where he will have to spend some time at the hospital with us again. We don't know whether to take him there when we go, or, how to tell him what's going on because, as I said, he is a bright child. I am afraid he may already have picked up on just enough to make it scary for him.

Dr. W.: You don't want to scare him, and you are concerned for the effect the situation will have on school for him. I think those are important issues for the family to look into.

Mrs. E.: We just didn't know at what point we should tell him.

Dr. W.: David, how do you feel about the treatments and what the doctors have said so far?

Mr. E: Well, I have complete confidence in the doctors. They are curing this kind of thing everyday. I'm not worried about it. I think they know what they are doing and that they'll take care of me.

Dr. W.: Okay. So you are leaving it to them? Leaving it in their hands to take care of.

Mr. E: Right.

Mrs. E.: He is but...

Dr. W.: You're not so sure?

Mrs. E.: Well, he is not really getting that involved in the details. He just more or less goes ahead and does what you've got to do. But I am not so sure about these guys. You know, I don't know that they are doing everything that they can do right now. We'll just have to see at our appointment tomorrow what they decide for treatment.

Dr. W.: So you're not so sure about these doctors in particular or doctors in general?

Mrs. E.: Well, I don't really know these doctors.

Dr. W.: You have a *protective skepticism.*

Mrs. E.: I had doctors in the past that I feel like could have done more than they did.

Dr. W.: Are you speaking of your first husband's situation?

Mrs. E.: Yes, as a matter of fact. I sometimes think they could have taken an extra step maybe prevented that second heart attack. I don't want to take any chances with David. We've just gotten our family back together a few years ago. The only experience I have had with hospitals, except for the experience of when my ex-husband died, is Heath had a broken arm shortly after David and I got married. That was an Emergency Room kind of deal and it was over with quickly. It's like they don't take that good of care of you.

Dr. W.: You and Heath handled that situation okay; it went fairly smoothly?

Mrs. E.: Yes, it was quick. But I wasn't too thrilled with the treatment he got. I just didn't think they gave him the care they should, especially for a child.

Dr. W.: So you had some problems with that treatment?

Mrs. E.: Yes, I guess I questioned what they were doing.

Dr. W.: Did Heath handle it okay?

Mrs. E.: Yes, but he was upset. I guess the whole thing was scary for him. He was just upset. The whole thing upset him quite a bit.

Dr. W.: Being at the hospital, being hurt?

Mrs. E.: Yes.

Dr. W.: It must have made him feel better knowing Mom was nearby.

Mrs. E.: Well I hope so. He didn't have to spend the night. But being there was enough for him.

Dr. W.: So your experience and Heath's experience, up until

this point, with hospitals, besides your two children being born of course, is your first husband's situation there and then Heath's broken arm, which was in the Emergency Room? They were both traumatic.

Mrs. E.: Yes, everything was wild. Pretty much we are all healthy except for those instances. It seems sometimes that they could take more care. Check into things a little bit further. I'm not comfortable with it.

Dr. W.: Okay. Tell me about your concerns with telling Heath about David.

Mrs. E.: I think with the way things have happened in the past, it is going to be very upsetting to Heath no matter when we tell him, or how. Like I said, we have just gotten our family back together. He's got him a new dad and it's very hard to replace someone in your life that you've lost. He and David are very close.

Dr. W.: You did say David had adopted him?

Mrs. E.: Right, and he has been very good for Heath. I just think it's going to be devastating for Heath to have to lose his dad again if something like that were to come about. I know that's something that crosses your mind when you hear "cancer" — is that you are going to lose that person. I think that it is really unfair. I think that his dad was here one minute and gone the next. He didn't really get to see his dad. He was here and then gone so quickly that he didn't really have time to see him before he died. I don't think he is going to be able to deal with it if it happens again. It's just not fair.

Dr. W.: Well, when you and Heath were alone after your husband died, you dealt with that okay?

Mrs. E.: Yeah, it took some time. We stuck together and did a lot of things together and supported one another.

Dr. W.: It is apparent that Heath has felt taken care of by you or he would not have been secure enough to do as well in school as he has.

Mrs. E.: Yeah, as far as I can tell he has been pretty stable. He was certainly glad to have David when that came about though.

Dr. W.: So David helped him out a whole lot when he joined the family?

Mrs. E.: Yeah. Both of us kind of turned to David to fill a

void that was there, that we were so used to having.

Dr. W.: And now you and David have a child as well, a daughter.

Mrs. E.: Yes. Mandy is wide open and a lot of fun but she can really wear you down.

Dr. W.: I bet so.

Mrs. E.: Don't you think that David ought to be more concerned about all of this? About his kids and me and what could happen.

Dr. W.: (Pauses and looks at Mr. East).

Mr. E: You know something like what I have or what they say that I might have -- there's no doubt in my mind that this is going to be alright. And it seems to me that it would make matters worse to sit and worry about something that's not going to happen. That could have a detrimental effect and there's no use doing it. Because I am going to be fine.

Mrs. E.: I know, but if someone doesn't check into all of this, it could happen.

Mr. E: I'm here now and they are going to look at me tomorrow. I'm doing my part and I'm just trying to convince you that I am going to be fine.

Dr. W.: David, do you feel that Heath should not be told what is going on?

Mr. E: I don't think we should worry Heath with things that might happen or could happen. If we get positive proof that there is something bad going to happen with me, then we can approach Heath and discuss it with him. Why scare the kid, he's had a bad time in his life as it is. There is no need to go telling him "You know, I might die here in a few weeks. I hope I don't, but...." Why scare the child with something that may never be?

Mrs. E.: The thing that worries me, Mike, is like I said, Heath is a really smart child. He may already have some idea that there is a problem. Even if he doesn't he may hear me on the phone with my mom telling her of my concerns with the treatments that are coming up, or we don't know what treatments, or about David not being assertive enough with the doctors - even to mention the treatments. Heath is smart enough that he is going to know that something is up. And rather then him decide in his mind himself how bad it is or what, I'd rather give him some of the facts. I don't mean medical school here or anything. I think he needs to know enough that he can feel comfortable that they are doing something for his new dad.

Dr. W.: I hear your husband saying that he thinks you should only tell Heath what you are sure of. So as not to scare him. Is that correct David?

Mr. E: Yeah.

Dr. W.: You're not saying to keep him in the dark but only tell him what you know. Is that correct?

Mr. E: When we get solid facts about my condition, then we can tell Heath. But we don't need to speculate with Heath about what might happen. He just needs to know what we know, not what we think or suspect.

Mrs. E.: I know, but you need to tell him that there are treatments for it and what kind of treatments. And not make him think that they are going to zap you off somewhere and put you in a hospital room, and he isn't going to see you again during the treatments. He needs to know that he will see you again while they are giving you the treatments and that you'll have normal functioning and that there will be some side effects with whatever they are going to use as a treatment.

Dr.W.: A lot of those points seem to make sense to me as well.

Mr. E: That's fine once they determine what kind of treatments and what they are going to do, then we will discuss that with Heath. But I don't think he needs to know things that we aren't sure of.

Dr. W.: Does Heath know where you are now?

Mrs. E.: No, he is in class.

Dr. W.: Okay. This sounds like an agreement on what to do, which is to tell Heath, but a difference on how to go about it. While it is a good idea to talk to him together, in this case it may make sense for one of you to do most of the talking.

Mrs. E.: Well David, do you want to tell Heath then? Why don't you tell Heath and I won't say anything, but I do want to be in there with him when you tell him.

Dr. W.: Your being there is essential, Teresa. It does sound like a good idea to let David present the information.

Mr. E: That's fine. I can tell Heath and I am going to tell him just the facts that we do know so far. As long as you really think you can stand there and let me do that without scaring the child to death about what could happen.

Mrs. E.: Okay. It may not convince me but I'll sit in there and let you talk to Heath in that respect. As long as you agree after we see the doctor that we can bring Heath with us and come back and talk to Mike.

Dr. W.: That is another good idea. I would like to see you all again together with Heath. I also think you have a very important point as well Teresa. This talk with Heath is not meant to change your mind about anything but to give Heath some information so his mind will be eased and he can concentrate on school again.

Mrs. E.: Yeah. That is what's important. I don't want his grades dropping any more, and I don't want him to drop out of soccer.

Dr. W.: You may be right that this grade adjustment may be simply due to other things on his mind. It is part of our job here at school to be aware of this change and help by being understanding and supportive of your efforts at home. David does this plan sound acceptable to you?

Mr. E: Yeah, that's fine.

Dr. W.: Okay, I think we have a good plan. Let me make sure that we all understand what your homework is. David, you are going to explain to Heath what you feel like the doctors have told you and what is going on. Teresa you are going to make sure you are there to show a united front and to report to me a balanced view of things when you all come back. Then when all of you come back to see me, Heath will already know what David has told him. At that time all three of you will sit down with me, and we'll find out if there are additional concerns that Heath has and see how his school performance is progressing.

Mrs. E.: Yeah, I think that is a good idea.

Dr. W.: I do have one other assignment to add to your task. I think it would be a good idea for the two of you to meet together and write down the main points that David is going to cover with Heath. That way you can be sure not to leave anything out, and Teresa you can know ahead of time what David is going to say. Teresa, do you feel like you are going to be able to avoid asking Heath questions to make sure he's okay? Because it is a natural instinct for a mother to say "Now Heath, are you okay with this or are you worried something is going to happen to David?" It will be easy to give him leading questions out of your concern for his well being.

Mrs. E.: I think I can keep the negative out of it.

Dr. W.: I think so too. So I will see all of you when you come back in. David, can we make it next Monday, same time?

Mr. E.: Sure.

Dr. W.: You can call in between if you want to. You realize that?

Mrs. E.: I really appreciate that.

Dr. W.: Good luck at the doctor's tomorrow.

Family Counseling Session #2
Mr. and Mrs. East and Heath

Dr. W.: It has been about a week since the last time we talked. Heath I'm glad you could join us this time, of course, we see each other around school from time to time right?

Heath: Yes, sir. Its good to be here... and not in math.

Dr. W.: I know what you mean. Can someone fill me in on what has happened since our last visit.

Mrs. E.: David talked to Heath and told him...well...oh I don't know how it went.

Dr. W.: Heath, why don't you tell me how you think it went.

Heath: I think it went pretty good. Dave told me that they are going to put him on radiation and cure it.

Dr. W.: So you think he's being straight with you?

Heath: Yeah.

Dr. W.: Then you are not particularly worried about it right now?

Heath: Nope.

Mrs. E.: I think he's more worried than he is letting on. I just think he's afraid to tell you that he's worried.

I think he's more afraid than he's letting on.

Dr. W.: Mom says that you aren't being straight with us.

Heath: I think she's still worried about me and my first dad.

Dr. W.: Go on.

Heath: How he died, you know. I believe in the doctors and that Dave'll be all right.

Dr. W.: Do you think about your first dad very much?

Heath: Not really. It happened a long time ago.

Dr. W.: So you haven't thought about it much lately?

Heath: Not at all in a few years or so.

Dr. W.: What do you remember about it?

Heath: Just that I was in a hospital.

Dr. W.: How do you feel about going back to the hospital now? Does it make you feel any particular way?

Heath: Not really.

Dr. W.: Have you been to the hospital with your mom and David yet?

Heath: Yes sir. Dave's had a treatment and I went then.

Dr. W.: Your mom mentioned something to me about you having a broken arm a couple of years ago and you having to go to the Emergency Room. Do you remember that time? Was it all right for you?

Heath: I haven't really thought about it much. Mom was pretty upset with the nurses.

Dr. W.: Teresa, you don't think Heath is being straight with us?

Mrs. E.: No. I think he's more scared than he is letting on. He's just trying to be tough.

Dr. W.: What makes you think that? What have you seen that makes you think he is not being straight?

Mrs. E.: I think he's just not letting out his true feelings. I think he is hiding his feelings.

Dr. W.: And you think that it is harmful, and it is not good for him to hold his feelings back? What kind of things do you think might happen to him if he held his feelings back? How would it make him feel?

Mrs. E.: That he will be real upset when all of this comes to a head. I think he is going to be more afraid later of things that happen.

Dr. W.: So it is more important to deal with the reality of things now rather than try to push things back and not admit it?

Mrs. E.: Yes, that is what I want him to do.

Dr. W.: You don't think David is dealing with his feelings appropriately either?

Mrs. E.: No, I don't think he is being true to his feelings either. How are you going to get better if you don't deal with your feelings? How can you respond to the treatments if you haven't dealt with what might happen?

Dr. W.: So you think that by David's not admitting how he feels that it could effect the course of his treatment somehow? That it could make him not be healthy or make him not have a good treatment outcome.

Mrs. E.: Wait a minute, are you talking about them or about me?

Dr. W.: I'm sorry, am I being confusing?

Mrs. E.: Sounds like you are talking about me.

Dr. W.: Would I be correct if I were talking about you?

Mrs. E.: I don't know. I'm upset and these two are acting like it is no big deal.

Dr. W.: But you are showing us your true feelings. You are sharing your true feelings.

Mrs. E.: Well, maybe that's what I am talking about. Oh, I don't know.

Dr. W.: So maybe when you talk about Heath not showing his true feelings and David not showing his, you're struggling with some of your own at the same time.

Mrs. E.: I guess maybe I can't imagine that it's not bothering Heath because of what he went through before. Because it was very traumatic for me, it would be hard to understand that it didn't upset him.

Dr. W.: You're right. And it would be hard for some of us who haven't dealt with that to understand how you feel about it. That can be frustrating.

Mrs. E.: Yeah.

Dr. W.: Because David hasn't gone through that. So he may not understand how scary it can be for you.

Mrs. E.: It's almost like he's acting like nothing ever happened. I am realizing the reality of it, that he could very well die and I would be without him.

Dr. W.: Because that has happened to you before.

Mrs. E.: He's not even acknowledging that that could happen.

It's very real to me that it could.

Dr. W.: Because you have experienced it.

Mrs. E.: Yeah. I feel that Heath is probably sitting more where I am sitting.

Dr. W.: But you feel that he is not admitting that.

Mrs. E.: I think that either he isn't admitting it or he doesn't realize it. That he's keeping his feelings hidden.

Dr. W.: David you haven't said anything.

Mr. E.: I was just thinking. I can understand where Teresa is coming from because she has been through something like this before. She knows how she felt then and what could happen. But myself, as far as I am concerned, yes I have cancer. But they treat people with cancer everyday and they can get rid of this. I don't see the point of worrying about what could happen, because what's going to happen will happen. All the worrying in the world is not going to change it. I'm not the least bit worried, I think they will take care of it.

Dr. W.: I think your wife is saying that they may take care of it and she's hoping they will, but that she has been in a situation once before where she has trusted and they let her down. So she is being a bit more cautious, maybe.

Mr. E.: Well, that's her prerogative, but I have complete confidence in the doctors that we have. Personally, I think her fears are unfounded. I think I will be fine. I can't convince her otherwise because of what she has been through. I guess she is just trying to get in touch with her feelings.

Dr. W.: Her feelings of being the "helpless protector." She is sitting here with her hands tied and there is nothing she can do. That has got to be really frustrating for you.

Mrs. E.: Yeah, it really is because I feel like he doesn't understand where I am coming from. The main thing that I want to do is to be supportive of him.

Dr. W.: So if you had something you felt like would be constructive to do, you would feel better about dealing with the whole situation? You would feel like you had some control? Like you could be helpful.

Mrs. E.: At least, understanding what they are doing and understanding about what this radiation does. He needs to check into what it is all about. I try not to overreact but I am not going to be comfortable unless I have a little more knowledge about what this thing can do.

Dr. W.: So given some information about this may be one thing to do to be less helpless and more protective and supportive. Maybe getting some information in writing or talking to someone from the Cancer Society. Have you made any moves in that direction?

Mrs. E.: No, I haven't.

Dr. W.: Then why don't we make that your next assignment. You could write or call to get some additional information or talk with somebody locally such as the American Cancer Association or the Cancer Patient Support group at the hospital. Can you think of anything else you might do?

Mrs. E.: I don't know. I guess I need to feel like he is behind me, too. I need to feel support in that area. That I have somebody on my side. That somebody understands where I am coming from. Somebody that either has been in this position (not actually the one with cancer that may want to be calm and deny what is going on). But that they feel that they are the ones that are sitting back helpless and wanting to help their loved-one.

Mr. E.: They told us at the hospital about a cancer support group you could go to. You didn't seem interested.

Mrs. E.: Yeah, I know about those groups. But I don't think you'll go with me, David.

Mr. E.: I guess I could go a time or two.

Mrs. E.: They said that family members of the patients go to the meetings a lot. They might understand. They might understand more where I'm at right now.

Dr. W.: Then your assignment David is to attend at least two of these support groups with Teresa once she has gotten information and made all the arrangements. How about you two having dinner out before the meeting?

Mr. E.: We could do that. It would be a nice change.

Dr. W.: Heath, what would you think about going to a group with some other people who have parents who have cancer that they are having to deal with? Would you want to do that or not?

Heath: I'm not sure.

Dr. W.: Certainly you and I can meet here at school to keep

an eye on things here so Mom and David will not have that to worry about on top of everything else. Is that agreeable?

Heath: Yeah.

Dr. W.: Okay. So you have a couple things to do Teresa that involve getting some additional information; maybe talking to someone and getting some questions answered. And going to a support group. Right?

Mrs. E.: Yes, I think that is definitely a start.

Dr. W.: David do you think you are doing all you can do right now if you attend at least two of those meetings with Teresa, and, of course, concentrate on getting well?

Mr. E.: Yeah, I'm just kind of leaving it in the hands of the medical people to take care of me, so I can help Teresa feel better about all this.

Dr. W.: All right. Heath, you know that if there are school problems you and I will handle them and take that load off Mom and David. Of course we will keep them informed of your progress.

Heath: Yes, sir.

Dr. W.: Another thing to remember is I'm still here. Heath, I would like to see you on Tuesdays and Thursdays. Why don't we have lunch together so I can catch up with how things are going with you and the family. I'll get with you and get the times later. I will be here for the next several weeks anyway, until school is out for the summer. I'd like to see everyone again in about three weeks to see how things are going. David, would the 21st be all right?

Mr. E.: Yes.

Mrs. E.: Okay.

Dr. W.: Heath, you'll be in school so if you want, you can drop in to talk with me anytime. You don't have to wait for our lunch appointment, all right?

Heath: Yes Sir.

Dr. W.: Okay. I'll see all of you in three weeks

Heath: Okay.

Mrs. E.: Thanks a lot for your time.

Dr. W.: Sure.

Family Counseling in the Schools:

Analysis

The overall conceptualization of this family's situation was based on the initial hypotheses that 1) Mrs. East is fearful of once again being left alone to take care of her children; 2) She has no trust in the medical profession; 3) She is angry at her husband for not understanding and sharing her fears and mistrust; 4) Mrs. East is addressing her feelings by misinterpreting her son's difficulties to be the same as those she is unable to recognize as her own; and 5) Heath's difficulties are minor if not nonexistent; if there are problems in school, they are expressions of the anxieties and tensions present between the mother and adoptive father subsystem. Consequently, if the tension between the parents—and specifically the anxieties and anger present in the mother—could be reduced, any school problems would also be reduced.

The school counselor working with Mr. and Mrs. East initially allowed a brief statement of the problem and then put the discussion of the presenting problem on hold in order to join with the family during the social stage of family counseling. This was accomplished by discussing topics of mutual interest such as soccer and by appreciating and sharing the parents' point of view (e.g., "It makes me feel old too." "I wish I had time to do some coaching."). The counselor showed respect by referring to the parents by surname until a level of comfort was reached. The counselor asked permission, at this point, to use first names. The comfort level was confirmed by the use of the counselor's first name by the parents. The counselor also made a point to support the parents as being good parents (e.g., "You have to be pretty good with kids." "It's the really good moms who have headaches and worries over their kids."). During the social stage, the counselor also gathered information about the family, its roles and relationships, so as to formulate hypotheses.

In the problem stage, the initial presenting problem is discussed. The presenting problem was actually two problems: how to tell Heath about his adoptive father's condition, and correcting any subsequent deterioration in school performance. The initial problem was addressed by the homework assignment made at the end of the first session. The school counselor continued to support the parents and in the second session the counselor joined the child in taking responsibility for solving any school problems, freeing the parents to concentrate on the situation at home without neglecting their parental duties.

The alert school counselor would have noted the obvious denial present in the father's assessment of his medical condition. This denial was intentionally not addressed for two reasons. The denial and/or adjustment to cancer and its treatment was not a part of the original presenting problem and, therefore, not an appropriate target for family intervention. Secondly, the overwhelming nature of a diagnosis of cancer may be more than a person can deal with at times. Their optimism, no matter how unrealistic, may be all they have to hold on to during the course of their treatment; therefore, this hope should not be taken away by a counselor or anyone else for the purpose of helping the client to "face reality."

During the interaction stage the school counselor began to explore, through *reflection, restatement,* and *summary,* the fears and anxieties of Mrs. East, as well as *communication patterns* within the East family. The school counselor began to promote a *realignment of family roles* by deferring to Mr. East for appointment times and final approval of assignments and future plans as a means of support for his position as father.

Both family counseling sessions ended in the goal setting stage with the family leaving with *homework assignments* to complete. It was important for the family members to have something to do regarding the presenting problem. The planning of the manner in which the task was to be completed was just as important. For example, in the first session, deciding who would tell Heath the information regarding his adoptive father's condition was more important than the actual content of the message. Tasks should be directive and clear in nature. The school counselor will need to anticipate obstacles and should address contingency plans when appropriate, such as having Mrs. East call about the support groups, and getting Mr. East to agree to go with her. Limiting Mr. East's commitment to two meetings made it easier for him to agree. The counselor anticipated that either Mr. East would find the group helpful and continue to go, or Mrs. East would feel comfortable enough going alone after two sessions should Mr. East choose not to continue.

Throughout both sessions, the counselor continued to *relabel* and *reframe* the comments of the family to underscore and encourage positive interpretations. For example Mrs. East's lack of trust of doctors was relabeled "positive skepticism" and Mrs. East was referred to as a "helpless protector" of the family. The counselor often attributed achievements to the parents that may not have been apparent to them, such as when he said "this sounds like an agreement," or when he pointed out that Mrs. East had provided good parenting when she was left alone to raise her son. The constant positive spin by the counselor on the parenting skills of Mr. and Mrs. East was intentional and important. It maintained the counselor as a part of the family system and made it possible for the parents to focus on action rather than them defending themselves as parents.

Writing Therapeutic Letters

The multidimensional issues presented by school children in family counseling often require unique approaches to solving problems. One such approach is the *therapeutic letter*. The writing of letters has been used in counseling in various ways.

Moreover, letters with a therapeutic message can be invaluable to school counselors engaging in family interventions. Letters can be used to reframe problem behaviors, to bolster and support recent advances by a family member, and to encourage families or family members to behave in a specific way. They also may be used for the purposes of motivation and direction in times of discouragement and for when counseling has ended badly.

If the counseling has ended on the wrong key, a letter may put things back on the right tone. Many cases that go this route simply need CPR (Counseling Progress Resuscitation). In these types of cases, if significant rapport has been established, the counselor can acknowledge that a *mistake* was made and that it is hoped that this will not continue to interrupt the counseling process. The mistake is often referred to as a *confession*. This may be followed by other therapeutic letter elements including *positive reframes, an unbalancing statement or motivator for change, new alternatives or options,* and *counselor availability* (see Omer, 1991).

While letters are not a substitute for verbal communications, they are generally received positively (Asch, Price, & Hawks, 1991). Although there could be the problem of other people in the household reading the letter, at times this possibility can be therapeutic. For example, if a letter in an official school envelope is sent to a young student, the parents are likely to open and read it. If this is a strong possibility, a message to the parents could be included in the letter. This may be useful when it is difficult for parents to hear a particular message about their family or child.

Generally, therapeutic letters should be short. The longer the letter, the more likely the addressee will not read the entire letter. Letters should typically begin with a positive, uplifting statement. For example, compliments and affirmations of a family's progress in counseling are good formats for beginning a therapeutic letter. Omer (1991) compares the beginning of the letter to the joining process in counseling. The joining portion of the letter is designed to engage the client, reduce resistance, confirm the client or family, boost self-esteem using the client's language, and sound themes of personal importance (Minuchin & Fishman, 1981; Omer, 1990).

Directives are generally embedded after a pleasant opening statement. Such directives may include direct messages to perform a particular behavior or activity, or may be indirect and only "suggestive." Finally, the letter should end on an uplifting, hopeful note. Examples of therapeutic letters can be found below:

January 15, 1989

Dear Mr. Smith:

I hope this letter finds you doing well and enjoying the New Year [joining]. I spoke with your wife and son this evening about their conference with John's teachers.

Since I know from talking with you that you are concerned and care about John's being successful at school, I thought I might take a moment of your time and share with you something that, I'm sure you will agree, would be helpful for John [joining; options], since we both want to make sure he does not become a failure [joining; unbalancing]. If you were to provide some

91

type of consequence for his staying after school due to unacceptable behavior, like not giving him $2.00 for lunch (he does not eat lunch anyway), this will help him to earn better grades, do his homework, and make the most of himself [options]. Again, since I know that you want to help John be successful and be all he can be, I thought I would make this small suggestion [joining; options].

I have enjoyed my contact with your family. You must be very proud of your efforts, for they have provided your family with a caring and worthwhile home [joining].

If you ever need to ask me anything about John's difficulty in "measuring up" at school as well as in life, please feel free to call me [counselor availability].

Sincerely,

J. Scott Hinkle, Child Counselor

February 22, 1990

Dear Mr. and Mrs. Cantrell:

As we agreed upon in our last session, I am sending you a written assessment of our sessions together. Overall, you have a very healthy, high functioning family [joining]. From the information you provided, our observations, and test data, the school staff is in agreement that Jim does not have attention deficit/hyperactivity disorder. In fact, it is unfortunate that AD/HD was ever mentioned. Jim's problem appears to be one of maturity and a very slight developmental delay [reframe].

It is our assessment that Jim is experiencing moderate difficulties with feelings of exclusion. In all likelihood, this feeling began with the birth of your second child, Meredith. This reaction is a very common occurrence within families. Jim's role was that of the "pride and joy" of the family for eight years. He eventually had to change roles for two new family members. Children have difficulty articulating their feelings about a new child in the family. Rather, they tend to act-up.

In addition, your family has experienced many changes in

the past three years. As we all know, stress accompanies change, even positive change. A new business has necessitated a rigorous work schedule making it difficult for Mr. Cantrell to spend time with the family, and especially with Jim. Likewise, Gilda is mothering two new babies which demands a lot of attention. We want to commend you for being the super parents that you are [joining]. Your concern for each of your children is apparent. You genuinely care about your children doing well and being successful [joining]. Often, when we parents have high expectations for our children, we can unknowingly set up situations wherein our children have difficulty succeeding [reframe]. This situation may pose some difficulty for children.

We suggest that in addition to the positive things you do as parents, that you consider spending time celebrating Jim's simply being Jim [options]. We mean this not in terms of expectations of performance in school or structured activities, but just participating in Jim being successful at being himself. One of the most beneficial things to assist Jim in this attitude would be for him to experience some quality, one-on-one time with his parents [options]. It would be especially beneficial for Jim to spend time with Dad [options]. It also would be helpful if this time was high in success and low in stress. Such time may be spent fishing, hiking in the woods near your home, or even working on the van together [options]. Anything that you both enjoy would assist Jim in developing maturity and a "place" in the family.

Finally, you put a tremendous amount of energy into your children. Although this is positive, we believe your marriage misses something as a result [reframe]. It may be helpful to also focus on each other; thereby, getting more of your needs met through each another rather than through the children [options]. By arranging for child care, you can get the break you deserve [reframe]. Also, you will be even better role models for your children by teaching them that parents are intimate and value each another's attention.

We have enjoyed your family and look forward to seeing you next week [counselor availability].

Sincerely,
J. Scott Hinkle
School Counseling Staff

Family Counseling in the Schools:

April 16, 1993

Dear Robert:

It was wonderful meeting with you and your parents this week. It seems that your family is behind you all the way this new school year [joining].

It was very nice to hear that your parents are following through with a homework hour this year. They were very convincing in their plan to turn the dining room into a "library" so you can be tutored while your parents unwind from their hard day at work. You must be proud of your parents since they want to help you be successful in school even when they are tired [unbalancing].

I look forward to seeing you in Mrs. Thomas' class [counselor availability]. I really enjoyed your drawings of the animals (when did you go to the zoo)?

Sincerely,

J. Scott Hinkle
Michael E. Wells
Child Counselors

November 1, 1994

Dear Jeremy,

I have been thinking about you often since the last time I met with you and your family. It was nice to see the progress that you have made in school and I am sure that your parents are proud of you [joining]. I realize that the uncovering of family secrets has not been pleasant for you, but we both know that you have the courage to deal with many unpleasant things in your life [joining; reframe]. That is why we disagreed on your revealing your sexual orientation. I must admit that I was mistaken about your tenacity and clear thinking on the matter [confession]. It was premature of me to indicate that you may be stating that you are gay only to upset your mother who is typically a little overbearing and domineering [confession; reframe; unbalancing]. Actually, you have convinced me that a satisfying sex life is more important than family and friends [unbalancing]. However, we both know that there is no substitution for direct communication, regardless of how much courage it takes [joining; unbalancing; options].

I am confident in your newly found confidence and wish you the best in your future family interactions, especially with your mother. I hope you will forgive me for not understanding the urgency of your family issues and you will find it possible to speak with me again [confession]. I am ready to speak with you on your terms whenever you can fit me into your schedule [counselor availability].

Sincerely,

Scott Hinkle
Counselor

Family Counseling in the Schools:

Chapter Six

Family Assessment and the School Environment

Although not clearly advocated by strategic or structural family counseling theory, assessing families by way of family structure can be quite helpful. Furthermore, perceptions held by the child and family regarding the school system may be beneficial (Aliotti, 1992). It is important to include an assessment of family system dynamics when working with student learning problems and behavioral difficulties. Because of their liaison between students, families, and teachers, counselors working within the school environment are ideally suited for such assessments. School counselors can utilize brief intervention models that focus on family assessment and parent-teacher interface (Nicoll, 1992).

Assessment of families will aid the school counselor in discovering and understanding family problems, will uncover some of the contributing stress factors, and will facilitate treatment planning. Holman has (1983) suggested that four areas of investigation are essential in assessing families. These areas include identifying

1. the problem,
2. the family system,
3. the family and its environment, and
4. the family life cycle.

Each area can be assessed in a variety of ways. Often the most unobtrusive method of evaluating a family is through an interview. The family evaluation should begin with the scheduling of the first appointment. As noted previously, which family member is responsible for committing the family to a specific appointment time and who in the family (if anyone) must be consulted before an appointment can be set are important assessment questions. Who is responsible for making sure that family members are present for the meeting? The answers to these questions provide the school counselor insight into family hierarchy, rules and roles, and communication pathways. Information about family members who could not or who refused to make it to the meeting may be equally revealing.

The school counselor usually has access to the records of the student of concern, but counselors should gather information on the perspectives of the student, parents, siblings, or other family members. Direct and indirect questions, as well as open-ended statements, can provide useful information. As with any clinical interview, the school counselor will be continually observing for non-verbal expressions, demonstration of affect, inconsistencies between verbal responses and non-verbal messages, and any additional information provided through observation of the family. Family counseling provides the opportunity, not present in individual counseling, to observe clues to such information as family hierarchy and roles, communication styles, and problem-solving strategies. Who speaks for the family, or from whom is permission to speak sought, are important clues to the inner workings of the family. Something as subtle as the seating arrangement chosen by the family can provide helpful information for the school counselor.

Since it is typically not possible to observe family interactions as they occur in the family's natural environment, the school counselor may choose to employ the use of *evaluation tasks*. With evaluation tasks, the counselor assigns the family a task in the office. Observational assessment of the family during the completion of the task is then made.

This process can be accomplished by having a co-counselor or a colleague observe through a one-way mirror, or by the school counselor leaving the family alone to work on the task and observing through the mirror. Videotaping for later analysis is often very effective and can be used in the place of a one-way mirror. Videotaping has the added advantage of allowing for repeated viewing of the family interactions for assessment purposes.

There are various ways to begin assessing a family, including observation and initial questioning. Some helpful questions may include, How and how soon do you anticipate the problem to be solved? How do you think counseling will help you deal with the problem? What made you decide that now is the right time for counseling? The answers to these questions may provide an initial idea about the families expectations and their readiness for change (Talmon, 1990).

Should the school counselor desire a more formalized process, there have been specific inventories developed to assist with the process of family assessment. In their *Handbook of Measurements for Marriage and Family Therapy,* Fredman and Sherman (1987), present a number of such inventories: (Several sources may be found in Appendix A.)

The Family Task Interview (Kinston, Loader, & Miller, 1985). Family members complete seven tasks: 1) plan a family activity of at least one hour duration, 2) build a tower from available blocks, 3) discuss preferences of family members (i.e., likes and dislikes), 4) sort a deck of cards, 5) complete a story involving a missing family member and a subsequent call from the hospital, 6) explain the meaning of a saying chosen by the parents (parents are then to explain the meaning of the chosen saying to the children in the family), and 7) discuss the interview process with the counselor.

The *Inventory of Parent-Child Conflict* (IPCC) (Olson & Ryder, 1977) and *The Inventory of Parent-Adolescent Conflict* (IPAC) (Olson, Portner, & Bell, 1977) include the parent(s) along with all the children involved in the counseling sessions. The assessment task challenges the family members to examine a number of provided case studies and discuss and decide which individual in the case study is responsible for the presenting problem or difficulty.

Families are requested to talk about changes they would like to see in their family when implementing the *Beavers-Timberlawn Family Evaluation Scale* (Beavers, 1985). The last ten minutes of the sessions are used (preferably from video tape) to rate the family on five dimensions: structure, mythology, goal-directed negotiation, autonomy, and family affect.

Unfortunately, most schools do not have access to facilities that include observation rooms or videotaping capabilities. However, the school counselor may wish to use activities that involve families in a typical office setting, without many additional materials. These activities are not only excellent therapeutic exercises, they also aid in providing additional information for the continuing assessment of the family.

Family Counseling in the Schools:

Creative school counselors will no doubt develop exercises with which they feel comfortable and find successful in their work. Nevertheless, there are three approaches which have been used widely by family counselors in a variety of settings, namely *ecomaps, genograms,* and *family sculpture.* These strategies were initially collected and presented by Hartman (1979) in her book, *Finding Families*; they were intended for use as family assessment approaches in adoptions.

Ecomaps

The ecomap (Hartman, 1979) is useful in determining the needs of families in counseling. The ecomap assesses how well-connected families are to their surrounding environment. School counselors often find the ecomap useful in determining a family's counseling needs. The ecomap provides a concrete, visual representation of the system in which a family operates. Since the entire family develops the map, the school counselor can observe and note differing assessments by family members regarding how a part of the system is or is not supporting or helping the family as a whole. By drawing the different systems and subsystems and graphically displaying their level of connection to the family, the family members and the school counselor can concretely see the composition and operation of the family system. (Holman, 1983).

The construction of an ecomap is simple. The family is represented by a large circle in the center of the paper. Individual family members may be included by drawing each one inside the larger circle. Position within the circle and approximation to other family members can be used to signify the individual's role in the family (convention suggests squares for males and circles for females). A discussion of this placement may be quite revealing for the family as well as for the school counselor. Additional circles are then added to represent other systems in the family's environment. School, church, extended family units, parents' work settings, the children's circle of friends outside of school, and sports teams or those systems from outside activities, such as dance class or scouting, may be included. The ecomap may be referred to from time to time during family counseling to help illustrate relationships or pressures involving the family or its individual members.

Figure 1. Ecomap

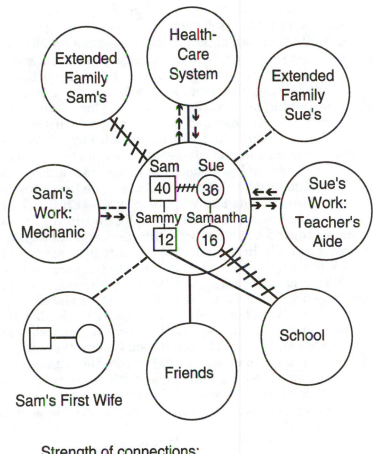

Strength of connections:
_____strong_ _ _ _ _tenuous ┼┼┼┼ stressful
———→ flow of energy or resourses

Ecomap of the Southern Family
    This ecomap is of the Southern family: Sam, age 40, Sue, age
36, and their children Sammy, age 12 and Samantha, age 16.
This map was prepared during an interview with the entire

Family Counseling in the Schools:

family. As viewed from the map, Sam and Sue are having marital difficulties. Sue enjoys her work as a teacher's aide in a local kindergarten and has been spending more time lately preparing classroom materials for the teacher she assists. This job provides Sue a source of self-satisfaction as well as a good income for the family. Her own children have always done well in school until this past year when Samantha began to neglect homework and lose interest in school. Her grades have dropped and she has begun talking about quitting school. Sam works as a mechanic but has become dissatisfied with his job over the last several months. He has had continuing problems with back pain and a recurring ulcer, both of which have caused short hospital stays and numerous visits to the doctors in the past year. This problem has resulted in missed work days and an additional financial burden on the family. Sam has never gotten along with his parents and while they visit with Sam's family several times a year, the visits usually end in an argument between Sam and his father, while his mother admonishes Sam for trying to bully his father. Sue's family lives several states away. While the family's relationship with her parents is not as volatile as it is with Sam's, they are not very close and may go more than a year between visits. The Southern family is fairly isolated socially. They mentioned a few friends that live in their neighborhood, but they see them only incidentally as they do yard work and have planned no social events with neighbors in years. Sam was married briefly just after he graduated from high school and still remains friendly with his ex-wife. She has been remarried for five years and has infrequent contact with Sam, although, he listed her among those he considered friends.

Genograms

Helping a family produce a genogram (Bowen, 1978; Holman, 1983; McGoldrick & Gerson, 1985) can be most instructive for the school counselor as well as for family members. A genogram is based on the idea of a family tree and typically includes the present generations and at least one prior generation of the oldest family member's. The genogram can be drawn on a single sheet of paper, on poster board, or on a large chalk board. As noted with the ecomap, it is customary to use squares to represent males and circles to represent females. Occupations, avocations, causes of death, and other events or descriptors important to the family may be included. The genogram provides family members with a sense of unity and togetherness in their perception of a common past. It also helps to identify patterns and traditions within a family. This may be especially helpful if step-parents or step-children are present in a family. The appreciation and acceptance of the fact that although individual family members have different backgrounds, they still have much in common can be both illustrative and instructive for the family and counselor.

Figure 2. Genogram

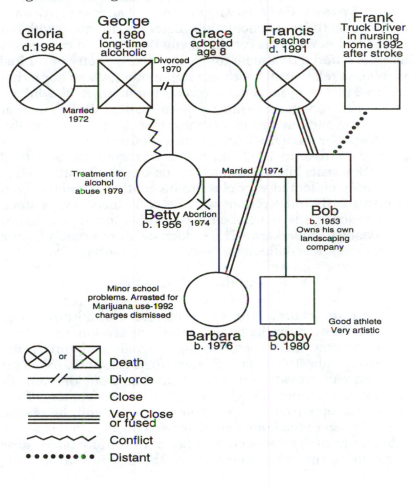

Family Counseling in the Schools:

Genogram of Bob and Betty North

Bob and Betty North married at the ages of 18 and 21, respectively. They decided to get married when Betty discovered she was pregnant. She subsequently obtained an abortion without Bob's knowledge. Bob was angry and hurt but they married, nonetheless, and subsequently had two children. The children are Barbara, age 19, and Bobby, age 15. Barbara has had some minor school problems most of her life including being retained in fourth grade. Bobby is an average student who divides his free time between sports and drawing sketches. He is very good at both according to his parents.

Betty's parents divorced when she was 14 after many years of drinking on the part of her father. Betty's relationship with her father had never been very good and deteriorated completely after he entered treatment for alcohol abuse. Betty never had much of a relationship with her step-mother whom her father married just two years after divorcing her mother. She did not attend her step-mother's funeral when she died. Betty's mother lives alone and has a good relationship with the North family.

Bob's father was a truck driver and was often away from home. He had a stroke in 1992 and has since required almost total care. Bob visits him in the nursing home each Christmas. Bob is an only child and very close to his mother, Francis. Even after his early indiscretions with Betty, Francis always stood by her son. She developed a close relationship with her granddaughter, Barbara. The sudden death of Francis from a heart attack was difficult for both Bob and Barbara.

Family Sculpture

If there are small children or less literate or withdrawn family members present in the family counseling session, the school counselor may find it useful to employ family sculpture (Duhl, Kantor, & Duhl, 1973; Papp, Silverstein, & Carter, 1975). This exercise can provide a means of learning about the family's structure and functioning, as well as give the members of the family the opportunity to see how their roles and the overall construction of the family are perceived.

In family sculpture, each member of the family takes turns positioning the other members of the family into a living sculpture which represents the family. The sculpture often reveals the relationships and roles played by family members and also, perhaps, something about lines of communication and family processes. The role that the sculpting member sees for him or herself often surprises the other members of the family and can provide invaluable information for the school counselor. Even the order in which each family member takes a turn at sculpting, and the manner in which this turn is determined, may be quite revealing. It is important that the school counselor ensure that each sculptor has a free reign in completing the sculpture without interference or resistance from others in the family.

Figure 3. Family Sculpture

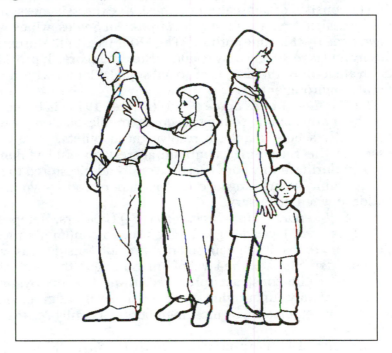

Activities such as these foster a cooperative environment during the counseling process. Once the school counselor has the family members' cooperation, goal setting, and a willingness to achieve these therapeutic goals, becomes more likely. Furthermore, ecomaps and genograms can provide a focal point for further assessment and counseling with the family or with the individual student if continued family sessions are not possible. Meanwhile, the information gathered during these assessment activities provides an ongoing evaluation of the family and helps in marking the progress of the family counseling.

There may be times when a more formalized assessment is required or desired by the school counselor. There have been many such appraisal instruments developed for family assessment that would be practical for use in a school setting. A small sampling of those available include the following:

The Family Relationships Index (FRI) (Holahan & Moos, 1981) consists of subscales of cohesion, expressiveness, and conflict taken from the *Family Environment Scales,* which was developed by the same authors. The FRI is used with the entire family and is relatively easy to administer and score. It provides an evaluation of the degree of social support found within the family environment.

The Conflict Tactics Scale (CTS) (Straus, 1979) is based on the theory that family conflicts become troublesome only when the family seems unable to resolve the conflicts. The CTS assesses the reasoning, symbolic aggression, and violence present during family conflicts. It is orally administered to the entire family using language that is understood by younger children when necessary.

The *Self-Report Family Inventory* (SFI) (Beavers, Hampson, & Hulgus, 1985) was designed to be used in conjunction with the observations of the counselor to provide "insider" as well as "outsider" views of the level of functioning in the family. It is based on the constructs proposed in the Beavers Systems Model of family functioning. The SFI is easily administered and can be understood by most members of a family regardless of their age.

Lowman's (1980) *Inventory of Family Feelings* (IFF) utilizes a systems approach in the assessment of family feelings. It is written in simple language to facilitate its use with children or less-educated family members. In IFF, family members rate each other. The family's typical communication and problem-solving patterns are then identified. The ability of the family and its members to give and receive positive feelings and affection also is identified. The IFF uses a unique charting system that can include extended family and actually becomes more useful with the addition of more individuals into the process.

The *Index of Family Relations* (IFR) (Hudson, 1982) is a self-report assessment which reveals the magnitude of family relationship problems. The IFR can provide information from the point of view of one or more family members. Since it is best used as a continual monitor of therapeutic progress, it should be administered on more than one occasion. The IFR is relatively easy to administer and score. However, the usual precautions for self-report tools are in order.

When working with school children, one of the issues to be considered is how much cooperation will be forthcoming from the family. A parent or, perhaps, even another family member, has the capacity to undermine any or all of a counselor's best efforts, including the attempts of other family members. Golden (1988) defines a functional family as "one that is capable of consistently implementing a plan of action in response to a child's misbehavior" (p. 179). Any individual counseling efforts carried out with an individual who is living in a dysfunctional family are likely to prove unsuccessful for all involved. Understanding this situation, Golden developed the *Quick Assessment of Family Functioning* (QAFF) (1988). This assessment is designed to meet the needs of counselors who have brief or infrequent contact with a student's family. As in most cases, a good interview goes a long way toward providing useful valuative information. A structured interview, as advocated by Golden, should provide many answers regarding the issues at hand, including insights on the functioning level of the family. The QAFF assesses families along five dimensions: (1) Parental Resources weighs the capabilities of the parents to meet the basic needs of the children; (2) Chronicity assesses how enduring a family's problems have been and how resistive the family has been to intervention; (3) Communication Between Family Members looks at communication, as well as the normal exchange of information, to determine whether the system is closed or open; (4) Parental Authority measures the effectiveness with which parents use their authority and the hierarchy and roles within the family; and (5) Rapport With

Family Counseling in the Schools:

Professional Helpers assesses the parents' history in cooperating with school officials and teachers, or others who have had occasion to work with the parents regarding the in-school children. The QAFF is easy to administer and was specially designed for use by school counselors.

The Clinical Interview

The clinical interview with the entire family is one of the least used assessment tools. The major portion of family information is gathered from interviews with mothers and children alone. To obtain information from mothers, and not include fathers, results in a less than comprehensive picture of family functioning and its relationship to school performance (Fish & Jain, 1992).

Following the initial interview, families should be asked to report on baseline behavior (Merrill et al., 1992). A family can record how many arguments they engage in or how many times a child does not bring his or her assignments home. This activity is typically an easy task for families and the data should be kept so as to record treatment outcomes. To analyze the data, simple time-series plotting can reflect treatment progress (see Hinkle, 1992; Tracy, 1983) and can demonstrate accountability.

It is helpful to ask parents to describe an average day in the family's life (Christensen & Marchant, 1983). Parents often ask if the counselor wants to hear about a weekday or a weekend. It is good to obtain information about both, especially school days. This information will provide descriptions of who wakes up when, who feeds whom, who coordinates activities, and what general problems arise as the day progresses. For example, it is common for parents to report that getting ready for school and bedtime are particularly difficult times of the day.

Clinical Diagnosis: Applications and Implications in Family Counseling

Diagnosis is becoming more popular among community counselors (Cowger, Hinkle, DeRidder, & Erk, 1991). However, its use in family counseling has been minimized. The current edition of the *Diagnostic and Statistical Manual of Mental*

108

Disorders, Fourth Edition) (DSM-IV) (American Psychiatric Association, 1994) has a modicum of diagnoses directly associated with family functioning.

Moreover, diagnosis is approached with varying degrees of ambivalence by many marriage and family counselors. Carlson, Hinkle, and Sperry (1993) have indicated that this ambivalence is mostly "due to the association of diagnosis with the medical model, which seems so foreign to the developmental model and systems theory model" on which counseling is based (p. 308). However, the authors also reflect that counselors can use a diagnostic system such as the DSM-IV without losing heart or soul. Furthermore, knowledge of the DSM-IV assists the family counselor in understanding the individual, marital, and family behaviors within a family system and helps with case conceptualization and treatment planning. For example, clients diagnosed with Borderline Personality Disorder are needy in their response to their families and to counseling. This information can be helpful in developing strategies for change within the family counseling context (Carlson et al.). Such information not only explains dynamics, but also helps determine the treatment style of the counselor. Knowledge of the DSM-IV's multi-axial format, including Axis IV *Psychosocial and Environmental Problems* and Axis V *Global Assessment of (Relational) Functioning*, assists the counselor in determining the level of family stress. To illustrate, Carlson et al. have suggested that families with *less stress* may be candidates to drop out of counseling.

The DSM System and Family Assessment. Three models of psychiatric diagnosis have been outlined by Harari (1990): categorical, dimensional, and multi-axial. These models' limitations include the loss of information concerning individual uniqueness, an emphasis on pathology, and a lack of consideration for social factors, such as family and other relational systems, as well as stressors in family life.

The DSM system, which is categorical, unidimensional, and multi-axial, has relatively few diagnoses associated with family functioning. This nomenclature is so specific and idiosyncratic that relationship problems are not addressed. In order to make a diagnosis, systemic and contextual information regarding a client's functioning are typically ignored. However, the contribution of such social factors to the client's diagnosis are meaningful and should be integrated both into the client's diagnosis and treatment plan. Models for such information have been offered for couples' problems (Sperry, 1989) and dual career couples' issues (O'Neil, Fishman, & Kinsella, 1987). Birk's (1988) integration proposal has suggested that an accurate diagnosis should include three components: 1) behavioral knowledge, 2) psychodynamic knowledge, and 3) the social systems in which the problem occurs.

Assigning a client a DSM diagnosis has been a controversial and historically uncomfortable process for many counselors (Seligman, 1986). Although some family counselors resist its use from an individualistic perspective, the DSM can facilitate treatment planning, can assist with the anticipation of the nature and progress of counseling, and can enhance communication among mental health professionals (Seligman). However, from a systemic perspective, treatment planning, counseling progress, and communication among clinicians lose their significance and value when a major, individualistic DSM diagnosis is made instead of a family or marital diagnosis.

Family-related DSM-IV diagnoses, however, are only assigned to individuals. These diagnoses are listed in Table 4.

Table 4. DSM-IV Diagnoses Associated with Family Counseling

    Parent-Child Relational Problem
    Partner Relational Problem
    Sibling Relational Problem
    Physical Abuse of Child
    Sexual Abuse of Child
    Neglect of Child
    Physical Abuse of Adult
    Sexual Abuse of Adult

Traditionally, disadvantages associated with using the DSM have included the promotion of a mechanistic approach to mental disorder assessment, a false impression that the scientific knowledge regarding mental disorders is more advanced than is actually the case, and an excessive focus on the signs and symptoms of mental disorders to the exclusion of a more in-depth understanding of the client's problems (Williams, Spitzer, & Skodol, 1985, 1986). It also has been reported that the DSM focuses too much attention on surface phenomena at the expense of clinical issues and human development (Vaillant, 1984). The minimization of an in-depth understanding of the client and family and the focus on surface issues reflects the DSM's lack of acknowledgment of systemic contributions to mental disorders. Although advantages to implementing the DSM have included the development of a common language for discussing diagnoses, an increase in attention to behaviors, and a facilitation of overall learning in psychopathology, the DSM's disregard of the vast literature on the association between systemic relationships and mental dysfunction hinders its overall objective of describing psychological and behavioral functioning.

One of the major criticisms of the DSM system is its exclusive emphasis on mental disorders as they occur in individuals (APA, 1991). This emphasis severely restricts the DSM's usefulness in the diagnosis, as well as the treatment, of problems that occur in the family. The DSM represents itself as a bio-psychosocial nomenclature; however, the social aspects are obviously much less important to the medical community.

The inclusion of *spectrum disorders* or overlapping disorders would be a helpful addition, at least conceptually, to the DSM classification system. The notion of "spectrum" reflects the theory that mental disorders overlap or exist on a continuum. To extrapolate, such a spectrum would be more beneficial if it included an axis regarding social context (Hinkle, 1992b).

The diagram on the following page depicts a continuum of child behavior, ranging from healthy functioning on one end to extreme personality dysfunction on the other end. However, it also takes into account the systemic nature of the presenting problem within a social contest. School counselors may improve their diagnostic processes with school children if they were to adhere to such a social concept of school behavior problems.

Family Counseling in the Schools:

Figure 4. Example of Spectro-Social Diagram of Child Diagnosis

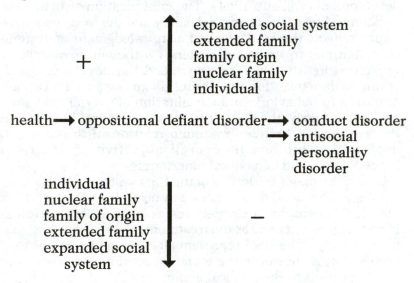

Conclusion

After a thorough assessment of the student's presenting problem, the school counselor must decide if a family counseling intervention would be helpful. All failed attempts need to be carefully assessed and analyzed for the reason for their failure. This positions the school counselor "one step ahead" when planning for family counseling. Amatea (1989) has suggested that specific action steps must be identified and they should be different from the ones used in the past. Although formal, quantitative, standardized testing is not necessary for all family counseling cases, qualitative or subjective assessment is always needed. Likewise, formal DSM diagnoses are not essential, but can be helpful in treatment planning.

Chapter Seven

Special Clinical Issues: Abuse, Anorexia, Substance Abuse, Attention Deficit/Hyperactivity Disorder, and Antisocial Behavior

The high cost of health care and the unwillingness of insurance companies to cover mental health services, combined with the increasingly hectic nature of family life and the stigma that continues to be attached to professional counseling services, contribute to the fact that only one-third of all the school children who need mental health services in this country actually receive them (Office of Technology Assessment, 1986). Because schools afford easy access to children, officials have begun to utilize the public schools as the most effective place in which to address public health issues (e.g., AIDS education, free breakfasts and lunches for poor children). Interventions at the public school level are more likely to be accepted by families who naturally distrust "outsiders" and by households too busy for or unable to afford professional services in the community.

Within this climate, school counselors are likely to be the onlyprofessionals in a position to help students and their families deal with many problems traditionally thought of as the purview of private practitioners. School counselors are in a unique position to offer family counseling for students suffering from physical or sexual abuse, anorexia nervosa, substance abuse, attention deficit/hyperactivity disorder, and antisocial behaviors. This chapter will offer information and some pointers on delivering family counseling to families of students faced with these problems.

Family Counseling in the Schools:

Abuse

The question of whether or not family counseling is an appropriate clinical response to child abuse has been intensely examined, particularly by those who strongly advocate that the non-abusing members of the family, whether victim or not, be protected from the abuser (usually by removal from the family). There is no question that an abuse victim's safety is a counselor's paramount concern. However, the opinion that the abuser behaves badly toward a spouse or children, independent of the behaviors of the other members of the family, would define abuse as a response outside the realm of the system. Perceiving the family as a complete and working system, whether functional or not, does not preclude the assignment of guilt, but it does make the family more likely to address the issues important to the healthy functioning of the family. The family approach highlights a family's communications. Such communication moves in many different directions at different intensities. The interaction of family members across all generations is the basis both for problems and for solutions from a family counseling perspective.

In his discussion of psychotherapy with sexually abused children, Friedrich (1990) writes, "behavioral problems represent the cumulative interaction of all members of a system over one or more generations, and they reflect the difficulties that families have in negotiating various transformations in the life cycle" (p. 168). He goes on to point out, however, that systems theory is evolving to a recognition of the different levels within a system when addressing incest or abuse. Individuals bring their own personalities to the family, either functional, dysfunctional, mentally healthy, or pathological (Langevin, 1983). The abuser certainly brings his or her own pathology into the family, perhaps developing it further from within the system. Other family members may be simply reflecting roles that have been imposed on them by the stronger personality and pathology of the abuser (Friedrich).

It is not realistic for the school counselor to expect to break the pattern of incest or abuse simply by getting the parents to talk more to each other. It is likewise an incomplete solution to remove an abusing parent and leave the remaining parent and children to sort out what is left of their family. As Friedrich

(1990) states, "devaluing the perpetrator and overvaluing the non-offending mother" (p. 169) leaves other long-standing dynamics between siblings and mother, and especially between mother and victim, unaddressed. The effects of ignoring all the interactions in the family, both before and after the departure of the abuser, except those between abuser and victim is woefully inadequate in helping the family heal and move on with life. This omission will almost certainly have long term effects as the children develop, begin relationships outside the family, and contemplate marriage and children of their own.

Family counseling as a treatment for incest or abuse should only be undertaken if the ultimate goal is to keep the family intact. If this goal is not possible (due to absence of the abuser from the family, adjudicated marital break-up, or otherwise), then family counseling with the newly created, single-parent led family may be most appropriate. This second family configuration is the one more likely to be encountered by the school counselor. Regardless, the counseling should encompass first and foremost the security and well-being of the victim. Counseling should address the circumstances which preceded the abuse, identify alternative and acceptable ways for family members to meet their emotional and physical needs, and provide a "shoring-up" of the parental subsystem.

A family counseling approach is just as appropriate when the abuse is perpetrated from outside the family. When one member of a family, especially a child, is victimized, the entire system is affected. The child feels vulnerable. His or her parents can no longer be counted on for protection. Parents may not even be counted on to believe the child's expressions of need if the initial reports of the abuse were made by the child and not believed by the parents. The child often feels that the abuse is a reasonable, negative consequence for some behavior on his or her part. If a child is victimized, family members feel some sense of blame or guilt that they were not there, that it was not them instead who was victimized, or that they had somehow driven the victim to others by not being a good enough parent or sibling. The stress and tension on a family does not stop with the discovery of the abuse or even with the conviction of the abuser (should that happen).

Moreover, there are questions regarding trust between all family members. Individuals in the family may feel that the

Family Counseling in the Schools:

child or sibling does not trust them enough to tell them about being violated, scared, and hurt. Anger at the victim for having put the family through the ordeal, embarrassment or, perhaps, publicity following discovery of the abuse, is not uncommon. These issues, along with constantly changing feelings, will need to be addressed in counseling.

It is not often that a school counselor will receive a referral specifically to address issues of abuse with a student. Children are quite resourceful in hiding evidence of abuse in order to avoid school officials' and outsiders' interference or difficult questions. A family in which abuse is occurring can be an incredibly impervious system. Therefore, it may be important for the child to protect the family from external forces.

An abused child is usually convinced that he or she is mostly, if not entirely, to blame for the abuse and may worry about being thought badly of by others such as teachers or school counselors. The child, or someone close to the child may have been threatened directly with further pain if the abusive activity is revealed. There may be unstated threats to family functioning or economic stability if the student believes that a parent or children may be removed from the family. The loyalty instilled in members of the enmeshed, abusive family is very strong. The fear and distress of abused children may be equalled by the feelings of guilt and embarrassment carried by the child. For these reasons it is often difficult for teachers, nurses, school counselors, or school psychologists to recognize a child who is being abused.

Several authors have offered lists of characteristics or signs common in children who have been abused (Adams & Fay, 1981; Hyde, 1980; Smith, 1990). Although these characteristics are not definitive in the identification of abused children, they do signal educators and counseling professionals that abuse is likely and that further efforts to work with the child in question are in order. Following is a compilation of signs offered by many experts in the field of child abuse research:

- Dirty or unkempt appearance
- Inappropriate clothing (e.g., long sleeves in warm weather; wearing coat in the classroom)
- Sleep disturbance
- Change in eating habits

- Reluctance to go home after school
- Reluctance to have school personnel contact parents (even about seemingly noncontroversial issues such as PTA membership or permission to go on a field trip)
- Injuries which are unexplained or for which explanations seem implausible
- Nervous or anxious behavior
- Strong reaction to being touched
- Frequent, unexplained absences or tardiness
- Shy, withdrawn behavior
- Frequent attempts to isolate self or avoid cooperative activities (e.g., working in pairs)
- Reluctance to be alone with someone
- Fights, arguments, or difficulty getting along with other students
- Overly cooperative or eager to please
- Dramatic change in grades or academic performance
- Sudden mood shifts or rapid changes in behavior
- Secretive, or evasive response to routine inquiries
- Regressive behavior
- Irritable or argumentative with teachers or school personnel

Once the school counselor has become convinced that it is likely a student has been abused or is being abused, some action must be taken. Most states have mandatory child abuse and neglect reporting laws and most school systems have policies regarding the procedure for school personnel to use in complying with the law. School counselors should know these laws and procedures and should act accordingly in reporting suspected abuse or in advising faculty in this regard. When a suspicion of abuse has been reported, the school counselor may find that he or she is in an even less effective position with the student and/or the family. Unfortunately, it is not possible to know how a family will react to an abuse investigation.

Even if the school counselor did not make the report, the family is likely to be very defensive with any school or agency employee and be generally angry about the whole process. Furthermore, establishment of a working relationship with such a family may not be possible. In most cases, however, the

Family Counseling in the Schools:

children in the family will continue to attend the same school. A consistent, supportive and open response by the school counselor towards the abused child may build an environment from which counseling may be beneficial. The counselor also may wish to take the initiative in contacting the parents whenever possible regarding school business. If these contacts are used as an opportunity to support the parents' efforts with the child and, if some of these contacts can be used to report positive responses by students, this effort may increase the likelihood of a more positive outcome. It may be that a direct and non-judgmental contact early in the intervention will prove helpful later. Following is an example of a possible first contact by telephone with a parent:

"Hello, Mrs. Easter. I am Don Westerly, the counselor at Jason's school. I called to discuss with you something a bit unsettling, but I know you to be the kind of parent who would want to hear this directly from me. It seems that we have some evidence that requires us to make a report to Social Services (or the agency required by local law) regarding possible abuse (or neglect) of Jason. I know this news will cause you distress and you will perhaps be angry at me or Jason's teacher. I called to let you know that we want to make things at school as good for Jason as possible. I feel like we can work together for what you and I both want; a healthy, happy Jason who is doing well in school. Please let us know if we can help. We will be back in touch soon to talk with you further."

This contact will give the parent evidence that the school counselor has not judged her (or him) as completely at fault or bad, and that the school counselor is willing to maintain some involvement with the family. It will be important for the school counselor to be involved with social or legal agencies as the situation progresses. Often times, abuse investigations result in families that are left intact, but which have been either recommended or court ordered to receive counseling. The school may be a less threatening and more convenient place for this counseling to occur.

Whether or not the school counselor has been involved in the discovery and report of abuse, dealing with an abusive family in family counseling will be a challenge. A number of authors have attempted to describe the "typical" incestuous or abusive family (e.g., Alexander, 1985; Boniello, 1986; Friedrich, 1990; Reposa & Zuelzer, 1983; Roberts, 1984). There are a number of characteristics that many of these families display. Families in which abuse exists are often very *isolated* and self-contained. They do not engage socially with neighbors, co-workers, or schoolmates. This tendency towards the "siege mentality" makes it difficult for the counselor to enter or join with the family. There may be a lengthy trial period with a school counselor before the family system becomes open to the counselor at all. This opening may only happen if the family is either compelled by law or some other strong force to stay in counseling through this period. Once in the system, however, the counselor may never enjoy full membership in the family system, which is all the more reason for the counselor to have good joining skills.

Abusive families expend a vast amount of energy in an effort to maintain the status quo. This desire for order and stability results in an *unhealthy homeostasis*. The family fails to adapt and change overtime and members of the family grow older and change as external circumstances change. The family may be so entangled or *enmeshed* that they do not respond to the cues that signal changes. The challenge to the school counselor is to help the family respond to changes adaptively without threatening the security and order so important to maintaining the family system.

Alexander (1985) writes of an absence of *negentropy* in abusive families. Negentropy is what enables healthy, functioning families to grow, adapt, and develop while avoiding the chaos and disorganization inherent in growth and change. Dysfunctional families, especially those in which abuse exists, do not have this ability and, therefore, react to changing situations with inconsistent and unpredictable responses. The results for the child in such a family is often a poorly developed identity and failure to successfully differentiate from the family. This failure to differentiate is primarily due to *inadequate communication* within the family. If the counselor can aid the family in improving communication and, thus, problem solving, then the family is free to grow more productively. Conflicts that continue require the family to put an inordinate amount of energy into avoiding or suppressing the problem, which, in turn, draws energy away from healthy pursuits.

Friedrich (1990) proposes characteristics of incestuous families based on a more multi-generational approach to understanding the family system. The characteristic pattern involves a *loss experience* by at least one parent. This experience could pertain to an actual physical loss of a parent due to death, an experience of abandonment or desertion due to divorce, or the withdrawal of the parent from his or her own family as a result of familial abuse. This loss experience can result in a parent being unable to form or keep strong attachments either with his or her spouse or with his or her children. Further issues to be found in some abusive families include poorly defined boundaries, confused family roles and hierarchies, and unrealistic or ill-defined goals and expectations.

When developing a treatment plan for an abusive family, the school counselor must be certain that the plan addresses the needs and safety of the victim and that it also supports the family unit. A family approach, which considers a systems theory base, will make it possible to discern the events which led to the abuse, and thus allows a picture of the extent of the abuse in the family, including other family members either directly or indirectly victimized. This approach also will make it less likely that the victim will be blamed for the discovery of the abuse.

As the school counselor begins to join with the family, it is important that he or she avoid the tendency to become protector and advocate for the "helpless" victim through displays of anger, condemnation, or contempt towards the abuser. The school counselor should not underestimate the importance of loyalty to the family unit and to individual family members. Unfortunately, the surest way for the counselor to remain outside the family system is to challenge this loyalty. A perceived attack on the family unit or any member of the family will often result in a displacement by the family of their own anger onto the counselor or the school. Having the family focus anger onto outside forces such as the counselor or Social Services workers blocks the chances for the victim to give up his or her feelings of responsibility for the abuse. As noted earlier, it is necessary for family counseling to address the needs of everyone in the family, irrespective of whether it remains intact or is reshaped as a result of the abuse.

In his discussion of treatment of sexually abused children and their families, Friedrich (1990) offered several *working assumptions* under which a counselor must operate. Many of these apply to the family counseling provided by the school counselor or school psychologist:

1) be willing to be active and directive with the family from the beginning.
2) the welfare and safety of the victim and siblings are paramount.
3) believe the victim and do not engage the abuser in denials.
4) be sure the proper authorities have been notified.
5) coordinate all counseling activities with Social Service agencies or, when appropriate, justice officials. This includes authorization for free exchange of information pertaining to the abuse between all parties involved.
6) It may be that remaining intact or reunification is not possible for the family and that option must be given its full weight.
7) Within these parameters, be willing to work with all persons involved.

The school counselor may have to insist on setting appointments quickly following disclosure of the abuse. The importance of doing so may be lost to family members as they sort out their initial shock and deal with their own individual responses to the situation. The school counselor may need to be quite directive in establishing a plan of action and early goals for the family counseling.

Once family counseling has begun, it is important for the school counselor to recognize that the family may view family counseling not as a pleasant or constructive action, but rather as a required consequence of a family tragedy. It may help to establish good lines of communication and expectations for honest exchange. Solid communication allows for discussion of the positive and negative reasons for counseling. Also, communicating gives each family member a chance to voice feelings about being in therapy. This will be an excellent time to explain how family counseling works. The counselor should discuss expectations of everyone involved (counselor and family members alike), issues of confidentiality, cooperation with other agencies, the counselor's theoretical approach, and the formulation of initial family counseling goals. In joining the family, the counselor must adopt and use the communication style of the abusive family. This process will include socializing before serious discussions occur. Although the use of certain terms may seem inconsequential, adopting the jargon of the family, as well as *reframing* negative comments or actions into positive terms or terms perceived as supportive, can be instrumental in achieving a place in the family system for the counselor. The school counselor also should develop an appreciation for each member of the family and the desired qualities noted in that individual.

The early setting of expectations and goals is essential to productive counseling when working with abusive families. Initial goals may need to be narrow and specific and easily attained so as to foster a pattern of success. For example, the school counselor would not want to encourage the family to work on a broad goal of improving parental communication as an initial task. Perhaps asking that parents consult with each other before giving permission for children to go to a friend's house may be more easily understood and attained by the family.

Some school counselors may find it practical or therapeutic to initiate individual sessions with the abuse victim and then gradually include other family members, beginning with the non-abusing parent. Friedrich (1990) and Barrett, Sykes, and Byrnes (1986) advocate that specific conditions be met before the abuser is included in the process. Friedrich does not begin family sessions until he is certain that the abuser has accepted complete responsibility for the abuse, has been involved in some counseling, and has been psychologically assessed. Barrett et al. suggest an "apology session" in order to include the abuser into family counseling. They caution that if there is evidence of any potential problems for the victim in doing so, this apology session should wait and the abuser should continue counseling independent of the family's counseling.

Others argue that family counseling should begin very early (Larson & Maddock, 1986; Madanes, 1990, 1991; Minuchin,

1974). Madanes suggests that the guiding principle for the counselor in such situations be that the family can have no secrets. This notion is promoted by obtaining each family member's account of the abuse. Even though the counselor should be careful not to place undue pressure on the victim, he or she should offer the victim the opportunity given everyone else so that the victim's account of abusive events is revealed only when the victim is ready. This is the *first step* in a process Madanes refers to as *reparation* and includes fifteen additional steps. While this approach is primarily designed to be used with a family in which the abuser is a member of the family, with some adaptations it would be appropriate with a family in which a member has been abused by someone from outside the family. *Step 2* requires each family member to make a statement regarding why the action of the abuser was wrong. While the abuser may have difficulty expressing reasons and may minimize the abusive actions or provide pat answers (e.g., it's illegal, or the Bible says it's wrong), it is up to the counselor to help facilitate others in the family to note the pain, loss of freedom, invasion of privacy, and violence associated with the abuse.

In *Step 3* the therapist also adds that the abuse was a violation of the victim's spirit or heart, causing what Madanes (1990) refers to as "spiritual pain." The abuser's spiritual pain is acknowledged in *Step 4* and the counselor expresses concern for the difficulty experienced by the abuser as a result of his behavior. Madanes equates spirituality with sexuality, noting that a sexual violation is a violation of a person's spirit. Having one's spirit damaged is much more harmful than a simple physical attack.

Madanes (1990) indicates that *Step 5* usually occurs spontaneously. It involves the discovery of sexual or physical abuse experienced by the victim or other family members at the hands of someone other than the identified abuser or even at some other previously undisclosed time. Abuse in a family rarely occurs in isolation. There is frequently some generational family history of abuse. The counselor indicates concern for the newly revealed abuse victim(s) and again notes the spiritual pain of the victim and the abuser. The counselor then discusses the pain experienced by the non-abusing parent (or in the case of non-parental abuse, both parents) and other members of the

Family Counseling in the Schools:

family in *Step 6.*

Step 7 involves an apology offered to the victim by the abuser. Madanes (1990) insists that this apology must be done by the abuser by getting on his or her knees before the victim. The humiliation of this act is a necessary part of the process and may have to be repeated before everyone can agree that the abuser is truly sorry. Forgiveness by the victim or others in the family is not required but may be given if the individual so desires. Madanes writes that a humiliating apology is therapeutic for the abuser and for the victims and should occur early in counseling. Other members of the family are then directed, in *Step 8,* to offer kneeling apologies to the victim for failing to protect him or her from the abuse. This allows the victim to be freed from blame and liberates his or her identity as "victim."

In *Step 9,* the family discusses the consequences of any further incident of abuse. The counselor encourages the family to be severe in their response. Usually, additional abuse should result in institutionalization or removal from the family. It is not until *Step 10* that Madanes (1990) suggests that the counselor see individually the child who was the victim of abuse. The counselor, while expressing concern and compassion reminds the child that bad experiences can lead to a "higher" compassion which allows one to understand more clearly the pain of others. It also is helpful at this time to put the abuse into perspective regarding the rest of the child's life and experiences, emphasizing the positive.

Next, in *Step 11,* the counselor devotes energies to finding a "protector" for the abused child. The initial thought in these circumstances would be to seek the mother as the protector. However, in many cases, the mother in an abusive family is weak or ineffectual and has perhaps already failed in her efforts to protect the child. It is better to identify a strong, independent, but accessible member of the family for this role. Perhaps someone outside the immediate family such as a grandparent or aunt or uncle would be most appropriate (Madanes, 1990).

The actual reparation begins with *Step 12* in which the family determines some act of restitution for the abuser (Madanes, 1990). This step would obviously be inappropriate if the abuser were not a family member. This act will be only symbolic since there is no act which could repay a victim for the abuse he or she suffered. The reparation should be something that will provide a long term benefit to the victim and some significant sacrifice by the abuser.

Next, in *Step 13,* the counselor takes the family into discussions of appropriate ways for the abuser to engage in more "normal" activities. This discussion may include talking about work or school, acceptable activities such a sports or hobbies, and development of friendships. Appropriate and inappropriate responses to sexual feelings are discussed or are perhaps assigned to a parent and child pair (e.g., father-son) for further discussion. This step may not be necessary in cases of abuse from outside the family; frank sexual discussions are difficult for many parents under the best of circumstances. The counselor may find that the parent greatly appreciates the counselor's support and guidance during this phase. Repair of the bonds of love and affection to pre-abuse levels may be impossible. However, in *Step 14,* it is the counselor's task to attempt to restore the positive emotional feelings as much as is possible. The love between parents is especially important to repair. Madanes (1990) points out that mothers may be angry at the offender as a result of the abuse or she may be angry at the victim. In either case, the counselor must help the mother to remember the love she once felt for her family members and encourage her to regain that feeling in order to aid in the overall healing of the family.

Step 15 involves efforts by the counselor to return the abuser to some role as protector of the younger members of the family. A full sense of trust and dependence on this individual may be difficult, but some return to the traditional hierarchy in the family should be sought. Finally, in *Step 16,* the counselor supports the abuser in self-forgiveness. This is never an easy task. This plan may be more successful if the abuser is encouraged to do good deeds. Donation of time or money to local efforts, such as prevention of domestic violence or protection of children, will help to discourage feelings of despair when remembering previous acts or when inappropriate urges reappear.

While the school counselor may choose to use some other approach in dealing with the abusive family, it is important that certain basic principles be considered. The parent-child relationship is important for healthy family functioning and

Family Counseling in the Schools:

optimal development of the child. This fact is especially true in an abusive family. The relationship with the father or the step-father, who is often an offender, will temporarily cease when he is removed from the home or removed from a position of power and authority after the discovery of the abuse. Should the offender be another family member or someone outside the family, the father's role as protector has been seriously threatened. The relationship between the father and his children will be affected regardless of his role in the abuse. In many abusive families, the mother's role has been diminished, often to the point that the mother is equal to the children in the hierarchy. Building her power in the family and enhancing her skills as a parent is essential to a return to normalcy for the family. One way in which the school counselor can help to *empower the mother* is to help her identify specific behavioral symptoms in her children she would like to modify or alleviate. Once identified, a straight-forward behavior management approach can usually be employed to address the desired behavior change. With support from the school counselor, the mother can successfully begin her newly enhanced role as parent.

If there exists a history of abuse in the mother's childhood, which is often the case in incestuous families, this issue may have to be dealt with first. This occurrence in the mother's history would likely mean that the mother has few friends and, perhaps, poor relationships with her own family. Building a support system for the mother will give her confidence to claim her role as parent without her having to fear the inevitable separation from the counselor. Helping her to recognize that she is not like her own parents is usually a positive development. A support group or group counseling arrangement specially for adults abused as children may be a good start for her. The use of positive reframing by the school counselor will likewise reinforce messages of competence and strength that may be new to the mother. Establishing the idea that her goal has been to be a competent parent all along is helpful. She now has the chance to complete that goal without being blocked by the situation created by the abuse.

The relationship between parents and children may have been impaired before the abuse began and almost certainly was affected by the presence of abuse before it was revealed to others. Often, this parent-child conflict involves several children. It is almost certain that the mother-daughter relationship will be strained if the daughter is being sexually abused. The daughter will have the issues of a lack of protection from mother and if the abuse is incest between father and daughter, the mother will have difficulties regarding her daughter being more desirable to her husband than she. Friedrich (1990) notes that in incestuous families, male children may be inappropriately idealized, resulting in discipline that is inadequate, whereas, female children may be devalued and overly disciplined. Helping the family gain a balance will depend largely on the functioning level the mother is able to achieve as a parent. One important realization to help a parent attain and understand is that misbehavior on the part of their children is a measure of the child's need for parenting. Abuse in a family results in confusion for all the children and creates an inability to regulate feelings and emotion; this fact is especially true for victims of abuse. This control and regulation of one's emotional responses is primarily learned through interaction with healthy, functioning parents. The abused child should be helped by the counselor to express his or her anger. The abused child often targets anger at the non-abusing parent who did not prevent the abuse from happening. While helping the child to express this anger, the school counselor also must support the mother in accepting the anger from the child. *Reframing* this tolerance of the abused child's anger, as a provision of support and a demonstration of good parenting, will make it more likely for the mother to accomplish acceptance. When the mother feels capable of taking care of her children and protecting them, and the children feel confident in relying on their mother, progress has been made.

When reaching the final step advocated by Cloé Madanes (1990, 1991), the abuse-related therapeutic process is over. However, this does not end the need for counseling intervention. Abuse can smolder in silence and reappear when resistance is low. For that reason, a long-term expectation for counseling should be stated by the school counselor. Sessions may occur a month or two apart in order to keep up with the family's progress. This plan may prevent the re-occurrence of abuse or allow for early detection should it occur again.

Family Counseling in the Schools:

Anorexia Nervosa

Anorexia is a disorder that more and more families are being forced to face. The clinical definition of anorexia nervosa is a refusal to eat. The stated reason for this refusal is usually a desire to lose weight and/or a lack of hunger. Accompanying this problem is a distorted body image and a multitude of physical consequences (e.g., cessation of menstruation and excessive weight loss). Since most cases of anorexia nervosa occur in adolescent girls, very often the school counselor or school psychologist is the first mental health professional to have contact with the student or her family. Treatment of anorectic individuals can yield varying success rates. Often the primary treatment is hospitalization and forced feeding. Family counseling is one mode of treatment available to school counselors that has produced successful results (e.g., Lieberman, Minuchin, & Baker, 1974).

Studies of family interactions and common features of families of anorectic students have found what Minuchin and his colleagues have termed the "anorexigenic" or "anorectic" family (Minuchin et al., 1978). This terminology, based in a family systems approach, proposes that certain family conditions and interaction patterns are at the root of anorexia nervosa.

As noted previously, Minuchin (1974) views the family as a system interacting with other subsystems operating within and outside the family. Part of the function of the family is to foster the healthy development of its members. One's sense of identity comes from the messages received from interaction with various groups. The family is certainly the earliest, if not the most important, of these reference groups. It is in this context that a child gets his or her first chance at independence or autonomy. Autonomy is possible because the individual knows that the family is there to support those initial tentative attempts at independence. As a child develops and becomes more and more independent, the family transactions provide crucial knowledge and assurance that the family support is still there. This is how the process works in healthy, functioning families. As the children grow up and leave home to start their own families, they will develop new transactional patterns made up of negotiated compromises and some unsettled conflicts or disagreements. These new transactional patterns comprise the familiar patterns or interactions for this newly formed family.

When children are brought into the family system, their own personality interacts with the family's rules and traditions. Their personalities alter and adjust based on the accumulated feedback provided from the family as a whole and from, specifically, the spousal and parental subsystems. As the child develops, more time will be spent away from the family, which increases the importance of the social system outside the family. This external information is then brought back to the family where the child integrates it into his or her emerging identity. The family may choose to blend the new information into its transactional patterns.

There are two characteristics of family functioning that family systems theorists believe are essential to healthy growth and development (Lieberman, Minuchin, & Baker, 1974; Minuchin, 1974; Minuchin, Rosman, & Baker, 1978). First, the boundaries, and diverse strengths of these boundaries, found in the various subsystems are part of the family. Secondly, a family must have the ability to react to continual demands for change. Every family has a variety of boundaries that define the subsystems within that family. The boundaries in an enmeshed family include a high level of involvement between one or more family members. This *enmeshed* family can become totally turned inward, creating its own self-contained system. Within this type of family there is a blurring of boundaries and an intensification of communication and concern among the individuals in the family, which reduces the ability of the family members to recognize individual identity.

At the other extreme are families with rigid boundaries. The communication in these families is minimal and difficult when it does occur. In these *disengaged* families, a high level of individual distress is necessary before the family's protective, supportive mechanisms come into play. Even then, these mechanisms may not accommodate the level of stress present. Highly *enmeshed* families behave in just the opposite way by being overly protective and hyper-responsive to any stress experienced by family members. In either situation, the formation of a strong, competent identity is made difficult.

The other task of a healthy family is to maintain the equilibrium of the family and its functioning. Equilibrium is guarded by responding appropriately and reacting to the constant changes which occur in a less than static world. One constant source of change within a family is the growth and development of the children and, to a lesser degree, the adults in the family. This changing situation makes it necessary for the family system to adjust and accommodate continually.

The Anorectic Family

A young adolescent who develops anorexia nervosa has probably been a part of a highly enmeshed family (Minuchin et al., 1978); or, as Kog and Vandereycken (1985) describe it, the family has a very tightly knit family structure. This pattern of family interactions places considerable emphasis on loyalty and self-sacrifice for the good of the family even if it results in a detriment of personal gain or development. The end result of efforts expended by a child in such a family is expected to be approval or acceptance (i.e., love) rather than skill acquisition or self-satisfaction.

Anorectic families are typically child-oriented. The energies of the family go towards taking care of the child, and there evolves a high level of alertness to the needs of the child. Correspondingly, the family's vigilance is easily adopted by the child, who then develops a hypersensitivity to his or her own needs, especially those relating to physiological functioning. This focus on somatic issues is typical of all members of the anorectic family. Kog and Vandereycken (1985) note a higher incidence of weight and eating problems among members of the anorectic child's family. Minuchin has suggested that in families with an anorectic child, everyone in the family often will have concerns or preoccupation with diets, eating habits, table manners, or food fads.

Families with an anorectic child have included the following circumstances: a mother whose diabetes is primarily controlled through diet; a father who constantly chided the overweight grandmother regarding her eating habits; parents who insisted that no activity or event involving the children could interfere with the family's dinner hour; and the grandmother who insisted that all of her grown children, in-laws, and grandchildren must be at her home for Sunday dinner every week. When the family reacts to a loss of equilibrium through somatic difficulties, the entire system reacts to protect and care for the "weakened" family member. Once again the need to address a change or conflict is diverted to care for the individual who is "sick." If the anorectic child serves this purpose, the family depends on its continuation. No matter how the parents or siblings may complain or feel burdened by the anorectic child, it is important to continue the total control and protection. Anorexia becomes a part of the child's identity, perhaps the only aspect of his or her identity that is different or separate from his or her family. The family myth may hold that all will be well once the child begins to eat appropriately again.

The enmeshment in anorectic families evolves to a point that any affront to the patterns and rules of the family becomes a challenge to everyone in the family. Acts of self-sacrifice on behalf of preserving the family order are highly praised. Adolescence brings the conflict between family loyalties and the gravitating draw of peers to a peak, creating a heightened conflict. Instead of shifting focus outside the family, the anorectic child doubles his or her efforts to understand and respond to the parents. In the anorectic child's attempt to alter the parents, he or she is simply increasing the level of involvement with an already over-involved family. The strong external boundaries present in anorectic families may hide the weak, blurred boundaries that exist within. There are often cross-generational coalitions that develop between parent and child or parent and grandparent which are formed against the other spouse. The child is usually a part of this conflict.

In an ideal situation the school counselor applying family counseling may choose to see all members of the anorectic's family for each session. There are situations, however, in which working with only a part of the family can be effective. It is important for the school counselor to keep in mind that family counseling targets the family and not the individual. When using systems theory, the school counselor will always be able to identify at least one subsystem as a unit of intervention (Minuchin, et al., 1978). The school counselor may first see everyone in the nuclear family. Further exploration, however, will reveal family rules and patterns of interaction, extended family, social networks, and other subsystems which need to be addressed. Likewise, if the school counselor works with an individual, the individual will be viewed in relation to his or her position and role in the family. As Minuchin and his

Family Counseling in the Schools:

colleagues (1978) have indicated, the individual is viewed as being "... in the web of significant relationships in which people interact" (p. 80).

The school counselor should make efforts to join with the anorectic family. One method for joining, or bonding, is to ask the family about their interests. If dad fishes, then the counselor should show interest in fishing, and so forth. In order for an intervention to be effective, the identified patient (i.e., the child exhibiting anorexia) must be an active participant in the counseling process. Discoveries and conclusions are best when made by the student rather than by the professional. The school counselor, by virtue of having joined the family's system, will activate change by interpersonal transactions within the system. He or she will change the system and be changed by it as a result of active participation. When utilizing a family systems approach, the school counselor not only sees the family as directing the behavior of the anorectic child, he or she also sees the anorectic child as directing the family's behavior.

Medical attention is necessary for some cases of anorexia nervosa and should be utilized when health functioning is in jeopardy. Salvador Minuchin, working with a variety of clinicians, has developed a number of approaches to working with anorexia nervosa from a family counseling approach (Lieberman, et al., 1974; Minuchin, et al., 1978). School counselors will find two of these approaches particularly helpful.

The Family Task

The Family Task (Minuchin, Rosman, & Baker, 1978) entails giving the family a set of recorded instructions to follow. The counselor leaves the area and observes through a one-way mirror or videotape, intervening only when necessary.

Recorded Instructions

1. Suppose all of you had to work out a menu for dinner tonight. You would all like to have your favorite foods for dinner, but in putting this menu together you can have only one meat, two vegetables, one drink, and one dessert. We'd like you to talk together about it now and decide on this one meal that you would all enjoy. Remember, it can

only have one meat, two vegetables, one drink, and one dessert. You must end up agreeing on this one meal that everyone will enjoy. Turn off the recorder and go ahead with your discussion.

2. All right now, we're ready for the next task. In every family things happen that cause a fuss now and then. We'd like you to discuss and talk together about an argument you've had; a fight or argument at home that you can remember. We'd like you to talk together about it. You can cover what started it, who was in on it, what went on, and how it turned out. See if you can remember what it was all about. We'd like you to take your time and discuss it at length.

3. We're ready for the next task. For this one, we'd like each of you to tell about the things everyone does in the family: not only the things that please you the most and make you feel good, but also the things each one does that make you unhappy or mad. Everyone try to give his or her own ideas about this topic.

4. Here is the next task. On the table you will find a folder with two picture cards in it. Each of these pictures shows a family scene. We'd like you to make up a story together about each of the pictures. We'd like you to tell what is happening in the picture, what you think led up to this scene, and what the people are thinking and feeling. Then make up an ending for the story. First make up a story for picture one, and when you're finished with that, make up a story for picture two. Remember, discuss the pictures and make up the stories together.

5. We are now ready for the last task. We have something we want you to make together. On the easel we have made a model for you to copy. In the folder in front of you there are enough pieces for you to put it together. The pieces are divided into bunches. There is one bunch for each of you to start with. Make your copy on the table and stay seated. Remember, it's for the whole family to work on together.

Preparation for the Session

1. Family members are asked to seat themselves as they wish

133

at the table, as long as all are facing the camera (or mirror), full or profile.

2. On the table is placed the tape recorder containing the Family Task cassette, a folder with the picture cards, and a folder with the color-form model pieces in envelopes. The model to be copied is taped to the wall facing the family.

3. Be sure to distribute the pieces used in task No. 5 according to the number in the family prior to the start of the task.

Verbal Instructions

1. Explain about the videotape, cameras, microphones, and one-way mirror. Tell them you will be watching.

2. "We have some things for you to do today, for you to do together as a family. The instructions for each of these are on this tape recorder." Explain the mechanical use of the tape recorder, how to turn on the play button, how to stop it, etc. MAKE SURE YOU LOOK AT ALL FAMILY MEMBERS WHEN EXPLAINING. "First, listen to the direction for the first thing to do. After you have finished the first task, go on to the second, and so on. Any questions?" The counselor leaves the room.

3. If the discussion for task Nos. 2 or 3 lasts excessively long and seems interminable, as will happen on occasion, go back in and suggest that the family proceed to the next task. In these cases, the task has usually been more or less completed, but the discussion goes on ruminatively.

4. If for the last task the family does not grasp the task about copying the model and starts making up their own creation, you may go in and tell them to copy the model. Give them a couple of minutes first, because sometimes someone from the family will call this problem to the attention of the others and then they will shift to copy the model. However, if it is clear there is no internal disagreement about the task and everyone has the wrong idea or the one who thinks that they should make his own version "wins," then you can go in and set them straight.

This task is an exercise in building family communication and cooperation. It is also an opportunity for the school counselor to assess family functioning along a number of dimensions.

The Family Lunch

School counselors will find it useful to work with the student as well as the anorectic families during mealtime and may wish to employ treatment techniques adapted for use in the school from a procedure known as *The Family Lunch* (Liebman, Minuchin, & Baker, 1974). This program has a number of phases which contain specific goals:

1. Informal lunch sessions including the school counselor and the anorectic student, for the purpose of assessing the degree of negativism and anorexia.
2. Application of an in-school operant reinforcement paradigm to initiate weight gain.
3. Family lunch sessions to accelerate and reinforce weight gain.
4. Application of an at-home operant reinforcement paradigm as a family task to prevent weight loss.
5. Family counseling to change the structure and functioning of the family. This counseling can be conducted by the school counselor as well, or may be referred to a professional outside the school setting.

To begin the process the school counselor arranges to have lunch with the student on a regular basis (at least three times a week) if not daily. Initially the school counselor will give messages regarding hunger and eating. The counselor (referred to as male in this example) can say that when he was hungry his stomach hurt and he had a light-headed feeling. He would say that it feels good for him to eat and be satisfied. No attempt should be made to get the student to eat his or her lunch. The school counselor may ask permission to eat some small portion of the student's lunch such as a carrot or stick of celery and then should offer to share his lunch with the student. This procedure enables the school counselor to assess the degree of negativism and anorexia manifested in the student. It also provides an opportunity to relate to the student on the issues of sharing and eating food, thus avoiding a power struggle over the act of eating. The school counselor should take advantage of the opportunity to talk with the student by gathering family

Family Counseling in the Schools:

background information in an informal manner.

Following the initiation of the lunch sessions with the school counselor, the counselor should implement (with the student's cooperation) a plan in which the student has access to activities he or she enjoys contingent upon weight gain. The student should weigh-in each morning with the school counselor present. If he or she has gained half a pound or more since the previous day, then he or she will have access to the agreed upon activity. Arrangements with the administration to miss class and engage in the chosen activity should be handled by the school counselor. If he or she has gained less than a half pound, then he or she must attend all classes and continue his or her assigned routine. The student should discuss the menu items available (within the limits of the school cafeteria) and have whatever he or she would like for lunch as long as it is a well-balanced diet. The school counselor may wish to bring in outside items, such as fresh fruits or vegetables or bakery items, to supplement the lunch. This would all, of course, be planned with the student. The school counselor should explain the procedure to family members and suggest that they discuss it with the student. Any questions are to be directed to the school counselor rather than to the student. The school counselor may need to emphasize that the program at school is to be negotiated between the student, counselor, and parents. Once they have given permission, the parents will have no other role in the school eating plan.

Once some weight gain has been achieved, the anxiety levels of all involved will have been reduced and it will be time to initiate the family lunch. The family lunch session should be held in a private area (e.g., conference room or vacant teachers' lounge) and should include the school counselor, the student, and his or her parents, as well as other siblings, if possible. A teacher or other school staff member with whom the student has a good relationship can be included at the student's request. This group will demonstrate a united front as school personnel and parents work together in support of the student and his or her best interest. The goals of the family lunch are, first, to enable the student to eat in the presence of his or her parents without the development of a power struggle, thus providing an entirely new experience for them with respect to eating, and, second, to redefine the presenting problem and dismantle the family's myth that they are fine except for the presence of their medically sick child. This latter formulation, which forces the student into the rigid role of being the sole repository of all the family's problems, is a recognition of the interpersonal transactional conflicts that exist between the parents and the child. This knowledge will decrease the student's centrality and the manipulative power of his or her symptoms.

At the end of the first lunch session, a weight goal is established. The initial weight gain and family lunch session will start the process of disengaging the child from his or her role in the family's dysfunctional transactions. This process is continued by the assignment of an operant reinforcement paradigm, which the parents will carry out. Providing the parents something to do at home will further reduce their anxiety and their feelings of helplessness. The parents should be fully supported by the school counselor and the administration in this undertaking. The school counselor should tell the parents that it is their responsibility to enforce the paradigm and that working together usually results in success. If the child refuses to eat and loses more weight, this indicates that the parents are not working together. The school counselor should remind the student that it is his or her responsibility to follow the paradigm. The authority for the paradigm remains with the school counselor. If there is a crisis, the parents should call the school counselor; they are not to acquiesce to the child's refusal to eat. This procedure gives the student increased responsibility and autonomy. As long as the student follows the procedure, the student can have complete control over the area of eating.

An example of such a paradigm would include a provision that the student must gain a minimum of two pounds a week in order to maintain normal activities. If he or she gained less than two pounds from Friday to Friday, he or she would not be allowed out of the house during the weekend and could not have friends come to the house. In addition, a member of the family would stay at home with the student. This produces a great deal of stress in the family system, causing the members of the family to join together to ensure that the student ate. If he or she gains between two and two and a half pounds, he or she would be allowed to be active on either Saturday or Sunday, but not both days. He or she should be given a choice of days and activities. If he or she gains more than two and a half pounds, activities on Friday, Saturday, and Sunday should be allowed.

Once weight gain has progressed in a gradual manner, the family subsystem as a whole will need some reorganization. Family counseling at this stage would be aimed at changing the structure, organization, and functioning of the family and the quality of the interpersonal relationships in the family. As previously noted, the school counselor may be best suited to continue this process (the family task described above can be utilized as a part of this process), or a referral to an outside professional agency, including medical monitoring, may be appropriate. It is certain that once the student gains weight and begins to eat regularly, the entire problem for the family is not fully solved. Yet, the family has made a good start in that direction.

Substance Abuse

When a child abuses alcohol or drugs, the abuse is often treated as an isolated event. There is certainly more to a substance abuse problem than can be seen on the surface. Substance abuse affects the entire family, and may also disrupt an entire community or school. It is not an easy task to determine which factor is primary in alcohol and/or drug abuse. Kaufman and Kaufman (1979) have noted that the most important causes in the current generation are societal, and involve the dysfunction of family and community. For example, the Kaufmans have reported in a survey of 20 young women in a residential drug treatment program, that the women had experienced sexual abuse by their father, father surrogate, or older brother before the age of eleven. Certainly a consideration of family factors makes sense when a school counselor addresses substance abuse problems in school.

Moreover, when families are asked to take their drug-using adolescent children to outpatient clinics, 85% do not follow-through with the recommendation (Foote, Szapocznik, Kurtines, Perez-Vidal, & Hervis, 1985) and, of those who capitulate, 50% drop out after two sessions (Arbour & Bramble, 1985). Bry and Green (1990) have reported that while families, may have resisted previous recommendations for therapy, they are often familiar with visits to the guidance counselor. Receiving family therapy in the school can become incorporated into the response class of "visiting the counselor" and may be called "counseling" instead of therapy. In this way, troubled families that may have been unreachable for other therapists may attend treatment at school (p. 91).

In these cases the objective of counseling is to help the parents help their adolescent do better in school, rather than an activity related to "unhappiness, family dysfunction, gripes between family members, or 'mental' problems" (Bry & Greene, p. 91). Counseling can be scheduled right after school or in the early evening when the parents have finished their work day. In this way the counseling fits the families schedule rather than the counselor's (Bry & Greene).

A number of studies have attempted to characterize common features found in families of substance abusers (e.g., Kaufman & Kaufman, 1979; Steinglass, 1987). The features all point to family counseling as a reasonable approach to intervention for the school counselor.

1. Substance abuse by at least one of the parent figures is very common and may result either in direct modeling of the abuse by the child, or in inadequate parenting which leads the child to substance abuse.
2. There are cross-generational alliances formed which serve to separate the spousal subsystem.
3. The substance abusing child serves as the symptom carrier for family dysfunction.
4. The abuse by the child maintains the homeostasis in the family.
5. While the parenting may be inadequate, the presence of substance abuse by the child reinforces the need for parental control and for the continuation of parenting.
6. Focus on the child's substance abuse acts as an effective means for parents to avoid acknowledging or addressing marital difficulties.
7. Generational boundaries are diffuse. The substance abuse of the child and the subsequent crisis it produces may offer the only catalyst for any joint action by the family.

Family Counseling in the Schools:

Weekly family counseling sessions have been found to effect the way families deal with drug problems among school-age adolescents. Bry, Conboy, and Bisgay (1986) found that by following family problem-solving, parents have learned to discuss between themselves the consequences for the drug behavior rather than attack one another. Families prefer problem-solving among themselves when compared to other treatments (e.g., medication, behavioral contracting) (Mittl & Robin, 1987). Some families have even significantly decreased drug use and decreased school failure after family problem-solving (Bry et al.).

In general, families with substance abusing children tend to contain enmeshed mother-child relationships, fathers who are considerably disengaged, and sibling subsystems which include a combination of siblings who have either individuated from the family or who are enmeshed with the identified patient. These enmeshed siblings are often substance abusers also and buy drugs for each other, as well as cover for each other with parents and other authorities. Clear boundaries between the substance abusing child and his or her parents are rarely found. The combination of an enmeshed mother and a disengaged father creates a complex circumstance for the child, and it is not surprising to find that such families frequently exhibit marital difficulties. The most typical pattern is that of a male child enmeshed with his mother. This alliance results in the father feeling separated from the family and reacting by way of further disengagement, violence towards the members of the family, or a combination of both. Enmeshment may become extreme resulting in the mother's inability to separate from the involved child without somatic, suicidal, or psychotic responses. Providing protection for the child from trouble with the authorities is the only area on which parents can find common ground. The family may initially deny the existence of a substance abuse problem while, at the same time, may need the problem to avoid focusing on marital discord or other problems within the family.

Pressure for change in the family of a substance abusing child is usually absent. In a family system, the substance-abusing child has many functions. He or she is likely to be the symptom carrier of the family dysfunction which helps to maintain the status quo (*homeostasis*). The child's difficulty reinforces the parents' need to control and provide parenting (inadequate or not). The substance abuse provides a "site" for family battle so that marital conflict can continue to be denied. The child is not viewed as an individual and the family feels helpless. Any blame for the family's difficulties is usually focused on some source outside the family. The child may be overprotected as the family focuses all of its conflict managing resources on the substance abuse problem of the child. The special role of the child is to provide the family with a problem upon which to focus, thus alleviating the need to address other issues. The role of the child becomes one of family stabilizer, an admirable role to be sure.

It is important to remember that the unit for intervention is not the student, but that it involves, at least, the parental subsystem. It can be assumed that the adults in this family are communicating through the child. This creates problems for them particularly when the child is not available. An initial goal of the school counselor is to remove the child from this triangle, allowing the child to function normally while maintaining family stability. At this point, there is no concern for exploring insight or expression of feelings. There are guidelines which are appropriate for school counselors wishing to utilize a family counseling approach to counseling families with substance abusing children. These have been adapted from those offered by Haley (1979).

1. The school counselor should have the entire family present for the first session. This task may require a considerable investment of energy on the part of the school counselor.
2. Blaming is counterproductive. Parents, or supervising adults, should be put in charge of solving the problem. The school counselor should convince them that they are the best qualified to provide the help the child needs. This fact requires the family to communicate about the child, as they have been, but in a more constructive way. Specifically,
    a) Discussions should be limited to dealing with and solving the problems associated with the child's substance abuse. Other family issues should be excluded from discussion. Consequences of further

        drug or alcohol use by the child should be addressed.

b) The past and supposed causes of the substance abuse are omitted or ignored. The here and now is the focus.

c) If necessary, the school counselor should join the parents against the student. This should be done even if it appears to make the child too dependent for his or her age or if it appears to be depriving him or her of independence and personal rights. Once "normal" returns, rights and privileges can be restored.

d) Marital conflicts or conflicts between family members other than the substance abusing student may surface and should be ignored. If family members insist, the school counselor should tell them that those issues must wait until the identified patient is back to normal.

e) Expectations of normal functioning of the child should come from everyone. Normal functioning would include continued school attendance, keeping part-time jobs, or responsibilities at home. These expectations should be immediate.

3. Improvements on the part of the family will result in the family becoming unstable. Parents may even threaten separation or divorce. At this point the student would usually begin to have problems again in order to return homeostasis to the family. If the school counselor has successfully allied with the parents, they will turn to the school counselor, leaving the student to continue his or her improvement. The school counselor must either move the student out of the conflict and allow it to go on directly between the parents, or help the parents solve the problem which allows the student to remain free of the relationship.

4. The school counselor should enter into this process with the expectation that it will require intense but brief efforts. As soon as positive changes occur, the school counselor should begin to plan for termination. Not all of the family problems will be, or should be expected to be, solved. A newly established contract to address other family issues can occur. For example, many families with substance

abuse may also exhibit child neglect or even physical and sexual abuse.

Our suggested approach for the school counselor in providing family counseling to the family of substance abusing students is based on the above guidelines. From the beginning, the school counselor should promote the idea that the solution to the substance abuse problem is actually a family solution. The school counselor may wish to make the telephone contact to set up the initial family meeting while the student is in the counselor's office. As noted, this process may take a considerable amount of time and energy but it is the basis for any success that is to be achieved through family counseling. It may first be necessary for the school counselor to convince the parents that a problem exists. Often, the denial process has had a long time to develop. The school counselor also may find resistance from the student when the issue of including the family is presented. It is imperative that the school counselor avoid any tendency to place blame; he or she should stress the need for a joint effort. Through the use of *reframing*, family behaviors can be characterized as helpful and well intentioned (e.g., "He is protecting his family like a father is expected to." or "Her intentions are to do what a good mother would do."). Reframing avoids the problems associated with attempting family counseling in the face of resistance.

Initially, the family counseling sessions should concentrate on setting goals for treatment. The school counselor should help direct the family to appropriate goals. Certainly one goal of counseling should be to help the student cease his or her substance use. Should other issues arise, the school counselor should challenge their relevance to the issue at hand. If no relevance to the substance abuse problem can be shown, the issue should not be addressed. The major role for the school counselor at this juncture is to ally with the parents in an active stance against the substance abuse. The parents should not be allowed to get into issues involving marital conflicts. A united front is very important. If mother is over-involved with her child, it helps to put the father in charge, for the time being. This plan may involve encouraging father-child activities. This arrangement may not feel comfortable at first and may need to begin in the school counselor's office before it is transferred to the home. During this time the school counselor will want to provide subtle support for the mother as the father and child begin to form a different relationship.

It is expected that the student will, in response to the family counseling efforts, cease his or her substance use. Stanton and Todd (1979) have suggested that this process takes about three to four weeks once the family counseling has begun. As the student begins to show improvement, it can be expected that a family crisis of some kind is going to occur. Most often this crisis will involve a marital conflict that surfaces as the child's "sickness" disappears. It is at this time that the child may need to "develop" a problem in order to save the parents' marriage. The school counselor's alliance with the parents should help deflect this pressure and allow the child to continue his or her progress. If other family problems surface, as they often will, the school counselor should refuse to address these issues unless they are related to the substance abuse. It is important to keep the focus on the major therapeutic goal which is to eliminate the problem of substance abuse. Should the student relapse, the question of accountability has to be addressed. The family will have to take responsibility for any relapse. The school counselor will not find the family ready to accept this responsibility without a considerable amount of resistance. Stanton and Todd write that the counselor "should help the family either to accept it or to effectively disengage from the addict so that he must accept it on his own" (p. 62). Ultimately, the parents must return to the executive position in the family and gain influence over their substance-abusing child (Haley, 1980; West, Hosie, & Zarski, 1987).

The final sessions of family counseling are primarily for the purpose of disengagement of the school counselor. If there has been a successful period of abstinence from the alcohol or drug use, then the family can turn its attention to other issues such as the student getting a job, improving grades, and staying in school, or disapproving of activities away from home. These concerns can be addressed through small, easily attained goals such as having the student finding two or three appropriate job listings. The counselor should involve the parents in this task while, at the same time, reminding them not to become overly involved. Parents might also begin at this point to deal directly with any marital problems. The school counselor may find this is an appropriate time to provide a referral for marital or further family counseling outside the school setting so as to address longer term issues. Usually, if the family counseling has proven to be successful then the issue of termination is not difficult. There may need to be some follow-up on a monthly basis for a while, but the family will be ready to resume responsibility for family functioning without much resistance.

Not all school counselors will feel comfortable with this approach. The school counselor will, of necessity, play a very active and often directive role in the counseling process. The school counselor will need to be supportive, energetic, and available to the family during the month or two that the described process should last. Flexibility will be an absolute necessity when dealing with substance abuse problems and the school counselor may be required to suspend some personal, moral, or religious beliefs to accomplish joining with the family. The family is likely to be quite demanding of the school counselor's time and energy. While a school setting is one appropriate place for family counseling to occur, the school counselor should insure that the parents are ready to meet the expectations of such counseling. Being available to the student on a daily basis certainly provides an advantage that counseling in other settings does not.

Attention Deficit/Hyperactivity Disorder

When a child has a chronic problem, such as attention deficit/ hyperactivity disorder (AD/HD), there may be significant family tension and a disruption in family functioning (Feetham & Humenick, 1982; Ross & Ross, 1982). O'Brien (1992) has indicated that usually "children and their families have been aware of and attempting to cope with the problems of AD/HD for a long time prior to seeking treatment" (p. 109).

Lewis (1992) found AD/HD prevalence rates ranging from 5% to 14% with more boys having AD/HD than girls. In addition, as many as 15% to 20% of children with learning disabilities have AD/HD (O'Brien, 1992; Silver, 1990). AD/HD is presumed to be a neurological disorder that affects motor functioning, impulse control, and the ability to pay attention (Silver, 1990). Two factors, although possibly independent of one another, that could indicate a poor prognosis are aggressive symptoms and a

145

Family Counseling in the Schools:

harsh family environment (Marshall, Longwell, Goldstein, & Swanson, 1990; Milich & Loney, 1979). Children with AD/HD may feel angry and devalued and may manifest irritability and a depressive mood. These children at times ridicule themselves, before their peers and family members have the opportunity. They sometimes blame many of their problems on AD/HD, thereby making them free of responsibility for their behavior (O'Brien). A review of the literature revealed that children and adolescents with AD/HD may have difficulty with academic achievement, antisocial behavior, drug use, and even arrests. Other problems include oppositional behavior, low self-esteem, and poor peer relationships (see Anastopoulos, Guevremont, Shelton, & DuPaul, 1992). Moreover, attentional and behavioral problems usually result in long-term problems for school children and their families (Lewis).

Family problems may include negative parental perceptions, parenting problems, poor parent-child communications, and sibling difficulties. Unfortunately, AD/HD children's problems may work synergistically with family difficulties to further deteriorate the family atmosphere (Hechtman, 1981). Many parents with an AD/HD child view their family as extremely chaotic or rigid, resulting in the belief that there is little opportunity for change. Parents of children with AD/HD typically have difficulties with discipline which include power struggles, management of defiant behavior, poor socialization, and reciprocal interactions that seem to maintain problems (see Anastopoulos et al., 1992; Lewis, 1992; Lorber & Patterson, 1981; Tallmadge, Paternite, & Gordon, 1989).

Although there is no consistent counseling approach or educational curriculum for treating AD/HD, treatment is generally multifaceted and features special education, behavior management, and family counseling. In addition, about 80% of children *accurately diagnosed* with AD/HD respond favorably to some type of medication (Silver, 1990). Co-existing learning disabilities should be identified and an educational plan developed to treat the academic deficiencies. Once this has been accomplished, family counseling in the school can assist the family in understanding AD/HD, in planning behavioral management, and in improving communication. It is important for the family to be perceived by the counselor as sharing in the problems as well as the successes of the child with AD/HD

(O'Brien, 1992).

Assisting families with an AD/HD child improves communication and may facilitate enhanced family functioning (Lewis, 1992). The stance that the parents take regarding the child with AD/HD is an important initial consideration in family counseling. This parental stance can range from the concern that something is terribly wrong with their child, to blaming the school, to seeing the fault as the child's. Because of the array of possible perceptions of the parents, it is crucial for the school counselor to remain empathic and to recognize the parents' frustration and attempts to cope with the AD/HD child within the family environment (O'Brien, 1992). Recently, parent training has become popular in addressing AD/HD (Newby, Fischer, & Roman, 1991).

Parenting programs have various formats. Barkley (1987) has focused on the social processes within the family that may be responsible for developing and sustaining non-compliant behavior. Consistent consequences, plans for reducing parental stress and conflict, utilization of timeouts, and nondirective playtime are hallmarks of the Barkley parenting program. Fifteen to twenty minute daily playtimes are designed to increase the quality of the attention parents give the child. Parents are asked to attend to positive rather than negative behaviors, which should improve the general relationship between parent and child. Parents need assistance in viewing the positive side of their children's accomplishments, as well as in seeing their AD/HD children in a realistic light. Parents may be angry with the school or school counselor, or they may feel guilty and ask the counselor what they have done wrong (O'Brien, 1992). Children may be openly rejected and considered for residential placement. In addition, siblings of the child with AD/HD may feel that a "double standard" is operating within the family, resulting in negative and provocative behavior, or even shame for their sibling with AD/HD.

In order to be successful with an AD/HD family, school counselors should establish a high level of therapeutic rapport, flexibility in applying interventions, and be able to deal effectively with a family's natural resistance to change (Patterson, 1982). Fenell & Weinhold (1989) have illustrated family counseling skills for child behavior changes that can

Family Counseling in the Schools:

easily be used by counselors working with families with AD/HD children. First, all behavioral problems must be clearly identified. In family counseling it is important for the school counselor to have the parents prioritize the problems in order of their disruption to family functioning. Next, goals for each behavior must be made and a relative action plan established. Finally, the plan must be implemented. Fundamental counseling skills will facilitate this family behavior change process. These include rapport building, information gathering, self-disclosure (especially if the school counselor has children), some degree of confrontation, interpretation, and closure. Since a number of children with AD/HD will demonstrate extreme defiance, a discussion of antisocial behavior in family counseling may be appropriate.

Many parents with AD/HD children emphasize the child's deficiencies. Braswell & Bloomquist (1991) have suggested that parents divert the focus of their thinking from the student's weaknesses to the student's strengths. Parents must be trained to focus on the positive rather than the negative; they should be informed that something can be done about their child's problem. A continual emphasis on deficiencies will undoubtedly affect the parent-child and other family relationships.

Parents can learn various methods for helping the child with his or her AD/HD problem. This may include behavioral management and, in many cases, cognitive-behavioral interventions conducted by the parents. Strategies for change may encompass modifying the home environment to accommodate the child's skill level. In just a few sessions, parents and child can begin making therapeutic changes within the family (Braswell & Bloomquist, 1991). Gard and Berry (1986) have reported that five essential parenting skills are crucial to child behavioral management: 1) positive interactions between parents and child, 2) reinforcement procedures to enhance specific child behaviors, 3) ignoring in order to decrease negative and oppositional child behaviors, 4) giving the child clear and consistent commands, and 5) using consequences to reduce inappropriate behaviors.

School counselors are in an excellent position to assist parents in learning behavioral management and cognitive-behavioral techniques. For example, parents must learn to accurately observe both their child's and their own behavior. Parents also need to be educated about inadvertently reinforcing problematic behavior. Additionally, parents need to recognize which of their responses to the child's impulsive or distracting behaviors are reinforcing. Children who are taught to "Stop, Think, and Plan" will do best in family environments that are supported by the parents. Parents also can be taught cognitive-behavioral methods which allow the child to solve his or her own problems (Braswell & Bloomquist, 1991).

Additionally, family counseling can enhance family problem-solving processes. This includes learning how to define problems, considering alternatives and options and then choosing the best one, implementing a strategy, and, finally, checking to see if the plan is working. Braswell and Bloomquist (1991) have developed a five-step problem-solving process for families with AD/HD children.

1. Stop! What is the problem we are having?
2. What are some plans we can use?
3. What is the best plan we could use?
4. Let us do the plan.
5. Did the plan work? (p. 192).

The school counselor can help the family learn how to negotiate plans and how to reinforce the AD/HD student for appropriate participation and cooperation (Braswell & Bloomquist).

Braswell and Bloomquist (1991) have indicated that communication problems are a major source of difficulty for families with an AD/HD child. Such problems include arguing, interrupting, vague/ambiguous statements, blaming, speaking tangentially, dominating conversation, poor eye contact, and destructive verbalizations. Skills training in communication helps the family realize their destructive patterns of verbal interaction while they learn new communication skills. Counselors working on family communication should model appropriate communication, teach the family different ways of speaking, and provide the family with recurrent feedback. It is often helpful to videotape communications skills training sessions and play them back for the family in order to provide direct feedback (Braswell & Bloomquist).

Family Counseling in the Schools:

Antisocial Behavior

Children in school will at some time or another engage in some behavior which either conflicts with society or with society's expectations. When this antisocial behavior becomes repetitive or develops into a pattern of social or personal conflict, the school counselor is often called upon to address and change this behavior. Antisocial behaviors include stealing, lying, and running away. Although society, including parents, disapproves of these behaviors, elements such as competition, winning, and some degree of nonconformity are rewarded. Often times "getting caught" has been portrayed as the real "sin" rather than the act itself.

Family sanctions or models provided by adults may be a basis for the beginning of antisocial behaviors. Mom instructing her son to tell a caller that "Mom's not home" makes lying acceptable. When a daughter sees her dad eat grapes from the produce section of the market, she learns that at least some stealing is allowed. These are all innocent examples. If parents actually engage in more blatant antisocial or illegal behavior, the child will certainly take notice and may be expected to imitate these behaviors. Many antisocial behaviors result not from specific parental models, but from the child's feeling disengaged or alienated from his or her parents. When needs for affection, consistency, or stability go unmet, the child will turn to members of his or her peer group, whose moral values and ethical codes are not as well established. As noted earlier, children may respond to a family break-up with antisocial or at least undesirable behaviors. We have already examined how a child may be placed in a family role that requires him or her to be "disordered" in some way in order to preserve homeostasis and keep the family together. The child's identity is likely dependent upon his or her role as troublemaker, problem child, or worse.

Once a problem area has been identified, the first task is to help the family accept the need to work with the school counselor towards a solution. This task may include convincing the parents that there is a problem and a solution and that they are an essential part of the solution. In general, the school counselor will need to join with parents and provide them with models and directives to improve parenting skills, as he or she facilitates more functional patterns of communication within the family.

Over time, most children will display some antisocial behavior. The vast majority of these children will grow into law abiding citizens. Parents need to be reminded of this fact. It also is important that parents avoid the tendency to label children as "bad," "delinquent," or as a "troublemaker" because of some limited antisocial behavior. Parents should know that such children can be successful. Parents may require help in determining which behavior to address. Trying to correct a multitude of behaviors at once will probably prove frustrating for the parents as well as for the child. It can be helpful to have the parents focus on one specific behavior. Meanwhile, the school counselor should concentrate on marital problems or family conflicts which the counselor has hypothesized as the basis for the problem (Wells & Hinkle, 1990).

While using the strategies noted earlier to achieve improved family functioning, the school counselor will want to give the parents specific guidelines regarding the identified problem and how to address it. Shaefer and Millman (1981) have provided some specific direction to be used in response to particular problem behaviors. These guidelines, along with encouragement and direction from the school counselor, should provide the parents with a concrete manner in which to respond.

1. Individualize. Parents should make certain that they tailor their responses to the individual personalities, preferences, and characteristics of their child. Parents know better than anyone what will, and what will not, work with their children. It is important for parents not to attempt cookbook remedies. Successful measures used with one child may fail with another. And what works with a certain child in one situation may not work with that same child if circumstances are different.
2. Be specific. When setting rules and expectations, it is essential that everyone understands the rules and expectations in the same way and can agree on their meaning. This agreement also should apply to the statement of consequences for both positive and negative behaviors. Making clear and easily understood *rules* and

regulations will benefit both parent and child in the smooth day-to-day operation of the household.

3. State the reason. The importance of understanding the rules is necessary, as is understanding the need for a specific rule. If children perceive that a rule was established solely to benefit the adults in the household, or was decided arbitrarily, the potential for rule breaking is certainly greater.

4. Expect obedience. When any request or directive is delivered from a parent to a child, the child is much more likely to comply if the adult conveys the expectation that the child will obey. Many times children desire structure and control, even when they protest against it. Allowing the child inordinate freedom places an undue burden on him or her. By providing structure and direction, the parent can alleviate that burden.

5. Make few demands. It is not necessary to try to anticipate every eventuality in setting rules. Parents who are fair and flexible provide a well functioning model for their children. Setting a multitude of rules also makes it difficult for parents to be consistent in enforcing all of them.

6. State rules and provide praise impersonally. It is much better for a parent to say, "hitting others is not allowed," than to say, "Jason, you are not allowed to hit your sister." In the same manner it is better to praise the efforts of a child, (e.g., "This room looks very neat and clean now.") than to associate good works with the goodness of the individual (e.g., "What a good girl. You cleaned your room."). The latter approach, while seemingly benign, can lead to the logical conclusion that if she does not clean her room, she is no longer a good person.

7. Make direct statements. The more specific and brief the directive, the less likelihood of confusion. "Pick up your shoes please," is much better than saying, "What are these shoes doing in the floor again," or coaxing with, "I sure would like to have this floor nice and clear."

8. State rules positively when possible. Express rules in a prescriptive rather than a prohibitive manner. For example, say "walk when you are in the house," rather than "stop running." Say, "dirty clothes go in the

hamper," rather than "stop throwing your dirty clothes on the floor."

9. Be aware of your tone. The way in which parents say things when they state a rule or give a directive can determine the way in which a child will respond. There is little place for sarcasm or put downs when parents interact with their children. An irritated or disgusted tone in one's voice is very likely to draw opposition from a child.

10. Give a choice. When giving a child a directive it may go easier, as well as teach responsibility, if the child is offered some choice. For example, a parent might say, "Do you want to take your shower in the upstairs or downstairs bathroom?" This question leaves no room for not bathing but does give the child some choice.

11. Be flexible. The rigidity of the house rules should be flexible enough to bend if a special circumstance calls for it or as the child develops and is able to handle more independence.

12. Be consistent. Being flexible does not mean being wishy-washy. Once a rule is set, it should be enforced as strictly one day as the next and only altered if circumstances really warrant, not just for the convenience of the parent.

13. Be reasonable. Make sure that in the zeal to gain control of behavior, the parent does not make the consequences more serious than the behavior warrants. The loss of a privilege, time alone in a room for a short period, extra chores, or some form of restitution (i.e., making up for the damage done by repairing, replacing, or paying for a replacement) are all effective consequences. Corporal punishment is usually not helpful for the child or the parent and seldom has more than a short-term effect.

In addition to the general suggestions above, there are some responses specific to individual problem behaviors. If *stealing* is the problem, parents should know that stealing can occur for many reasons. Younger children may not have developed an understanding of individual ownership. Older children steal to obtain desired items, to demonstrate an independence from adult authority, or to impress peers with their daring or bravado. It is not uncommon for stealing to occur in the aftermath of a

153

separation, divorce, or death of a parent. To address stealing, parents should make sure they confront the child immediately by telling the child they are aware of the stealing and will administer appropriate consequences. Asking a child if he or she did something when parents already know the answer usually sets up the child to lie and leads the child into deeper trouble with parents. At the point of discovery, confession in not necessarily helpful. The consequence that makes the most sense is either restoring the stolen object to its rightful owner or restitution. Restitution may involve monetary compensation, replacement of the object, or provision of some compensatory act (i.e., working for the injured party), all of which should be accompanied by an apology. Any consequence imposed should result in some inconvenience or loss to the child. School counselors must not forget that stealing sometimes occurs because of a dysfunctional transactional patterns in the family or due to a parent-child relationship that is lacking. While parents respond as prescribed, the school counselor should continue to work with the family to repair the relationship or communication patterns in the family.

The one characteristic that parents appear to prize above all others in their children is honesty. The *truth* is, however, that children frequently engage in *lying*. Very young children may be unable to reliably distinguish reality from fantasy. Older children, once able to recognize the difference, will either blame others for their actions, invent stories that never occurred, elaborate the facts of a real incident, or simply reverse the truth (e.g., a child says that the dog has been fed when in fact it has not). The reasons for lying are as varied as the lies that children tell. A child will often be motivated to lie in self-defense, so as to avoid punishment or embarrassment. Lying may be a means to deal with unpleasant realities through denial or it may be due to a failure to trust an adult to deal fairly when told the truth. Following the models of familiar adults, or fulfilling a self-image as a liar, can result in children lying. They may lie to get attention or to demonstrate loyalty to a peer. Whatever the reason, lying is a behavior. When practiced frequently by children, it is upsetting to adults. Parents can help to prevent lying by not insisting that children confess to their behaviors. This notion was noted in the previous discussion of stealing. It also is important for the school counselor to help the parents realize how influential their own behavior is on the behavior of their children. The school counselor should promote open communication between all members of a family. With better communication between parents, as well as between parents and children, it is possible to identify what the child gains from lying and to develop more acceptable ways for the child to obtain what he or she seeks.

It is not difficult to imagine all the reasons why a child may run away from home. Running away is often the last of many behaviors of a child with problems. Fleeing from home is a desperate act, often undertaken as a means of communication rather than as a real attempt to leave. Parents can prevent running away by watching for signs that a child is having difficulty and by responding to these signs. Children who do not receive affection or praise may turn to peers or to the streets in search of acceptance. Children often threaten to run away or they leave signs that are easily read to indicate their intention. Parents should not challenge the child by telling him or her to go ahead and leave or act as if they do not care if the child leaves. This is a time to express concern and affection: "I sure would miss you and I would worry about you if you left." Next, present an option for communicating with the child: "Can you tell me what's bothering you —maybe we can work things out." Parents should remember that there is a need for further autonomy that comes along with development.

If a child has run away and returned, the school counselor should help the parent avoid taking immediate punitive action. Any sort of extreme reaction either totally punishing or totally capitulating is unproductive. The real answer for the family of a runaway is to establish a functioning system of communication. It also is necessary to examine the role played by the run-away child. Just as with substance abuse and many other problem behaviors, the child may act to preserve the family homeostasis by bringing a large amount of negative attention upon him or herself.

Conclusion

Family counseling, particularly family counseling based on systems theory, assumes that every family member plays a part in the disruptive or undesirable behavior of any one member.

Family Counseling in the Schools:

The identified patient may be signaling that the family is in distress; that the family is acting to close family boundaries and isolate itself from the surrounding community. The school counselor who understands these processes may be the one hope for a complete and lasting solution to the family problems brought to school by students.

Chapter Eight

Issues of Divorce and Marital Conflict

It has not gone unnoticed by anyone in the field of counseling that divorce is a common issue. School counselors, by virtue of their primary work with children, encounter divorce as much or more than any other segment of the counseling profession. It is surprising, then, that it has not been until recent years that any systematic attempt by school counselors to address this particular issue has occurred.

When a married couple separates and eventually divorces, there are many emotional and practical adjustments which must be accomplished. The children's adjustments are as difficult as those of their parents, but the child's accomodations differ in many ways from those of the adult. A series of studies of children in divorcing families found six tasks necessary for adaptation to the changing situation in a divorcing family (Papalia & Olds, 1992; Wallerstein, 1983; Wallerstein & Kelly, 1980):

1. Accepting the reality of the marriage break-up. Younger children may have difficulty comprehending the situation beyond any arguing they may have witnessed. If there is some understanding of what the implications of the divorce are, a child may become muddled with feelings of fear or apprehension. This fear can be associated with being left alone, with not having both parents present, or with the guilt of having some responsibility for the break-up. Older children may deal with the situation through denial or they may retreat into beliefs of parental reconciliation.

2. Disengaging from marital conflicts. It is a challenge for

children in a divorcing family to get on with their usual activities and separate themselves from the turmoil that is often present with divorcing parents. They also may be so upset that they stop working in school, playing with friends, or participating in sports.

3. Addressing loss. The loss of a parent is traumatic if due to death, but when that parent is lost, regained, and repeatedly lost again, the impact is multiplied. This situation is the case in many divorced families. However, there are many more losses than these for children experiencing divorce. They must deal with the loss of a life style, both economically and functionally. Family routine, ritual, and tradition are all changed or lost with the absence of one parent from family activities. Also lost, for at least the initial months or years following a family experiencing a divorce, is a sense of security that comes from two parents working (i.e., employment, or child and home care) to maintain their family, paying the bills, and protecting the children from all outside threats.

4. Addressing guilt and anger. As previously alluded to, most children feel some sense of responsibility for the divorce of their parents. Children are aware that divorce is the choice of at least one, if not both, parents and, is therefore, not inevitable. In addition, anger may be directed at themselves as well as at parents who have subjected them to the trials of living in a divorced family. This anger often goes on for years, sometimes never subsiding.

5. Accepting that divorce is permanent. Often children hold on to the hope that their parents will reunite even in the face of overwhelming evidence to the contrary, including remarriage by one or both parents. It may, in fact, take a physical as well as emotional separation from parents to accept the reality of divorce. This acceptance may not happen until children reach adolescence, go away to college, move into their own accommodations, or marry themselves.

6. Developing positive expectations for relationships. Children from divorced families may find it difficult to overcome the fear that they will fail at any relationship they attempt, just like their parents. This belief can result

in an avoidance of intimacy or in the development of only superficial relationships, along with the poor self-concept and the depressive mood that such relationships foster.

For school children, the resolution of these tasks may hinge on a number of factors which need to be addressed in family counseling. The child's own ability to deal with stressful situations in general, as well as divorce in particular, depends on different variables. Some of these variables can be facilitated or enhanced through family counseling with the school counselor. Papalia and Olds (1992) have identified five specific factors that can effect the resilience of a child, and which can indicate a child's ability to rebound from stressful situations. These factors are (a) elements of the child's personality, such as adaptability, high self-esteem, support from family and other adults; (b) experience gained in dealing with stressful situations; (c) the number of sources of stress; (d) the overall amount of stress to be dealt with; and (e) availability of "compensating experiences," which include successes in other areas of life.

While all children may need to accomplish these tasks in order to adjust emotionally to divorce, it is not the case that all children from separated or divorced families need counseling. Understanding and feedback from a supportive environment at school, a mature and thoughtful approach taken by parents, along with the reasonable passing of time, may be all a child needs to make necessary adjustments. Richard Gardner (1982) notes that "divorce per se does not necessarily produce psychopathology in the child" (p. 39). He goes on to point out, however, that "the child of divorce is more likely to develop such reactions (psychopathology) than the child who grows up in an intact, relatively secure home" (p. 39). Other researchers have recorded school behavior problems, academic difficulties, delinquent behavior, and friction with peers in children from divorced families (Hetherington, 1986; Kelly, 1987).

While most school counselors would agree that children of divorce would benefit from counseling, a child's ability to benefit from a counseling relationship is different from actually having *a need* for such intervention. Therefore, an important task for a school counselor is to determine whether or not counseling is needed.

Family Counseling in the Schools:

Many of the anxious and depressive feelings that children may experience in a divorce are temporary and specific to circumstances. Support or a friendly smile could be all that these children require; therefore, family counseling is not necessarily warranted in such cases. Children in this temporary, adjustment period may engage in behaviors that alarm parents, family members, or teachers. The students may write stories about divorce in response to an English assignment or show inordinate interest in stories or movies about divorced families. For the parent, this response may be especially painful, but for the child it is often therapeutic to release the feelings of sadness, depression, or anger through the attention to such stories. This reaction is adaptive and does not necessarily indicate a need for family counseling. Should this interest reach unusual levels, so that it takes up most of a child's time, distracts from schoolwork or other interests, or develops into an obsession, then counseling becomes more appropriate.

School counselors should be attuned to the fact that parents often ask mental health or school professionals to speak with their children so that the parents can receive counseling for their own concerns. With the child or children as *identified patient(s),* adults can address their own adjustment issues while having the satisfaction of being a good and caring parent as demonstrated by their willingness to participate in counseling. The school counselor will need to be careful not to challenge this parental belief while also avoiding the trap of joining the parent in identifying the child as "the one with the problem." It is generally not a good idea to "treat" a child in the absence of a problem. On the other hand, it may be useful for everyone to examine and perhaps modify the family's functioning as a unit.

As previously noted, should adjustment difficulties persist for the child, reconsideration for family counseling is in order. Gardner (1982) suggests that four to six weeks following a divorce or separation is a "reasonable" period of time to expect adjustment problems to occur. Should such behaviors as fighting, tantrums, or acting out at school or home persist beyond 1 1/2 months, family counseling may be needed. This time frame holds true if persistent depressive mood is present for longer than a month. School counselors will remember that the symptoms of depression in children does not always follow the same pattern as depressive mood in adults. Young children may manifest depression through overly active or aggressive behavior, while an adolescent will react to depression with negativism, antisocial behaviors, and protestations that he or she feels misunderstood. There are situations when the child's response to the separation or divorce is so intense that it would be unwise to wait for several weeks to see if problems dissipate. The intervention necessary in these situations does not require immediate family counseling, but it will, most likely, initially involve support and reassurance from a trusted adult such as the school counselor.

In the event of a separation or divorce, some children may warrant intervention by the school counselor because they have already displayed some difficulties prior to the announcement of the marital break. It may be that the previously existing problems were, in fact, rooted in the marital conflict and began to manifest themselves before the marital problems; or, there may be existing psychological difficulties which are merely exacerbated by the stress of the separation or divorce.

Another area for the school counselor to note in determining the appropriateness of intervention is the student's peer relationships. The ability to refrain from fussing or fighting with peers is usually retained even if sibling disagreements escalate following the parents' marital break-up. If a child is unable to control his or her feelings to the point that an unusually high number of arguments or fights occur with peers, perhaps the child's difficulty in adjustment is severe enough to require intervention by the school counselor. Certainly the observations and trained eyes and ears of an experienced counselor will go a long way in making the determination about the need for counseling. In the same manner, parents are not always seeking their own gratification if they request help from the school counselor. Parents typically have a reasonably good feel for the usual behaviors of their children and may be able to "sense" trouble before it is apparent to others. The school counselor is usually well served to consider parental requests when they occur.

In addition to standard counseling and assessment concerns, the school counselor must be able to determine the point in the separation process that the family in question finds itself. Bohannon (1973) has proposed six different stages or *stations* through which individuals pass during a divorce. Family members neither enter the stations at the same time, nor do they spend the same amount of time in each station; however, in order to achieve some level of stability, each station must be entered and successfully completed by families facing divorce.

Initially, couples will find themselves in *emotional divorce,* which typically occurs prior to any physical separation. During this time the couple is beginning to feel more negative than positive emotions about the partner. The waning of excitement, expectation, and caring are accompanied by feelings of being betrayed or lied to, since one's dreams are not coming true. The partner who feels this may vacillate between these negative feelings and denial in an attempt to convince himself or herself that the trouble is not real. An increased attempt to "patch things up," or act as if nothing is wrong may ensue. This acting can be confusing for the children since their allegiances may be questioned by one parent or the other. Also, a parent often turns to the children for confirmation of his or her feelings or for validation of anger or resentment towards the other parent.

The next station is *legal divorce* in which the couple are actually separated and the divorce is recognized outside the family. The parents often react with depression, a combination of resignation and relief, and feelings of ambivalence and guilt. Children may have a different position in the family structure as parents depend on them more for emotional support and as the family's roles are readjusted. Many of the major decisions for the adults in the family have been relegated to attorneys or a judge and the adult's power may feel diminished as a result. Children suddenly find themselves with adult responsibilities as the family struggles to realign itself.

As the family begins to consider and implement economic rearrangements, such as alimony, and/or child support and custody, the family moves into the station called *economic divorce.* This period is often more difficult and scary for the children since the sole support on which they depend is now threatened. Depending on the age of the child, the economic impact may be experienced as a loss of extra treats, or a loss of desired luxuries, or the potential loss of a future (e.g., an opportunity for a college education). The need for reassurance by the children may come at a time when the parents are least prepared to be supportive since they themselves are feeling insecure and uncertain.

The fourth station is the time when the school counselor is most likely to find him or herself involved. This station is called the *co-parental divorce and the problems of custody*. Divorced parents often return to court for battles involving custody, child support, or visitation. The participants may choose to discredit each other in order to strengthen their own case. Parents or grandparents may attempt to enlist children in this process from one side or the other. The fact that the children are required to develop a split in allegiance is only part of the problem the school counselor may see reflected in school behavior. Children also are learning about the ugly side of adult behavior as they watch trusted individuals lie and scheme against people that the children love. This realization can make the child doubt the love his or her parents have professed. It also may serve to provide a jaded view of those that have been, and continue to be, role models. These custody issues often come for children at the time when they are developing their own morals and internal rules of interaction with others. To find a child lying to a teacher, showing a lack of respect, or plotting with one child against another should not be surprising if that child is in the fourth station of a divorce.

As the family moves into the fifth station, *community divorce and the problems of loneliness,* parents commence to make or seek new friends and begin new activities. The new life that has been carved out for the family will gradually settle in and the parents may start pursuing long-desired activities that they never pursued when married. There is a strong signal to the children that their former life is gone forever and this life may, in fact, have to be mourned as an additional loss. The parents may become more self-centered and concerned with their own healing, creating in the children a sense of abandonment. The non-custodial parent may, in fact, encourage a child's feeling of anger and depression in order to turn the child against the parent with which he or she lives. An increasingly common situation is where the children do not live with either parent; they reside with grandparents while parents attempt to "get their lives together." During this stage of the divorce, the parents may rarely see the children as mother and father concentrate on their own adjustment and enjoy their new freedom. The children may exhibit acting-out behavior, depression, or a lack

Family Counseling in the Schools:

of concern for grades or personal accomplishment.

Psychic divorce is the final station through which Bohannon (1973) suggests that divorced families pass. This stage should involve the acceptance and final adjustment to a new life circumstance. A realignment of identity for the parents, as well as a chance to reorganize family hierarchy and roles for the children, is necessary. Difficulty can develop when all members of the family do not reach this point at the same time. The school counselor may be instrumental in helping the children and parent communicate effectively in order to alleviate some of the misunderstanding and conflict that can develop. Working independently with the child is an inefficient way to improve family communication.

School counselors can count on being asked to address at least one, if not all, the possible situations that accompany families experiencing marital problems. The school counselor may be required to deal with single-parent families, most often headed by mothers -- many of whom may be entering the work force for the first time so that they can support themselves and their children. Children in these families may be spending more time without adult supervision or adult interaction. They may be assuming many parental duties or totally separating themselves from the family. Isolation is common among the adolescent children in a family that is divorced or divorcing. The family will likely be experiencing financial and emotional hardships that go along with single-parent child rearing. School counselors may be asked to deal with newly constituted step-families as parents re-marry, intact families on the verge of break-up in which the parents are making a last-ditch effort to keep a relationship going, separated families, or divorced families.

In this chapter, as well as elsewhere in this book, we have presented specific suggestions or guidelines for the school counselor to follow. These are not rigid procedures and, when used optimally, they will reflect the creativity and personality of the individual school counselor implementing them. As with any procedure the manner of presentation, the existing rapport between counselor and client(s), and the timing of the delivery will go a long way in determining the success of the endeavor.

Guidelines for Intervention

The Family Floor Plan

The family floor plan (Coopersmith, 1980) is an exercise that is often used as an assessment technique, but it works well when used as a means of facilitating family communication and giving feedback to the family regarding their efforts. Having one's own space, where that space is, and the degree that others respect the sanctuary of the space is an important aspect of a family. In using the family floor plan, the school counselor asks the parent or parents to draw a floor plan of their childhood home or the one they most identify with if there is more than one. The children are instructed to watch. Coopersmith provided the following directions and questions, which may be altered:

1. As you draw, note your mood for each room.
2. Let yourself recall the smells, sounds, colors, and the people in the house.
3. Is there a particular room where people gather?
4. When the members of your extended family visit, where do they go?
5. Are there rooms you could not enter?
6. Do you have a special place in the house?
7. Let yourself be aware of how issues of closeness and distance, privacy, or the lack of it are experienced in this house?
8. What is the place of this house in the neighborhood in which it stands? Does it fit or not?
9. Let yourself recall a typical event that occurred in this house.
10. Let yourself hear typical words that were spoken by family members (p. 142).

These questions and directions are meant to encourage memories of the family's rules and procedures for usual operation. It indicates the roles of family members and how they may relate to roles of the parents in their family of origin. It provides shared experiences that can be helpful in the therapeutic process. Alternatives to this procedure may include having the children draw their current house floor plan, encouraging the children to ask their own questions while parents draw, or instructing all family members to draw their current or some previous home as a group project. In any use of this technique, a vast amount of information may be gained. Family members will also have many opportunities to examine their roles in relation to each other, the implicit rules of the family, and the areas of the home which are viewed as "hot spots" for conflict. Additionally, places of safety and support may be discerned in light of separation and divorce.

Generational Support

In a family in which the two-parent system has been disrupted, regardless of previously existing generational boundary violations, it is important for the school counselor to find ways to support the defining of the roles and places of the different generations in a family. There should be an observable difference in the way a family perceives a parent as compared to a child or, a grandparent. The school counselor may have to help establish a hierarchy or lend support to a hierarchy with weak definition of boundaries. Moreover, many counselor's interventions are subtle and unobtrusive.

A counselor can strengthen a parent's role by addressing family questions directly at him or her and then seeking confirmation from other members. This approach may include asking a parent's permission to give a task to one of the children. If differing perspectives emerge, giving the parent's perspective more weight can strengthen that parent's position within the family.

Such simple things as where family members sit may be symbolic of family position and can be altered by school counselors. The school counselor can place parents or grandparents together in one place and the children together in another. Giving mother or father the counselor's padded, swivel chair while others sit in the chairs brought in from the outer office is a subtle but effective support for the *generational boundaries* in the family. It may be necessary to help the parents in defining roles by suggesting a reassignment of chores and by differentiating between the adults' tasks and the children's tasks. It is important to encourage parents to meet with the school counselor, or with adult friends, to seek alternatives in discipline rather than delegating this task to the children. It is important to discourage parents from allowing older children to parent the younger ones. Even if older teens baby sit for younger siblings, encourage the parent to set down rules before going out rather than leaving that in the hands of the older child.

Joining a Subsystem

There will be times in dealing with a divorced family in which the school counselor will encounter a dysfunctional organizational system: the children will hold more power than the single parent; there is a dominant grandparent who treats the parent and the children equally; or there are members of the family (siblings or a parent and child) who are too enmeshed or involved and have separated themselves from the rest of the family. Should any of these situations occur, the school counselor may wish to engage in joining one of the subsystem groups in order to strengthen that group, with the long term goal of effecting a change in the overall family organization.

Initially, the school counselor will determine which subsystem is in need of strengthening and will then move to add the power of the counselor's role to that subsystem. There are a variety of ways to bring about this alliance. Some of the following have been suggested by Sherman and Fredman (1986):

1. The school counselor can suggest that members of the targeted subsystem sit together and then he or she joins this group. As noted above, this also will help to delineate the boundaries of the subsystem.
2. The school counselor should make certain that the members of the subsystem get full attention when speaking and that the comments of the subsystem are given extra consideration. The counselor will need to intervene at times to ask that the other members of the family acknowledge what has been said by the members of the targeted subsystem.
3. The school counselor should avoid taking on a parenting role but may need to encourage or guide the parent(s) to assume that position within the family. Encouragement should focus on the parents assuming the parental role within the counseling session.

Family Counseling in the Schools:

4. It may be necessary for the school counselor to provide definition to the roles of the parent(s). This would include who makes disciplinary decisions. The counselor may have to help the parent(s) determine which child has which chore, what the role of the grandparents is to be within the nuclear family, and who is responsible for planning different aspects of the family's life. This division will almost certainly require some negotiation, which gives the counselor the opportunity to educate the family about this valuable tool regarding family functioning.

5. Feedback from the school counselor to family subsystems and members regarding how family power is used may be necessary. The counselor will explain how using this power has resulted in the opposite of the desired effect (e.g., An acting out teen may complain that he or she wants the parent to leave him or her alone yet the teenager continues to confront and engage the parent).

6. It may be necessary for the school counselor to remove a parenting child from such a role by asking the child to sit with the other children. Should the child continue to assume the role of parent, the counselor should stop him or her and guide the parent to take on the task the child was about to undertake.

7. The school counselor must inform the other members of the family about the appropriate role for different subsystems within the family unit. This includes the rules under which they should operate as well as the responsibilities they may hold in the family.

As subsystems in the family gain or relinquish power, it will be necessary for the school counselor to make adjustments in his or her alliances in order to maintain an appropriate balance of these subsystems. Once the family is in an organizational pattern which is conducive to healthy functioning, then the focus can turn towards gaining skills in conflict resolution and crisis management.

As noted earlier, the creativity and individual talents of the school counselor will determine to what extent these few techniques will be used. The procedures outlined elsewhere in this book, with refinement or adaptation for specific situations, will help the school counselor work with families that are separated or divorced. The actual changes that occur within a family are the result of many factors, most of which are out of the control of the counselor. Nevertheless, a willing family working with a competent school counselor can accomplish many positive results. Divorce is one of the most devastating events taking place in today's families. As a result, divorcing parents need to adapt their parenting skills in order to promote child growth (Palmo et al., 1984). Some divorcing couples will avoid closeness by distancing themselves from one another; however, others may regulate closeness by initiating conflict (Bowen, 1978).

Peeks (1991b) has presented a procedure for divorced or divorcing parents. It suggests that separating or divorcing parents share with their children helpful information about the state of the marriage. This includes information about their love for the children, the potential finality of the marriage, the continuation of parental roles, and that the divorce is not the children's fault and that they are not to blame. Such information can be delineated in a family counseling session as illustrated below.

The Worst Boy in School
Counselor: Jim Fuller
Supervisor: J. Scott Hinkle
Counseling and Consulting Services
University of North Carolina at Greensboro

Bill had been referred to the university clinic by his principal and school teacher because he was the "worst boy in school." In fact, the principal had indicated that Bill was the worst student with whom he had ever been associated. A fifth grader, Bill lived at home with Mother and Brother, a third grader. His parents had been divorced for three years. It was at the time of the divorce that Bill's behavior began to deteriorate.

Following two sessions of information gathering, it was *hypothesized* that Bill was misbehaving because he was simply *out of control* and that his behavior was metaphoric of the mother's loss of control over her life. During the third session, I deliberately sent Mother and Brother to the waiting room. After an informative conversation with Bill, we had a private talk with Mother. I told her that after talking with Bill, who, by the way, had been very helpful, it became apparent that he misbehaved because he was losing control. I also shared that we thought his attempts to get his parents back together, by meeting to discuss his behavior, was a great sacrifice on Bill's part. Mother agreed.

Subsequently, I told Mother there was a sure method for reducing his being out of control (and, metaphorically speaking, her's as well). Consulting Peek's (1991b) procedure, I recommended that Mother, as well as Father, discuss their divorce with Bill and Brother. Again, Mother agreed. In separate sessions, Mother and Father shared with their sons that they would always be their parents, that they loved and cared for them, and, that regardless of the boys' behavior, the parents' marriage was over.

Within one week Bill's school and home behavior improved remarkably. His grades rose and Mother made an unsolicited appointment for individual counseling.

Analysis: This case utilized both behavioral *metaphor* and parents communicating with their children. Mother was feeling out of control since she lost her husband to another woman. Bill's misbehavior was positively *reframed* to be both protective and helpful. When the parents *took control* and told their sons that they would not re-marry, but would always be there for them as parents, Bill's misbehavior was no longer needed by him, *or his mother.* By telling her sons that she and Father would not be together again as a couple, Mother publicly closed the relationship and made a counseling appointment to discuss career issues and relationships with other men.

A Primer to Couple's Counseling

Many school student's behavior problems may be a function of parents' marital difficulties which have not yet deteriorated to the point of separation and divorce. These couples may need to discuss their issues with the school counselor as they begin to relate to their child's school problem. Follingstad (1988) has suggested that the counselor ask if there is a commitment to the marriage. Is the couple motivated to remain in the marriage? This issues should be dealt with early in counseling. If one partner already has "one foot out the door," a more direct discussion about the commitment in the relationship is required. If an outside affair is occurring, many counselors believe that this must discontinue for discussions about marriage counseling to proceed.

Counselors also should ask if there is commitment to *work on the marriage*. Previous attempts to improve the marriage may leave the couple hopeless. Are there aversive behaviors which block couples communication? This may include embarrassing one partner in front of the other, turning statements into power struggles, and blaming a partner for problems in the marriage. It is best for counselors to deal with this directly. Also helpful is a *positive reframe* — an explanation of how each partner originally had good intentions, but through misunderstanding and misperception, both now feel that they must defend themselves or attack the other (Follingstad, 1988).

Are there beliefs regarding the marriage that need restructuring? Such beliefs may include roles, rule-making, expectations of oneself and partner, personal independence, and beliefs that personal identity may conflict with marriage goals.

The key to restructuring beliefs for the couple lies in the ability of the counselor to convey that the couple's current situation is understandable based on past learning history and family of origin issues—changes in ideas will only come about when new beliefs make sense to them.

When a couple is in treatment, three systems need to be simultaneously considered: the individual, the interactional, and the inter-generational. The counselor has several important tasks: (a) inquire about the couple's expectations for counseling; (b) discuss administrative issues (length of sessions, lateness, missed appointments, telephone contact); and (c) the counselor's expectations in counseling (e.g., importance of balance; don't quote the counselor in a negative fashion during arguments and discussions at home) (Weeks & Treat, 1992).

A way to avoid triangulation in marriage counseling is to not begin a session until both partners are present. In order to join the couple from a balanced perspective the counselor should never confront only one partner, and he or she should be

Family Counseling in the Schools:

cognizant of the following:
1. Shake hands with *both* partners.
2. When socializing, make sure you are invested in "small talk" with both partners.
3. When asking about the presenting problem, try not to let one partner monopolize the conversation for too long.
4. Make sure each partner knows that what they have to say is important to the counselor.
5. Opening attempts at assessment should be balanced and fair (Weeks & Treat, 1992).

If the counselor sees the one partner individually in the beginning of counseling, then the other partner should also be seen separately. If individual sessions are deemed necessary, make them as equivalent as possible in frequency and time. If one partner appears for a session when both partners were expected, it is up to the counselor's clinical judgement whether or not to see that partner individually. If so, the next session should be an individual one for the other partner. If potential couples counseling began as individual counseling, it could be problematic to see the couple and a referral outside the school should be considered.

Conclusion

The quality of the parents' relationship always affects their children's behavior. Bergman (1985) has wisely reflected that
1. All symptoms in children stabilize unstable marriages, and if a "small" symptom cannot stabilize a marriage, then a "larger" symptom is needed.
2. The greater the magnitude of the marital conflict, the greater will be the magnitude of the symptom.
3. The more covert or hidden the marital conflict, the more a symptom will be needed to stabilize the marital conflict so it can remain hidden and covert (p. 4).

School counselors need to consider the relationship of the parents (or custodians) of the student if effective interventions are to be implemented. From a systemic perspective, it is important to evaluate all the systems that affect a student's school performance, including the status of the student's parents' relationship. If this is neglected, individual types of intervention are typically futile and have little long-term effectiveness.

Chapter Nine

A Family Approach to School and Community Crisis Management

On any average day in any school, a school counselor must deal with issues involving violence, multicultural and multiethnic conflict, and general unrest and upheaval. It takes a skilled and persistent counselor to be effective and not to "burn out" under these conditions. When a school is faced with a crisis, the challenge to a school counselor becomes unimaginable. Even crises that happen elsewhere can ultimately affect students in school.

For most schools, the bulk of their crisis preparation is first-aid training for some of the faculty or coaching staff, occasional fire drills, and the observance of tornado awareness week once a year. The authors are reminded of the "duck and cover" drills of the 1960's. These drills did little to reduce fears or heighten preparation for students or teachers.

Of additional concern for the school counselor is the manner in which counseling is understood by most parents, teachers, and school administrators. While many professionals and parents now recognize the value of counseling, they have little understanding of what actually takes place in counseling. As in a magician's trick, someone is put in a magic closet and ends up somewhere else or comes out changed. No one knows what happened in the closet but the results can be impressive. These individuals are going to be making the referrals to the school counselor, often without any information regarding the appropriateness of counseling for a particular student. These also are the individuals on whom the school counselor must

Family Counseling in the Schools:

rely regarding observations of behaviors or behavior changes, and the timing of these behaviors relative to the crisis. The school counselor needs to know how a child is likely to react following the occurrence of a crisis; at what point intervention is most useful; and how adults in the child's life (teachers, parents, and grandparents) can best facilitate the child's coping abilities. Neither teachers nor administrators are trained to handle a crisis in the school and they usually turn to the school counselor for help and guidance. The school counselor has usually undergone no more crisis managementtraining than other school professionals but he or she draws on personal knowledge of people and their behavior to address the situation to the best of his or her ability.

A crisis is an event of inordinate and unexpected intensity, such as violence. It may result in loss of life, disruption of daily functioning, or overwhelming emotions, despair, and fear. Survivors of a crisis often find themselves consumed with fears or they imagine that they could have suffered the fate of the less fortunate. The survivors may feel guilty that they escaped while someone less deserving suffered. Petersen and Straub (1992) have offered the following as examples of crises that may face a school or school system:

- Eight year-old Sarah was an angry child of divorcing parents. Her classmates were often provoked into fights by her sarcasm. Sarah was in a small plane along with her mother and grandparents when it crashed, killing them all.
- Four high school seniors left a party early one Saturday night and crashed their car while speeding down a winding road. There were no survivors.
- The principal of a middle school approached his school early one morning to find the body of a student hanging from the bleachers. A suicide.
- A fire started in the library of a high school on Saturday. Over one-third of the building was burned and students had to be assigned to three other schools, resulting in the separation of friends, couples, and teammates.
- A second grade teacher's ex-husband rushed into her classroom and shot her in front of her class.

- Two students left their elementary school riding bicycles. They were never seen again. The abandoned bicycles were found a block away from the school.
- A tornado tore through a town clearing a path 100 yards wide. Several people were killed and many houses were demolished (pp. 3-4).

Johnson (1989) has suggested that there are three categories of trauma which may be experienced by school children: victimization, loss, and family pathology. Victimization and loss are the major issues most school counselors will have to address.

Victimization refers to situations in which an individual child or children are the targets of physical assault, sexual assault (either rape or incest), or robbery. It also is reasonable to include in this category, situations in which children have been victims of accidental or natural disasters or have witnessed the actions described above happening to someone else. (Sexual abuse is discussed in Chapter 7). When anyone, especially a child, experiences a crisis in which he or she is victimized, the initial response is likely to be a noted lack of response, often described as feeling numb or deadened. This response may be accompanied either by a sense of exposure or by a feeling of being unprotected and open for additional victimization. Following the initial shock there may be symptoms of a physical nature, such as disturbances in sleep or eating patterns, and somatic complaints, like stomach aches, nausea, breathing difficulties, and muscle fatigue. Additionally, the victim of a crisis may report hopelessness, lack of concentration, distractibility, and feelings of guilt or shame at having survived when others were not so fortunate.

As the individual is separated from the crisis event, he or she may alternate between periods of detachment from the event or other victims (if any), and periods of near total absorption with the event, or with locales and stimuli similar to that of the crisis. This response does not mean that the individual has forgiven him or herself; it indicates that the individual may begin to target other individuals upon whom to focus blame, anger, or contempt. Usually there is, with the passage of time, a return to an emotional state similar to that which existed prior to the crisis. A failure to return to normalcy is a signal that counseling intervention is warranted.

Loss as a result of crisis may include the loss of friends or family due to death, the long term loss of contact with a friend or family member due to hospitalization for treatment of illness or injury, or a sensation of loss which comes from the death of a person not close to the individual but somehow so similar as to suggest identification with that victim (e.g., death of a classmate not acquainted with the individual or of a person of the same age or sex). Additionally, a crisis may result in the loss of one's home, familiar places (e.g., school, church), homes of friends, or family, and/or the permanent or temporary loss of a way of life.

Dealing with loss involves many of the same processes as previously described. A student will pass through a period of disbelief or denial before experiencing emotional responses — anger, depression, and/or feelings of guilt or shame — to the loss. Finally, a person who has experienced a loss will usually come to some degree of acceptance and healthy acquiescence to the current realities. Elisabeth Kübler-Ross (1983) has delineated much the same process for children who experience the death of a loved one.

Children deal with loss differently. Their reactions depend on their emotional state prior to the crisis, their sense of security within the family, and their developmental stage. Pre-adolescent children will seldom have sufficient cognitive development to understand and accept a loss. These younger children who are much more likely to react to the absence of their basic wants and needs, deal with the loss through their own adjustment process. Isolation and refusal to be involved in any family activities are likely from children who find their needs un met.

Wass and Cason (1984) outlined children's concepts of death at different ages:

Life Period	Concepts of Death
Infancy	No concept of death
Late infancy & early childhood	Death is reversible: a temporary restriction, departure, or sleep

Middle childhood, late or pre-adolescence	Death is irreversible but capricious; external-internal physiological explanations
Pre-adolescence, adolescence, adult	Death is irreversible, universal, personal, but distant: natural physiological, and theological explanations

As stated previously, when viewing the family as a system, if one member of the family undergoes a behavior change, the remaining family members will also adjust and change. Many of the crises described above are such that the immediate effects will involve all members of the family. There are other crises, however, that can initially affect just one member of the family, such as the suicide of a school mate. In either circumstance, the family, as a unit, will be facing the crisis in one way or another.

A crisis strains the fabric of even the strongest, most functional family. Following a crisis, family routines are disrupted, roles may shift, and a great deal of emotion is experienced by the whole family or by a single member. If a stronger, more dominant member of a family is sidelined or lost as a result of a crisis, the communication pathways and usual routines of the family's functioning are disrupted. If a quiet, unobtrusive family member suddenly needs more attention or becomes the center of the family's focus, everyone must adjust their respective roles. Whereas when a capable, dependable member of the family becomes depressed or unresponsive, the expectations of the rest of the family are suddenly in doubt. For example, can this individual, previously the family's "rock," be depended on in the future?

Conventional wisdom says that during a crisis a family will pull together and support one another, functioning as one single-minded unit. In reality, this often is not how a family responds. A crisis can result in inordinate pressure on family structure. It also must be remembered that many families are not functioning optimally even before a crisis occurs. Families can react by pulling apart and blurring the lines of communication as separate alliances and resentments develop. Dormant family dysfunction may surface during the aftermath of a crisis making the stressors on the family greater than those which can be attributed to the crisis itself. A family, in order to regain reasonable functioning, must make the necessary adjustments following the [post-crisis] upheavals.

Most families will respond with cohesion during the first hours or days immediately following a crisis. Negative feelings, jealousies, or conflicted relationships are often put on hold. To illustrate, the family may be able to forget mom's drinking, dad's harshness, or even abuse towards the children, and other family difficulties. However, once the initial shock has subsided and things begin to return to normal, suppressed conflicts may re-surface; only this time these conflicts may be accompanied by heightened tension and stress resulting from the crisis. The family may eventually return to prior patterns, functional or not, with the added history of responses resulting from the reactions during the transition period. Families who are not capable of adjusting and returning to previous roles may have to form new patterns of behavior. For better or for worse, the family may find itself irreversibly different following a crisis.

The family may change the communication patterns they use in terms of who speaks either for the family or for individuals in a family. Furthermore, the communication lines between individual members may be altered as the result of the family's response to a crisis. Also affected are the family's problem-solving strategies, the negotiating processes used to make family decisions, and the alliances between family members.

The *emotional space* between members of a family is often at a fragile balance. A move by either member to close that space may be seen as smothering or as too *enmeshed*. Any attempt to broaden the emotional space could be interpreted as abandonment or lack of caring. In the aftermath of a crisis, a parent may move closer to a child emotionally, in order to protect or shield that child from further danger, or as an overcorrection to the guilt associated with not being a better, more protective parent in the first place. It is typical for parents to blame themselves for mishaps or tragedies that befall their children. The resulting "parental blanket" placed around the child can be experienced by the child as an intrusive and unwelcome move by parents. The subsequent response of the child can be one of quiet, yet resentful, surrender. After all, parents mean well. On the other hand, the child may react by actively resisting or pulling away from the new, unwanted closeness. The ripples of this push-pull situation can go on for some time before some agreeable compromise can be reached. If this new adjustment cannot be made comfortably for everyone in the family, then the family's energy is diverted from healthy functioning and growth.

A family with inflexible roles will function poorly in the face of change. This rigid response may be necessary to maintain the status quo in a family in which unplanned, uncontrolled responses are threatening. This rigidity may work well to hide the dysfunction in a family from the outside world. A family that is keeping secrets must not vary in the roles taken on by each member of the family in order to keep those not in the system from penetrating or learning about the family. This inability to change, however, can be devastating to the family system in the event of a crisis. A crisis can bring attention to the specific roles and responsibilities of each family member. A crisis also can highlight the breech of this agreed upon behavior should it prevent anyone from carrying out his or her expected role.

The school counselor, just by becoming involved, creates an imbalance in the family's system. The family's standard operating procedure has to be adjusted to include the counselor. Healthy families will adapt with little difficulty and will, in fact, gain valuable experience in making adjustments. Following a crisis, the school counselor can provide a focal point of calm and reassurance which may make it possible for the family to cope with the changes resulting from the crisis. Families with functioning difficulties may find the inclusion of the school counselor an additional source of stress, which will result in further closure and a heightened sense of the family as a fortress. The roles of the parents, in particular, may be shaken and the inclusion of a seemingly more capable adult will likely be viewed as threatening to the parent and disconcerting to the children. Reactions to the school counselor may vary from an anticipation of he or she being able to "fix" everything to a suspicion that the counselor intends to dismantle the family. The latter is especially true if the family has had any history of conflicts with public agencies or the school. The family may expect the school counselor, by virtue of his or her profession, to know all there is to know about how the family works. A counselor who

Family Counseling in the Schools:

speaks of things getting better may surprise family members who believe that things cannot improve.

A school counselor must be aware of these possibilities when entering or joining a family system, especially in the high-tension aftermath of a crisis. Johnson (1989) offers a number of *trouble shooting strategies for professionals.* Below is an adaptation of those strategies for school counselors who find themselves assisting a family in crisis:

1. What stage of post-crisis adjustment is the family in?
2. If conflicts among family members or between the family and the school counselor exist, did differences in mutual expectations create these misunderstandings? Would clarifying those assumptions assist the family?
3. Could misunderstandings about the role or intentions of the school or school system account for the conflict between the school counselor and the family?
4. Are there unspoken or indirectly spoken messages about expectations that the school counselor is missing or misinterpreting?
5. Could the conflicts, whether or not a result of misunderstandings, have their basis in any expected roles that may be incompatible, or different, now than they were before?
6. Could the school counselor's own conflicts be the result of a misunderstood expectation of roles?
7. Are there differences between the roles the school counselor expects (as a result of his or her own background) and the roles particular family members fill? Is the school counselor certain that such differences do not underlie the difficulties?
8. Could the family's resistance or unnecessary conflicts and problems be a means of resisting needed change? (Consider how the problem could function to avoid family change).
9. If the school counselor is experiencing difficulties with a particular family member, is the school counselor violating the family's rules and procedures regarding communication patterns and feedback systems?

10. If the school counselor is becoming entangled in a family conflict, is there any indication that he or she is being "triangled" by one of the members?

11. To what extent has the crisis strained bonds of affection, disrupted normal parenting functions, and challenged scripts within the family?

12. The school counselor should look closely at his or her own affection and affiliation needs to make sure that these needs are not being projected onto the counselor's assessment of the family.

13. Is the school counselor clear about his or her own values so that negative evaluations of the family on the basis of those values can be avoided? Is the assessment of the family based on the extent to which its values contribute to the development and well-being of each family member, and not on whether they match the values of the school counselor? Have the values of the family shifted as a result of the crisis?

14. In assessing parenting skills, is the evaluation based upon the school counselor's bias about parenting styles? To what extent has the parenting style in the family changed or deteriorated since the crisis?

15. Are all strategies planned with attention to their likely effects upon the whole family system?

A crisis can serve as a spotlight on a family. It can confirm or dispel long-held feelings of security and safety. It can call into question promises of love, endurance, and loyalties and can affect relationships between the parents, between parents and children, and between siblings. A crisis can highlight flaws in family members who have previously appeared flawless. It can elicit strength from the family weakling or courage from the quiet wallflower. These revelations not only cast these individual members in new, perhaps unsought, roles, the new roles may threaten the positions of others. The entire understanding of family process may come into question.

Conclusion

The school counselor must always enter this potential family "mine field" with caution; he or she must put aside previously

Family Counseling in the Schools:

held perceptions of how families "are supposed" to behave and be willing to enter as a part of the system.

Family counseling skills are even more important when working with families in crisis. In one particular incident, application of family counseling techniques in the school was called for when a high school student experienced behavior problems at school and was eventually suspended. Although a number of significant problems occurred at school, the majority of the student's problems were associated with difficulties at home. In this case, the mother had been consulted, but the father exhibited detachment regarding his child's problems. Out of frustration and an inability to communicate with his father, the student came to school and shot a teacher, a student, and then committed suicide. The student's family had been in crisis for several months as a result of the parents' marital difficulties. Joining or entering this family, exploring family issues, and potentially discussing the marital relationship with the parents, may have benefited the family by reducing tension, enhancing communication, and changing relationships. It also may have prevented the violence that devastated the school and community.

Chapter Ten

Getting Started

Having read the previous chapters, you may find yourself asking how you can add a family counseling approach to your services. Carlson (1987) notes several essential resources which must be present in order for a school counselor to implement family counseling in his or her school. First, the school counselor would need to seek and secure the support of the school principal and other appropriate or influential members of the school administration and school system. The support of fellow school counselors, psychologists, exceptional children program staff, and certain elements of the community also would prove helpful. Secondly, adequate training, of which this book may be a part, would need to be arranged for school counselors and psychologists interested in conducting family counseling in their school. Thirdly, there must be available financial resources to allow for direct services to students above and beyond the usual guidance counseling and psychometric services provided. Lastly, there must be a blending of family treatment with the traditional educational and academic process and the problems inherent therein (Carlson). The research indicates that families with such problems have success rates from between 70 and 90 percent when school-based family counseling is a mode of intervention (e.g., Gross & Mascari, 1991; Shore & Vieland, 1989).

The family counseling approach advocated in this book is one that requires an overall shift from linear thinking towards an interactive, interrelated, systemic approach (see Table 5 below as adapted from Amatea (1989)). It is essential that the school counselor perceive him or herself as a potent force injected into the student's family system -- a system which has, through functional or dysfunctional means, created a unique

Family Counseling in the Schools:

pattern of communication. This communication pattern includes hierarchies and rules which have taken family members to their current state with at least some degree of success. This awareness will result in the school counselor respecting the family members, their present interaction patterns, and the likely reluctance by the family to fully include him or her in the family system, at least initially.

Table 5. A Comparison of School-Based Family Counseling to Traditional School Counseling Approaches
(Adapted from Amatea, 1989)

Family Counseling in School Setting	Traditional School Counseling
Nature of the Dysfunction	
incongruent or nonproductive family hierarchy, maladaptive interactional patterns, problems with family and school structure	improper conditioning, poor environment, poor self-esteem
Nature of the Change Process	
modify family hierarchy and/or patterns of communication and interaction, change family structure	provide consistent punishment or reinforcement (praise), increase pressure on parents to take more control
Focus	
1) structure of family	1) history of learning including deficit patterns
2) assess family hierarchy from observed interactions during family counseling sessions	2) identifying solution through reinforcement & punishment history
3) here and now	3) past history and connection to present

184

Methods of Change

1) directive/cooperative	1) directive
2) establish goals, make family responsible for results	2) establish goals, make individual and or family responsible for results
3) reframe in order to gain motivation	3) motivation from reinforcement of success assumed
4) uses both direct & indirect methods of change	4) uses primarily direct methods of change
5) empowerment of parents	

Change Agent Style

uses direct, counselor-as-expert style, & indirect, cooperative style	uses primarily direct, counselor-as-expert style

Tailoring Programs

The basic elements proposed by Carlson (1987) and ourselves will be common to nearly all schools. The individual school counselor, working within his or her school, will need to tailor our approach to fit the setting in which the family counseling is to take place. There are, for instance, "unique characteristics" in smaller or rural schools that require different approaches to counseling as compared to efforts conducted in larger, more urban schools (Rose-Gold, 1991).

The smaller, more rural, and poorer school systems will have tighter budgets and smaller staffs than their larger, urban counterparts. The school counselor may be an important part of students' lives in such small systems. In these schools, school counselors are likely to find close relationships between school personnel and students, and their families. In situations where a student's family is not well known, the teachers and staff of schools in smaller communities are likely to know something

Family Counseling in the Schools:

about the family, including the accomplishments and problems of family members. In such settings, the parents of a student are likely to have attended the same school, with some of the same staff.

When compared to larger districts, the relationship between the school and the community is likely to be more intimate and perhaps more interdependent in small or rural systems. Rural schools may be remote from support services, such as mental health agencies, social services, or medical providers. However, while services may be physically closer in larger cities, their availability to students and families may be just as remote due to financial, ethnic, or cultural obstacles. Parents of minority students may not trust or feel comfortable with services provided by the community; these parents may feel more comfortable with their school and school counselor.

Starting at the Foundation

There are initial strategies school counselors may implement when first approaching problems with students. Such strategies will facilitate the beginning steps of family counseling and will maintain family counseling components as part of a comprehensive school counseling program (Rose-Gold, 1991). Early identification of student problems within a systemic context will give interventions of any kind a better opportunity to succeed. Early identification will also facilitate a family counseling approach. Families may be more willing to be involved if they collaborated with a school counselor, at the first hint of a problem, rather than waiting until the problem became large and complex and the consequences potentially more serious. Establishing a good relationship with parents or care givers early in a young person's tenure at the counselor's school will certainly increase the chances for success should a family intervention become necessary. Likewise, the inclusion of parents in all school programs will encourage a more cooperative attitude among students, parents, and school personnel. Such cooperation will foster better performances from students and may serve to prevent some school problems. When problems do occur, this established relationship will facilitate the family counseling process.

School counselors should establish and maintain contacts with human service and social service agencies that serve your school's families. These contacts will not only enhance cooperation between the school and the community, they will widen the circle of individuals that may support or participate in family counseling. Remember, that in a truly systemic approach, agency personnel involved with a family are a part of the family's system; therefore, it may be desirable to include these professionals in a family counseling session or treatment plan.

It follows that if improved communication and cooperation among school, family, and community is a goal, then improved in-school cooperation and communication is also necessary. Rose-Gold (1991) advocates the establishment of an advisory counsel within the school. Including teachers and support staff in the planning and establishment of family counseling in the school increases the possibility that these teachers will participate in the family counseling process when it becomes necessary.

School counselors will need to be constantly mindful of a basic assumption in family counseling that differs from traditional approaches in education and mental health. That is, when using a family counseling approach, the counselor views the behaviors of his or her students as adaptive responses to the system in which the youngster functions. Carlson (1987) has suggested that the behavior of a child cannot be considered "deviant" but is rather "dysfunctional for maximal development." We could add that it is "a good adjustment mechanism" considering the circumstances. Furthermore, a systems approach does not recognize a specific correct manner in which a family or any social system should be organized. It also is necessary to compare the system's pattern of behavior with the social environment in which it operates. More to the point, it is necessary to examine whether or not the individual student's development is enhanced or impeded by the manner in which the system responds. This underlying, systemic understanding must be incorporated into the thinking of the school counselor, and, subsequently, the counselor must help others within the educational process to utilize this way of thinking (systems theory, family intervention, and assessment) as well.

Family Counseling in the Schools:

A Note About Assessment

As noted in Chapter 6, an important element of family counseling is assessment. The school counselor, by choice or by policy, may have in the past left the responsibility for any student assessment to school psychologists or psychometrists. Since family assessment is an integral part of family counseling, the school counselor will wish to assess the family either him or herself, or in collaboration with a school psychologist familiar with the systemic components of holistic assessment. The assessment of families, it will be remembered, is interwoven with intervention and treatment. As the counselor moves through interventions, the responses of the family and the outcomes of the interventions confirm either the validity or the dubiousness of hypotheses which were formulated to explain the structure upon which the symptomatic behaviors reside (Aponte & Van Deusen, 1991; Carlson, 1987; Minuchin, 1974). Family structure is not easily and directly detected or observed; it must be discovered through observation of the interactional patterns of the family. Carlson (1987) has pointed out that hypotheses are ultimately evaluated by challenging the existing family structure and by observing the family's responses. Observation of the interactional patterns between families and other segments of the overall social system, such as the school, is another important part of the assessment in which school counselors should be prepared to engage.

School counselors may prefer to engage in less formal assessment procedures which incorporate a therapeutic component as a part of the process. Examples of this type of assessment are found in Chapter 6 and include the use of ecomaps, genograms, or family sculpture. These assessment techniques will allow the school counselor who is familiar with implementing interventions to engage in an activity in which they feel comfortable and in which the family may feel a sense of therapeutic productivity. In like manner, if a school counselor is more comfortable with direct, score-based, objective evaluations, they may wish to use such assessment instruments as the Quick Assessment of Family Functioning (Golden, 1988) or the Family Relationships Index (Holahan & Moos, 1981), as well as other assessments described in Chapter 6. School counselors will experience greater success in conducting family counseling if they keep in mind that family assessments should evaluate the presenting problem, the family system, the family's broader social system, and the family life cycle (Holman, 1983). The important point is that school counselors should prepare to use assessment throughout the family counseling process to establish hypotheses, confirm or reject hypotheses, and to assess progress as the family and the family's social system change.

Within these few pages we have attempted to provide a general overview of family counseling as it might be used in a school setting. We have presented information on how to address specific issues which a school counselor is likely to encounter (such as those discussed in Chapters 7 and 8). Some final general points can be further presented here that apply to any case in which a counselor wishes to utilize a family counseling approach.

Some Closing Comments

Successful use of family counseling approaches may require some didactic work as clients become students of the systemic way of thinking. The concept and techniques of family counseling need not be kept secret by the counselor. The elements of family counseling may prove even more successful when clients understand and put into practice the communication and interaction patterns being modeled by the counselor. When a mother uses reframing in discussing the behaviors of her son, the son may no longer hear himself described as a misbehaving or "bad" child; he becomes "energetic." As a result, the school counselor may find that he or she has an ally in the counseling process, while the children experience a more positive response from Mom. Mom subsequently finds a way to see other than negative behaviors from her children.

Behavioral problems can be a function of peer difficulties and a host of other problems, but issues within the family are a likely place to explore such problems (Silver, 1992). Although some behavior may seem eccentric, it may be metaphorically perceived as protective in nature (Haley, 1980). Many child problems will last for years if parents do not do something (Haley, 1980). For example, in some cases, a student's behavior may escalate until one of the parents takes charge of the situation (Grove & Haley, 1993). In other cases, the mother could escalate the problem behavior in order to get the father to take charge. Furthermore, reframing this situation can make the student's "direct" behavior and the mother's "indirect" behavior appear to be benevolently directed at helping the family.

Likewise, when parents have divorced, it is helpful for the counselor to help the parents clarify their relationship. For example, the parents often need to say something like "We're not getting back together." This is helpful in two ways. First it helps the children see the finality of the marriage. Secondly, if one of the parents also believes the couple may get back together, it also assists that parent with the closure of the relationship as husband and wife (Grove & Haley, 1993). It is better for the parents to communicate directly than to communicate metaphorically through the problems of the student (Haley, 1980).

Furthermore, schools need to be in step with the realities of divorce. Generally speaking, schools have not been in touch with the needs of children dealing with divorce. As Elkin (1985) has indicated, "Rarely does one find the word 'divorce' in school books" (p. v). If schools and school counselors were more involved, they could become a tremendous source of support for a family having problems and, at the same time, demonstrate to children that there are caring adults in the world, at least within the school environment (Elkin).

As school counselors become effective in assisting children with problems from a family perspective, issues regarding various family constellations will become important. Such family profiles are beyond the scope of this book; however, they are certainly worthy of a brief discussion.

For example, step-families (also known as reconstituted, aggregate, bi-nuclear, compound, consolidated, joint, meta, or re-coupled families) are becoming more and more common (Medler, Dameron, Strother, & DeNardo, 1987). Such families have problems similar to those of any other family, but they also have difficulties that are idiosyncratic to "composite" families. To illustrate, the step-family tree or genogram generally looks more like a "family forest" (Medler et al.). Issues that are of particular concern include dealing with loss, divided loyalties, belonging, membership in two households, unreasonable expectations, fantasies of natural parents, guilt over causing the divorce (Medler et al.), and the myth of instant love. Additional stressors for step-families include disciplining children and having a biological parent living elsewhere (Medler et al.).

Medler et al. (1987) have indicated that "rapid growth in the number of school-age children living in step-families indicates the need for school counselors to initiate programs to assist step-family members" (p. 54). This may include family counseling and parent training. Family counseling with these families will be similar to that with nuclear families; however, the goals will be somewhat different (Visher & Visher, 1979). For example, helping the adolescent and both families with issues regarding visitation (e.g., feeling pressured to visit or kept from visiting) can be helpful (Medler et al.). Additionally, the myth that time will take care of everything needs to be addressed. School counselors are in an optimal position to dispel this and other myths regarding step-family functioning. Moving from a nuclear family to one in transition involves new experiences (Poppen & White, 1984). This process can be facilitated by the school counselor working with the family.

Economic difficulties and inadequate living environments are other major issues that obviously need to be addressed when working with children in the schools. Additionally, family stress associated with children with disabilities, impaired parents, lack of social support, and placements outside of the home are important concerns for healthy family functioning. Matters regarding diversity, adjunctive treatments outside of school (e.g., alcohol- and drug-abuse therapy for parents or children), and coordinating service delivery systems will be required of the school counselor working with families (Tracy, Green, & Bremseth, 1993).

Our discussion regarding therapeutic letters was initiated by our observation that not everything that can be done to help families occurs in the session. Therapeutic letters can be utilized for a variety of reasons, including acknowledging mistakes that have been made as well as enhancing motivation. It is a good idea to consult other school counselors when writing a letter to a family in order to avoid writing indirectly about the situation that may need correcting. In addition, consultation

Family Counseling in the Schools:

regarding the letter writing may be helpful because the counselor is attempting a different stance or one that is contrary to what has been discussed at previous meetings with the family. If the letter writing's purpose is to heal a "counseling break," then the letter needs to be sent as soon after the fracture as possible in order to make an impact before things settle down. To be sure, "mistakes" are not professional misgivings or anything unethical; rather, the mistake is one of interpretation, insensitivity, or emphasizing the wrong point (Omer, 1991).

It is important to assist parents in defining their roles and family leadership, and in enhancing their communication. It takes months and even years to learn a particular trade (e.g., beautician, electrician, counselor), but people can become parents without any training. Helping with duties and feelings regarding these roles can be an effective way to improve family functioning, as well as school performance.

To conclude, experience has indicated that integrating family counseling into the schools is not an easy task (O'Callaghan, 1991). Mascari, Danzinger, and Gross (1992) have illustrated this point by describing three types of families. The family "from hell" plays "let's fight" from the beginning of treatment. This type of family is difficult for any counselor but may be more problematic for the beginning school counselor working with families. All the same, they need assistance and should be approached in some manner. The family "living in hell" functions in such deplorable conditions (e.g., poverty, illness, inadequate housing) that school issues take a back burner in terms of priority. This family also needs family counseling, which may include helping the family to access adjunctive services from the community. The family "visiting hell" is more workable since their distress appears to be temporary. This may be the easiest family for the school counselor to work with and may be the type of family that beginning school counselors approaching family counseling should attempt. Once experience and confidence are gained, more difficult family circumstances can be addressed.

Chapter 11 presents case contributions from school professionals; the cases in this chapter are actual cases that have been altered to protect the privacy of the student, family, and school. We believe that these cases nicely illustrate school problems and that they represent systemic

192

interventions utilizing the student's family.

Family Counseling in the Schools:

Chapter Eleven

Case Contributions From School Professionals

Case presentations of in-school counseling sessions offer an exceptional opportunity for learning about family counseling. The following brief cases illustrate many of the family counseling concepts discussed in this book.

Case 1
The Brothers Who Soiled Their Pants to
Save Their Parents' Marriage
Counselor: Michael Wells
Supervisor: J. Scott Hinkle

North Wilkesboro, North Carolina

Wells & Hinkle (1990) reported a case in which two brothers— Donny, age 8, and James, age 7—soiled their pants on a regular basis. A combined structural and strategic family systems approach was implemented based on the hypothesis that problematic elements of the family system were contributing to childhood encopresis. The family consists of Father, age 33, a small business owner, and Mother, age 32, who was not working due to long-standing somatic problems. The parents had been married for twelve years, the first marriage for both. Mother had been hospitalized at least once per year since the delivery of her first child and was often sick. Their sons were exhibiting encopresis. There was a great deal of involvement from the paternal grandmother, age 66, who convinced her son to call for a family counseling appointment. During the initial family counseling session, it was discovered that the parents had been sleeping in separate bedrooms for the last three years and that Father often sleeps in the boys' room. Early sessions featured

Family Counseling in the Schools:

a minimal amount of time spent in discussing the soilings.

From the first session the major theme of the treatment was the belief that the encopresis was a family problem with a family solution. In addition to obtaining a complete description of the presenting problem, the opening sessions included an assessment of the degree of motivation held by each family member to work for change. The parents' extreme frustration with their lack of an effect on the soiling and the persistent demands made of them for improvement by the grandmother indicated a strong desire for change.

The introductory interview revealed that the boys' soiling occurred only at home and only during waking hours. The parents reported trying rigorous behavioral treatments including punishment (spanking and taking away privileges) for soiling, rewards for not soiling, and making the one who soiled clean his own pants and his bedroom on the day of the occurrence, all to no avail. Following the social stage and problem formulation, an attempt was made to increase the day-to-day awareness of the soiling. We set up the expectation that no-soiling was just as likely as soiling, and the family was given the assignment of predicting whether or not each of the boys would soil during the next week. The predictions were made each night, and the results were to be written down and posted on the refrigerator.

During the second session, family members were asked to describe the family, talk about family roles, and share their perceptions of the roles of other family members. It was hypothesized that a number of dysfunctional elements were operating, including the parental disengagement; the perception by family members that mother was sick or inadequate; Grandmother was overly involved and domineering; and the younger son had a learning disability which required placement in special education classes.

By the third session, the rate of correct prediction of encopresis by the family was approximately 50 percent, with no family member predicting correctly more than 60 percent of the time (Wells & Hinkle, 1990). The actual incidents of soiling, however, dropped to zero for James and two for Donny. In the third session, the parents sat at opposite ends of the office, with Father and the boys on the sofa. It was suggested that Father and Mother sit together in order to facilitate conversation with the counselor and to enhance the family restructuring process. As expected, considerable resistance was encountered from the mother, but cooperation was obtained. The counselor said they made a very nice "family picture" with the two parents in the center and the boys on either side.

Most of the questions in this session were purposefully presented to Father with the preface, "Since you are the dad ,...." This direction was an attempt to establish some traditional family roles for the family and to assist Father in regaining power he had relinquished to his mother. Similar strategies were used to empower Mother and to establish the parents as a joint voice of authority in the family.

Mother and Father agreed to go on a date before the fourth session. It was necessary for the counselor to guide and prompt them through all the planning steps of the date, including the anticipation of and planning for obstacles, all the while reminding them that this activity would help the whole family and give them the needed break from the hard work of alleviating their sons' soiling. In order to include the boys in the homework assignment, they were given the task of observing their parents' attire prior to the date and reporting back to the counselor regarding how the parents were dressed and if they seemed to enjoy their date.

The boys also were seen separately during this session and participated in a "secret" with the counselor. James was instructed to tell Donny anytime that he soiled his pants. Donny, being the older brother, would then help James clean himself, wash the soiled clothing, and dress James in clean clothing. This plan was to be kept secret from the parents. Donny's seeking James' aid should he soil was not addressed. This procedure established Donny in the hierarchical role as older brother. The parents were told not to pay attention to their sons' soiling behavior, since the counselor was attending to it as an expert.

During the fourth session, the parents were again prompted to sit together. Their date was discussed and the boys commented positively on their parents' time away. Since the assignment was successful, it was repeated, and the family was praised for their progress and cooperation. The boys reported having one soiling incident each during the previous week.

Family Counseling in the Schools:

Mother and Father sat together without prompting for the fifth session and all subsequent sessions. The boys even indicated that their parents were sitting together at home. In the meantime, Father's mother had called a family meeting, including aunts and uncles, to discuss Donny's and James' soiling. The parents indicated they were unhappy with Grandmother's intrusive behavior. Mother said that Father should tell his mother the meeting would not take place. Father stated that he would. In order to clarify boundaries, he was challenged by the counselor to call his mother while in the office. He did, and he and his wife were pleased. No soiling was reported for either boy during the past week.

By the seventh session, Father reported sleeping in the bedroom with Mother. The counselor and the parents mutually decided to meet again in three weeks. Three weeks later, Mother reported being free of headaches. She had decided to go back to work. Three weeks passed between sessions eight and nine. School had started and each boy continued to do well both in school and at home with no reports of soiling.

Two weeks elapsed between sessions nine and ten. The closure session concluded that family counseling had been successful. Three months later, a follow-up session found the family functioning at the same, improved level with no incidents of encopresis.

Analysis: All nuclear family members were included in a family counseling process that utilized strategic homework assignments, predictions about family behavior, and the restructuring of family roles and boundaries. Initially, a more direct approach was used which consisted of record keeping by parents, predictions of soiling behavior made by all family members, and cooperative correction of any soiling incidents by the boys. This approach brought the encopresis under control and allowed the family to relax and focus on resolving the underlying problems through the family sessions.

A strategic approach also was utilized in order to address the entire family, rather than singling out the children and the encopresis. A number of family systems issues were evident: the disengagement of the parents, the role of the grandmother as "de facto" head of a house in which she did not reside, and the confused role of the children. Therefore, a structural family approach was used to restructure the roles of family members.

The encopresis was hypothesized to be associated with the role confusion among the brothers. Donny had regressed to the behavior of a younger child by soiling while James began to soil after Donny had taken his role as younger child. The soiling also may have been an attempt to relieve the tension of the stressful marital relationship of their parents. Mother's sleeping separately from her husband, physical complaints, and inability to obtain a job indicated significant relationship issues. These issues were hypothesized to be systemically associated with Father's enmeshment with his mother. After restructuring the family roles and boundaries, Mother's physical complaints significantly decreased, she found a job, and Father moved back into the bedroom with his wife.

Grandmother's external source of power often left the family with no real leadership. Therefore, restructuring was necessary to empower Father as leader of the family, a role previously assumed by his mother. The parents were encouraged to function once again as a mutually supportive partnership in leading the family.

Case 2
The Parents Who Didn't Want to Go to School
Counselor: Michael Kahn
Consultant: J. Scott Hinkle

Greensboro, North Carolina

Mrs. W, age 47, sought counseling for her 15 year-old, eighth-grade son, Joseph, because of his repeated failure to attend school (which resulted in his repeating the eighth grade). The school's pursuance of a truancy action brought Joseph and his mother in for family counseling. During the initial session, Mother reported that Joseph had been diagnosed with a developmental learning disability. Additionally, most of his friends attended a different school. The case was transferred to me after being managed by a counselor intern for approximately six weeks.

Joseph often would spend time at his father's business when he skipped school. Apparently, his father did not attempt, or was unable, to get Joseph to school. Father was not very involved in Joseph's life and Joseph's mother was not very consistent or credible with regard to discipline. She felt guilty about disciplining Joseph because of her divorce five years before. For the most part, Joseph was able to do what he pleased. Shortly after counseling began, Mother obtained a job requiring her to work from 11 p.m. to 7 a.m. Joseph was left at home alone because he did not want to stay at anyone's house. Mother reported that her ex-husband did not want Joseph with him in the evenings, since he had remarried and had a one year-old son.

During our first session, Joseph said that his life "sucks." He also said that his life would be better if he had a girlfriend and a driver's license. He seemed uninterested in talking to me, but was not overly resistant. He was apathetic, but willing to come to counseling. The first seven sessions involved discussions about school and home and some art therapy.

It was hypothesized that Joseph's problem with truancy was connected to his situation at home. His mother was subsequently invited to school. Unfortunately, she and Joseph failed to follow through with homework assignments. During the fourth family session, Mother reported that Joseph had chosen to skip his driver's test. Joseph said that he wanted to wait until he was eighteen. During the seventh session, Mother reported that Joseph was now staying at her son-in-law's when she was at work. However, Joseph was still skipping school. I felt that we were not making much progress.

Accordingly, I decided to take a more directive and strategic approach to the case. I called Father to arrange a family counseling session with him. He agreed to a meeting with Joseph and his ex-wife. During this session, Father agreed to care for Joseph on alternate nights.

The tenth session took place at school and included Joseph, both parents, the school counselor, the assistant principal, and Joseph's five teachers. After Joseph was asked to wait outside, Father and Mother presented a plan that was developed in the previous session. The school staff were ready to make it work. In addition, they were open to promoting Joseph to the ninth grade if he showed some progress and motivation. Joseph was brought into the room and the plan was presented to him with an emphasis on support and not punishment. The plan simply stipulated that if Joseph skipped school one day, one of his parents would attend school with him the following day— for the entire day. Each teacher agreed to have a desk available for the parent if it became necessary for them to attend school with their son to provide him support. Joseph and his mother, or father, depending on which parent attended that day, would meet with the school counselor at the end of the day. The teachers, the counselor, and both the parents indicated that they wanted Joseph to be successful in school.

Joseph attended school the day after the meeting. However, he failed to attend school the following day; he reported that he was upset with the difficulty of his math work. Unfortunately, neither parent followed-through with the proposed plan. Their excuses ranged from responsibilities at the father's business to previously scheduled appointments. Unfortunately, I neglected to discuss these and other potential barriers to success when the plan was first initiated.

Mother came without Joseph to the eleventh session. She reported that Joseph was now staying at his father's house and had not returned to school. She agreed to give the plan another try. The twelfth session had the parents and Joseph in attendance. This time we discussed the barriers to the plan. Father responded that he could not afford to spend the entire day at school. Mother said that she could not get Joseph to school the morning after he failed to attend school. Rather than discuss the parents' ability to cooperate, Father was asked to stay until 10:15 a.m. at which time Joseph's mother would take over. Father indicated that if one of his assistants at the business did not come to work, he would be unable attend school. In that event, the counselor asked Father to agree to let his wife fill-in at the business.

Again the parents did not follow-through with the plan. Subsequently, and without the counselor's knowledge, Joseph and his mother met with the school psychologist for an evaluation. The psychologist sabotaged the plan by telling Mother that the family plan would humiliate Joseph. Needless to say I was not happy with this situation. The results of the psycho-educational evaluation indicated that Joseph was at the third- or fourth-grade levels in most subjects. He was recommended to the ninth grade with a special tutoring arrangement and received tutoring during the summer.

Joseph eventually moved to his father's home and his mother

was accepting of this arrangement. She appeared to be pleased that Joseph's father was more involved in his son's life. She reported being angry about Joseph reaching the eighth grade with so many academic deficiencies. Mother began attending a support group for parents in similar situations. Following many cancellations, Mother ended her relationship with me one month after the twelfth session.

Following the summer vacation, Joseph began the ninth grade and began his skipping behavior again. The parents were asked to attend a family counseling session with Joseph's new teachers. In addition, the school psychologist was in attendance and was asked to help guide the session. The same strategy was attempted, but this time the parents were given the ultimate responsibility for Joseph's being successful in school. Every potential excuse was turned into a reframe concerning parenting opportunities and success versus failure. The school psychologist was asked to tell the parents how important it was for their son to attend school and improve his test scores. The parents agreed to the plan and agreed to meet with the school counselor and the school psychologist in one month in order to check on their progress.

Immediately after the session, the school counselor and psychologist penned a letter to the parents telling them how inspired they were with the parents new-found commitment to their son's education. Joseph skipped school one day during a four week period and both parents attended school the following day.

Analysis: The most important aspect of this case was the school counselor's tenacity. The counselor did not give up on the family and continued to survey the social context for a way to solve the problem. In hind sight, the counselor did not consider all the barriers to failure and an important component of the school team had been left out of the treatment plan. From a systemic perspective, this omission was a blunder that came back to haunt the counselor. The plan was a good one, so the counselor enlisted the school psychologist the second time around. The parents also were given more responsibility during the second attempt. The counselor knew that if the school did nothing when skipping began again, the family might get the idea that the school did not care about Joseph's attendance. Also, Joseph may have developed the belief that the people who said they would help him had deserted him.

This strategy, "circling the wagons," is based on love and protection. It was hypothesized that Joseph did not invest in school because he felt unimportant and unloved. When several caring adults, including his teachers, gathered to tell him that they wanted him to be successful, the strategy was effective.

Case 3
The Girl Who Sacrificed Her Education for Her Family
Counselor: Thomas A. Burgess
Supervisor: J. Scott Hinkle

High Point, North Carolina

(Although the family counseling sessions in this case did not occur at school, for reasons that are obvious, the school problem and its solution are worthy of mention. This case was previously discussed in the *Journal of Mental Health Counseling,* Vol. 15, No. 2, 1993).

The Bates family was court referred to a public family counseling agency for the chronic school avoidance of the fourteen-year-old daughter, Alma. In the previous school term, she was absent 150 of 180 school days due to reported chronic anxiety, depression, and numerous somatic complaints. Medication did not alleviate the identified patient's (IP) frequent illnesses and anxiety. Testing and behavioral observation reflected that Alma suffered from both avoidant behavior and social phobia with secondary depression.

Alma's parents did not cooperate with the school's attempts to alleviate the problem, suggesting that the family system was maintaining Alma's presenting problems. For example, when she attended class, her father would presume that she would become ill and waited outside the school to take her home. Alma's father had suggested that her absences resulted from the school's lack of concern and not from problems within the family system. Unfortunately, the parent's inability to have Alma attend school led the courts to threaten her removal from the home if the family did not participate in family counseling.

A thorough family assessment suggested that family members rallied around Alma whenever she exhibited any indication of

Family Counseling in the Schools:

anxiety or somatic discomfort about school. Family members hoped this attention would allay her feelings of anxiety concerning school and subsequently reduce her symptoms. This attention included taking individual walks with her and offering protective words of encouragement. It was hypothesized that this reactivity maintained Alma's excessive anxiety by attempting a first order change and indicated an enmeshed or overly involved family system. It was further hypothesized that the family's tendency to protect Alma served the systemic function of keeping the family together. Father had frequently reported that "caring families are involved in the day-to-day living of each member's life; anything less was uncaring." At this point the purpose of the symptom had been found and the strategic family counseling process began.

Initial family counseling interventions attempted to reinforce boundaries around the individual subsystems and draw attention away from Alma. This intervention included behavioral modification exercises to reduce the family's level of accommodation. While there was modest cooperation, the parents did little to decrease their excessive attention.

It was discovered that Mother checked on Alma every morning and began crying when the client expressed any degree of anxiety or somatic complaint. The directive intervention incorporated had two therapeutic fronts. The client was prescribed the symptom and instructed to become as anxious as possible at school in order for school personnel to understand better the source of her problem and thus allow them to proceed despite her parent's reaction. Alma was resistant to this plan and said that she could not go to school if her mother became emotional. Her reaction suggested that ignoring another family member's feelings was not acceptable, but she eventually agreed.

The parents' unwillingness to insist that Alma attend school was an indication that they did not care whether their daughter was placed out of the home (this was one of the possibilities that the juvenile court had outlined to the parents). The family was advised to meet every night to discuss what it would be like for Alma to be placed in a foster or group home. The following day, the school counselor reported that Alma was brought to school by her mother and that Alma remained all day.

After six sessions, Alma was attending school three days a

week until 1:00 p.m. At the seventh session, she reported that her anxiety was significantly reduced and that when she did become anxious she would focus on her school work and the anxiety would decrease. During this session, Alma presented a brighter affect, did not sit between her parents, and spontaneously engaged her mother in conversation. The school counselor subsequently reported that the father had telephoned and asked the school not to contact him when the client complained of anxiety. These positive changes indicated that the boundaries between subsystems had been strengthened, and new coping mechanisms were being implemented by Alma.

The family system adapted to a new level of functioning with Alma remaining at school until approximately 1:00 p.m., three to four days per week. She would complain of physical problems approximately one to two days per week, resulting in absences from school. At this point, the counselor predicted Alma would relapse, would refuse to go to school, and would develop an incredible number of physical maladies. This predicted regression was reframed as an attempt to test the parents' resolve about keeping her at school. This strategy addressed the family's high degree of reactiveness to the counselor and it challenged them to prove the counselor wrong. Mother, as well as Alma, quickly declared the counselor "crazy," while the father stated that the agency was trying to strip the family of any pride attained by Alma's improvement. However, after the prediction the client reported less anxiety and somatic complaints, and school attendance increased.

Twelve months following counseling, Alma was attending school regularly, rarely reported anxiety, and interacted with the counselor in a more relaxed manner. She had continued to differentiate from her parents and had enrolled in a driver's education program, a further indication of her ability to disengage from her family. Since she was not hampered by her previous symptoms, she had assumed the responsibility of further developing the social and life skills she had not acquired earlier.

Analysis: Family counseling demonstrated that the family's behaviors had benignly maintained or contributed to Alma's school avoidance. The directives allowed Alma to differentiate from her parents and replace negative reactions toward the phobic situation. Alma's, or her parents', inability to change would have resulted in the ultimate form of family disloyalty by engineering Alma's removal from the home.

In terms of reframes, Alma agreed to have more of the symptoms so that her behavior at school could be better understood. The parents were put in a position to discuss their daughter being removed from the home. This was the ultimate *disengagement* and resulted in some degree of improvement in *enmeshment* - Alma increased her school attendance.

Case 4
The Power Struggle
Counselor: Kenneth Simington

Winston-Salem, North Carolina

Jane was an eighth-grade student newly enrolled in our school. She lived with her single mother, Ms. P, who had been transferred to our city by her company. Jane's mother was an ambitious career mother who was moving up the company ladder. Mother's job required a considerable amount of out-of-town traveling, which meant leaving Jane alone quite often. When Mother was out of town, arrangements were made for a sister to look after Jane.

During the fall of the year, Ms. P called to inquire about boarding schools because Jane was failing several classes and Ms. P felt Jane needed more discipline. During our telephone conference, I scheduled an appointment for Ms. P to come in for a parent conference. Additionally, I arranged for her to meet with Jane's teachers. In preparation for our conference, I agreed to meet with Jane to discuss the situation. Ms. P noted that Jane was not in favor of attending a boarding school. She also indicated that they did not get along all that well but did not give specific details.

My interview with Jane reflected a mother and daughter locked in an intense battle for *control* and *power*. Jane viewed her mother as a peer, not a parent, and subsequently was not compliant to any parental directives. In the conference with Ms. P, she told me that the situation was so intense that the two of them had been in physical conflict. This conflict had been a result of Jane's failure to obey her mother. In fact, this incident is the one which prompted Ms. P to call the school requesting information about boarding schools.

My initial assessment was that the family was severely, if not chaotically, *disengaged*. Further, I believed that it was an under-organized family where the traditional *hierarchy* in the family had been destroyed. This family needed intervention quickly, otherwise, it would fall apart completely. Decreasing the amount of emotional distance between Jane and her mother might take time, but the threat of potential violence in the home required immediate attention.

For the first family counseling effort, I offered the mother support for the difficulty of the situation and assigned her one task. Do not for any reason engage Jane in physical confrontations. When Ms. P returned for the next session, she reported a marked decrease in the level of conflict (this would prove to be a mixed blessing). By engaging in physical fights with Jane, Ms. P was giving away the natural power that was part of her parental role. Jane used the fights to further erode her mother's parental authority, thus pulling her mother downward in the family hierarchy. When she refused to be drawn into the physical conflicts, Ms. P regained much of her authority as a parent. As a result, she improved her perceived credibility with her daughter and became a more consistent parent. This change also allowed Jane to invest her time in adolescence and school.

Analysis: This case focused on the most basic of family counseling strategies for families with child problems. Counseling elevated the mother's position above that of the child. This strategy was successful and the family made many positive changes.

Case 5
Parents Letting Their Child Parent
Counselor: Holly Craven

Thomasville, North Carolina

I met Sally, a ten-year-old student, while working as a School Family Counselor. In this position I worked as a liaison between the home and the school so as to ensure that students had

Family Counseling in the Schools:

successful school experiences. Some parents assume that as a counselor I am going to tell them how to raise their child. In order to let the parents know that I am not trying to "bully" them, I tell them that they are the experts on their child, and that I need their help in assisting their child.

Sally was referred to me by her fourth-grade teacher, who was disturbed by Sally's behavior. Sally had stolen many items in her classroom, had lied to her teacher as well as to her mother, was disrespectful, started disagreements with other children, and was controlling and manipulative. The counseling referral form indicated that these problems were of a chronic nature. Although I talked with Sally, her problems continued.

At the beginning of Sally's fifth-grade year, I met with Sally and her mother to begin family counseling. I initiated counseling by joining with the family. This effort helped me to obtain a perspective regarding the underlying issues in the family system. During the first few "visits," Sally, Sally's mother, and I discussed who lived in their home, what it was like to live in their home, their family interests, and background information about Sally's school performance. They were currently living with Mother's parents but were in the process of buying a house. I decided to meet with only Sally and her mother in order to establish a separate family boundary. Mother also preferred not to meet at her parents' home; so, we met at school.

Sally had reported that she felt her grandparents were actually her parents. She also openly shared negative feelings about her mother. It was my impression that Sally made such statements to play on her mother's guilt about living at the home of her parents. Mother would often be pulled into a disagreement when Sally would make comments of this nature. I decided to address this issue by confronting Mother about her feelings concerning Sally's remarks. I addressed the issue by pointing out to Mother the effect the statements had on her behavior and facial expressions during the family counseling sessions. I would try either to help Sally see her mother in a different light or ask Mother to have a discussion with Sally about the way that she expected Sally to talk to her. However, these discussions often turned into bickering as if they were sisters rather than mother and daughter.

Once the counseling goals were set, Sally and her mother

agreed that they would like to relate to each other differently. They also agreed to work together on helping Sally complete her school work. In order to help them interact differently, my objective was to establish a proper hierarchy in the family system. I believed that since they had been living with Mother's parents for so long, they had established a pattern of interaction that was on an equal level of power instead of a more functional parent-child hierarchy.

My first step in empowering Mother was to establish some independent adult time during the counseling sessions. Mother decided on the amount of time spent with Sally during each session, dependent on the level of Sally's disrespect to her in the early part of the session. This approach provided me with an opportunity to discuss Mother's parenting style as well as help establish Mother in a position of power. Mother admitted she was inconsistent with Sally, often letting her have her own way, and that she had essentially lost her credibility as a parent. We discussed what a healthy parent-child relationship should look like and what it would take to get her and her daughter to an improved relational level.

I taught Mother that children test limits and may rebel against them, but limits are necessary and actually provide a degree of safety. In order for Mother to set adequate limits for her daughter, she would need to become more consistent. For example, when Sally was given a consequence for her inappropriate behavior, Mother agreed to enforce the consequence rather than allow Sally to talk her into "backing off." Mother also agreed to practice not arguing with Sally. She had found this arguing to be very difficult because Sally knew what to say to upset her. Mother established, in the counseling sessions, what it meant to have control and power in her family. This understanding helped her to perceive how the *power hierarchy* had essentially been reversed. Mother also became adept at recognizing Sally's manipulations and learned how to deal effectively with them. Once she realized that she was being manipulated, Mother was able to stop the "bickering."

I took this approach with Mother because she was intelligent and quite logical in her thinking. We also discussed how her parents often undermined her parenting and how this undermining often led to family arguments. Even after Mother and Sally moved out of the grandparent's home, Sally often called her grandparents and initiated their involvement concerning matters between she and her mother. Although improvements were occurring at school and at home, Mother believed that boundary issues were still in need of attention, since arguments increased in frequency in the presence of the grandparents. I asked Mother if it would be all right for her parents to accompany her to school for her next visit. I explained to Mother that it appeared her parents continued to play a large role in the family even though they were not living together any longer. My rationale for inviting the grandparents was to *re-organize or restructure their family roles* so that they would support their daughter, and so that Mother could receive permission from her parents to become a parent herself. Mother reported many times that her parents were either "jumping in when she was disciplining" or telling her that she was not "doing it right." I asked Mother for permission regarding directives in order to provide her with a sense of power.

The grandparents attended the next counseling session. I used this session to have them express their theory of the existing problem and to "facilitate" a decision by all three of them as to how Sally should be handled. I took a risk and asked the grandparents if they thought their daughter was ready to be a parent. Fortunately, they both answered "yes." Then I asked them each to look at their daughter and, one at a time, tell her that they believed her to be a capable parent and that they were willing to let her be Sally's parent. Following this, we established how they would help their daughter to parent. They agreed that when the three of them were together with Sally, Mother would be the one to handle problems and that the grandparents would be supportive of their daughter.

One final thing occurred in the session. Grandfather reported that his wife and daughter argued. I allowed Mother and Grandmother to discuss this problem because Mother quickly shared that she was concerned about the contention between she and her mother. Grandmother admitted that she wished she had handled matters concerning Sally differently.

Afterwards, Mother reported that everyone was sticking to the agreed upon plan and that the family had made significant improvements. It may seem surprising, but during the remainder of the sessions, Mother and I worked on her confidence as a parent and not directly with Sally. I asked her to share what things she had accomplished and how Sally had responded. Mother's negative attitude about her inadequacies as a parent quickly moved in a positive direction. Additionally, I asked Mother to watch two videos on self-esteem and empowerment. Mother and I discussed ways that she could apply the films to her life situation. Sally's teacher also reported dramatic improvements in the classroom. I closed the counseling sessions by asking Sally and her mother if their goals had been accomplished. They responded affirmatively but understood that they would need to continue working on their parent-child relationship.

Analysis: Establishing rapport with the mother was important to the success of this case. The counselor indicated Mother was the "expert" on her daughter and that she needed the mother's assistance to help with Sally. The counselor hypothesized that permeable family boundaries were contributing to the problem. As a result, the counselor put the grandparents in a position to disengage from parenting their daughter. This also could be described as a *cross-generational boundary* problem. The counselor also utilized psychoeducation in coaching the mother about parenting skills including consistency and credibility. Finally, as an example of *equifinality* (discussed in Chapter 2), the counselor continued to help the family improve by only working with the mother.

Case 6
The Couple That Needed Help
Counselor: Holly Craven

Thomasville, North Carolina

Joe, an eight-year-old boy, lived with his mother and her boyfriend, Ted, at a trailer park known for its violence. His mother had been living with Ted for eight years. Joe had an older sister who was ten that lived with their biological father. Additionally, Joe had three sisters, ages seven, three, and ten, living with him.

Joe was referred for his violent behavior and loud outbursts in the classroom. His teacher had reported that it took very little for Joe to become angry. He fought on the school bus as well as at the bus stop. Joe had been labeled behaviorally/emotionally handicapped and was prescribed Ritalin for attention deficit/hyperactivity disorder.

His teacher and I met with Mother to discuss the family counseling program at school. Mother was willing to help since she essentially had little control over Joe's behavior. The first two sessions were spent joining with the family and gathering information about family functioning. Mother admitted that she was not consistent with her children and that she had become afraid of hurting them while angry. Ted was an important resource, but he was unable to make the scheduled meetings due to his work schedule.

Mother's counseling goals consisted of gaining better control of her temper and learning to discipline her children without spanking them. My goal was to get Mother to agree to deal with some of her family-of-origin issues that were keeping her so on edge. Just giving Mother someone to talk to seemed to help her calm down. This intervention eventually had a concomitant calming effect on Joe in the classroom.

Throughout the counseling, Mother and I continually focused on her consistency with the children and her ability to discipline without spanking. I also empowered Mother in her role in the family hierarchy and reinforced that she was more than a babysitter. This fact was established when Joe admitted that he had many of his outbursts because his mother would give into his demands.

Mother continued to share information about her family of origin. She explained that her past haunted her and made it difficult for her to make adjustments with her life. Also, when she became depressed, her children's behavior deteriorated. Mother agreed to some bibliotherapy and to keeping a journal. All of these issues brought up the importance of Ted, again. Mother agreed to try and get Ted to meet with us.

When I first met with Joe's mother, she was willing to do what she needed to in order to change her life. After assessing the larger system, I realized that she had no support. Her family counted on her to be there for them, but they were not there for her. Her boyfriend worked unusual hours and typically was not around when the children were home. As a result, there were three things I knew that needed to happen: let her know I was in control and could be a source of support for her; normalize things for her as much as possible; have her be strong enough to establish *boundaries* for her children and others. These interventions were designed to help her obtain a sense of hope. In fact, she saw her family as hopeless and she spent most of her time responding to things instead of making things happen. She had many problems that needed immediate attention and she had few skills to deal with them. Instead, she would become depressed or lose her temper. So, I explained that everyone had problems, that was just life, and if we worked on one thing at a time, it would not feel so overwhelming.

Mother immediately wanted to deal with her anger regarding Joe. I addressed this issue and asked what she did when she became angry. She explained, noting that it was interesting to her that Joe would engage in similar behaviors. I worked with Joe and Mother to set up appropriate ways to handle anger. I modeled ways to talk to her children. Her tone was loud and abrasive, which Joe would respond to in the same manner. I told her some other ways that people deal with anger and asked her to try one. She and Joe agreed to "take five" (time-out) when they became angry. Mother would help Joe recognize when he needed to "take five" if he did not do so on his own.

Mother and I spent time building a relationship. To help establish boundaries, I asked her if her children could go somewhere in the house that would give her time alone. She had not clearly established limits in her family; she would tell the children too much adult information. As a result, I felt Joe was very tied to his mother and acted-out many of her feelings. That way, her attention stayed focused on him and she did not get as depressed.

We tried to get Ted to meet with us, but it did not seem possible because of our schedules. Money was a problem for the family and jobs were hard to come by, so I did not feel I could ask Ted to risk a job so we could meet.

I asked Mother to begin reading a parenting book. She had a hard time being consistent, which I felt came from the weak family boundaries. She wanted to make everyone happy; so, if the children manipulated her enough she gave into their demands. However, as Mother improved her parenting skills, she reported feeling better about herself. I encouraged Mother to make decisions about what she wanted and what she would do to meet her goals. I did this to help her realize that she had control, if she wanted it. I put on the table the idea of Joe being in tune with her and asked if she had noticed that Joe seemed to have difficulty when she was upset. When she thought about that, she did see a pattern. This idea gave Mother something to keep in mind. Joe could be a good barometer for her; when he started having problems she needed to see what was going on with her and make necessary adjustments.

Finally, I was able to involve Ted. From a systemic angle, his commitment was important if things were to work at home. That session was chaotic and it became clear that Ted and Mother had relationship problems. Mother looked for Ted's approval in the session; she often asked Ted if she were right.

I set up a session for the couple alone. In that meeting, issues of trust, resentment, and alienation surfaced. Mother and Ted felt that the first thing they needed to do was spend some time alone. Ted felt that Mother needed to work on her own issues -- so they agreed that she would do that -- but he would need to support her. She worked diligently on her issues. She shared her most painful family-of-origin experiences and thought about how they continued to affect her. She started a journal so that she could release more feelings.

I hypothesized that the parenting team was not strong and the children knew it. I met with Mother and she reported that Ted was overwhelmed by the last meeting and was doubting the effects of family counseling. Ted, however, returned and I initiated a discussion regarding John Edward's *metaphor* of a guardrail. I explained that a guardrail is strong and provides a boundary or limit when it is hit; however, it gives and bounces back. Parents need to do the same for their children. They liked the metaphor and agreed to start working towards being "guardrails" themselves. Once we began discussing their relationship and their parenting as a team, many issues surfaced.

Mother and Ted agreed that the bottom line was that they were not connected as a couple. The first thing I did was to agree to help them make their relationship more solid. They decided to spend more time together and Joe agreed to watch the younger children so this could be possible. Mother also agreed to continue discussing her family-of-origin issues.

These simple family interventions resulted in remarkably

more times before the school year ended. Once Ted and Mother started working out their problems, Joe's difficulties significantly decreased. His special resource teachers had cut his time back significantly, and Joe began controlling himself in class as well as at home. Mother reported that she was pleased with the family changes and Joe's improvements at school. Interestingly, Mother continued counseling to obtain closure on her family-of-origin issues.

Analysis: Without Ted's collaboration, it was expected that any change would be short-lived. The counselor, therefore, strengthened the couple subsystem by insisting that Ted come to counseling. Once he began to attend, the couple addressed some of their issues which subsequently affected Joe's school behavior in a positive way.

Case 7
Counselor: Susan S. Crawford

Greensboro, North Carolina

As the counselor at an elementary school, I offer several types of support groups for the students. One set of those groups included children whose parents had either separated or divorced. Students became a part of the group through teacher, parent, or self-referral. The first indication I had that Rob and Jill were separated was through two teacher referrals, each requesting that this couple's children attend the support group. Rob was a 42 year-old male in his first marriage to Jill who was 40 years-old. They had been married for twelve years and this was Jill's second marriage. They had two children from this marriage and Jill had two grown children from her previous marriage. Matt was an eight-year-old, third-grade student and his sister, Julie, was a six-year-old first grader.

Outwardly, this family appeared to the school staff to be happy and healthy. The children were considered to be good students. I approached the referring teachers to inquire about any changes they may have noticed in the children. Both teachers mentioned that the children had become much more quiet and Julie was described as "clingy." Individual sessions were scheduled for the next day.

Family Counseling in the Schools:

I met with the children separately. Matt was reluctant to discuss his family situation and appeared sullen. He did mention that his mother had been sleeping in the guest room for several months and that his parents always "argued a lot." He agreed to attend a meeting of the support group and seemed to brighten once he realized that there would be group members in a similar situation.

My meeting with Julie was much the same, but I detected more anger than I had with Matt. She also mentioned her mother moving out of her parents' bedroom and that her mom "now had her own apartment, but she didn't stay there overnight." She was much more hesitant about joining a group until I mentioned that we did a lot of art activities and that some of her friends attended the group.

I encountered Jill in the hallway and asked if she could come and talk with me. She appeared eager to talk, although she seemed uncharacteristically flustered. We met for about 20 minutes and she discussed her deteriorating relationship with her husband. Jill disclosed that she was very interested in pursuing a new career in public relations and that she just didn't feel as close to her husband as she had in the past. She mentioned that they argued or did not talk at all and that she was concerned about the effect this relationship was having on the children. We discussed Jill's impending move and she said that she was planning on moving the following week. The children were scheduled to stay with her husband during the week, "to maintain stability," and with her on the weekends.

We discussed the children's involvement in these decisions. The children's role in decision-making was minimal, with little understanding on their part and lots of feelings of anger. Jill stated that she would come to school for family conferences and agreed to the idea of Matt's and Julie's attendance in the support group.

I asked Jill if she and Rob had been to couples counseling. Jill stated that they tried marriage counseling and that she simply did not love her husband and wanted to end the marriage. She acknowledged her love for her children but was sorry that things had not worked out with her first husband. She seemed reticent but also appeared determined to begin her new life.

I met with Rob several days later and saw a man who had changed dramatically. Previously, he had been full of confidence and energy. He now appeared despondent and cried openly when discussing the current situation and how he viewed his future. Rob stated quite plainly that "Jill will come around — this is just her mid-life crisis." We discussed the experience of marriage counseling and he said he felt it was beneficial to talk but that it did not lead to his desired outcome. Rob indicated that he felt he had done everything he could to make the marriage work and Jill was still determined to leave.

Individual sessions with Rob and Jill continued throughout the next three months on a fairly regular basis. When they were visiting the children during the school day, they would stop by and talk for a brief time. Rob became more resigned to the fact that Jill was not going to move back into the house. He began to date someone approximately four months after their separation; Jill began the same within two months of the separation. She never expressed any regret regarding her decision and continued to move forward with her life.

Prior to his parents' counseling, Matt had been mildly disruptive with minor acting-out behaviors. His grades had dropped drastically at first, but began to improve as things at home became more routine and stable. Matt willingly attended all support group meetings and was always willing to participate. After six months, Matt was returning to his former, more cooperative self but maintained a defensive attitude with both students and teachers. When his mother began dating, Matt seemed to accept this idea in a rather matter-of-fact way.

Julie had labile emotions before her parents came to see me. She refused to share with others and seemed constantly to stir up trouble among other children. Initially she was quiet during the sessions with the support group but would always participate in activities. After a few weeks of group counseling and discussing the family situation with her mother and brother, Julie began to smile more spontaneously and became less of an instigator. When her parents began dating other people, Julie would tell the group about all the "neat" places they took Matt and her and all the things they bought her.

Toward the end of the school year both children, when asked, would tell me that their parents were happier now and that things were going well. It appeared that parent-child communication was fairly open, judging from the openness displayed by these children, but it also seemed that the children

Family Counseling in the Schools:

were trying to protect their parents from unhappiness.

Analysis: The work with Rob and Jill was not "traditional family counseling," and the meetings to discuss their separation were not "typical school counseling." Still, it was clear that Matt and Julie were not adjusting well to their parents' marital difficulties and that individual and group counseling were not enough to make a significant impact on their adjustment and school performance. It was attempted, unsuccessfully, to see the parents as a couple. This was, however, diagnostic of the marital dysfunction and helped to plan effective counseling for Matt and Julie. The children's behavior reflected the parent's *disengagement.* The fact that the parents did not discuss their separation with the children was favorable in that they had not let the marital subsystem boundaries deteriorate to the point of letting the children in. However, following the separation, the children needed to negotiate different family *roles* and *rules.* This was effectively accomplished by meeting with the children and each parent on a regular basis (about every two or three weeks) for approximately three months. It is important to discuss family issues with parents and students because it improves academic performance and enhances the child's development.

Case 8
The Case of the Father Who Shared His Son's Pain
Counselor: Michael Wells

Surry County, North Carolina

I received an urgent call to see Justin and his parents at his elementary school which was in the school system for which I worked. It had just come to the attention of school officials that Justin's fifth-grade, male teacher had perhaps molested a number of his male students, including Justin.

At the initial family meeting, I attempted to calm the hysteria and provide the family with information regarding procedures and scenarios they were likely to encounter in the near future. I also collected some basic information about the family and the situation regarding the molestation and told them what my role would be in the process. I had previously spoken with school officials in order to clarify my role as a counselor to the family and not as an investigator of the abuse.

The family was understandably agitated. My goals were to alleviate some of the initial shock and assess the family's resources for getting through this situation. They were a family of four, including Justin and a younger brother, age seven. The marriage of Justin's parents appeared strong and the family seemed to be stable and well-functioning. The extended family consisted of both sets of grandparents and siblings of both parents; all were available for support. After exchanging pertinent information and obtaining reassurance about another session in three days, the family, having calmed considerably, left arm in arm.

Within twenty-four hours, Justin's mother had called and asked if I could see Justin individually for our next visit. She said he wanted to talk with me alone. I agreed to see him for a few minutes at the beginning of our next family session to explain to him why we needed to have all our discussions as a family. I told Mother how important a united front was for the whole family to face this issue. I emphasized that this incident had affected the entire family, not just Justin. I expressed my confidence that she and Father were willing to do whatever was necessary to help Justin, even if that meant turning over their parent-role to me. However, I pointed out that a transfer of authority would not be necessary and reinforced the message that they were in a much better position than I to lead the family through this trial due to their knowledge about the family and their love and concern for each other.

At the second session, I was able to determine from my brief contact with Justin that seeing me alone had not been his idea but his father's. Father had been *disengaged* from the family since the molestation had come to light. He had many "chores" in the garage and around the family farm which kept him away. I characterized Father's behavior as one of devotion to the continuation of the family and its possessions -- behavior expected of any good father. While Mother and Father were seated side-by-side, with the children sitting on the carpet at their feet, I commented on what a strong family picture they presented.

I mostly spoke to the parents and encouraged them to be alert for information regarding the abuse that Justin may want to share. I also reinforced their demonstration of belief in Justin and commitment to protect their children. All of this was intended to encourage and strengthen traditional family *roles* and *hierarchies*. It appeared that Father was having the most difficulty with the situation and I hypothesized that he felt inadequate as a father for not preventing and later avenging the violation of his son. I allowed him to chastise me, as a representative of the school system, for not knowing that this teacher was dangerous and should not have been hired. I apologized to him and acknowledged his complaints. I told him that I realized a decision to bring his family back was up to him and I hoped he would set another appointment to return. He did so, for one week later.

Shortly after session two, Father called to say he had taken Justin out for breakfast and asked for details of the interactions between Justin and his teacher. Justin told his father of incidents prior to the molestation in which his teacher made him feel "weird" and that since he was making the best grades ever, he was reluctant to tell anyone and "ruin things." He had not spoken of these things to anyone before. Father had not told his wife of this conversation, even though he had Justin's permission to tell both Mother and me. I strongly supported Father's initiative with Justin and highlighted the trust Justin showed in him. I deferred to him regarding *when* to tell Mother, without mentioning not telling her as an option. He decided to tell her at our next session which was scheduled for the next day.

In the third session, my questions regarding "how things were" were directed at Father. He then chose to tell his wife and younger son what Justin had told him. Father also revealed that he had been molested as a teenager by a stranger in a movie theater and had never told anyone. He said that as Justin talked about the "weird" feelings, the memories of his own molestation became more vivid. Mother and the boys were quick in their responses of concern and support for Father.

Subsequent sessions primarily involved encouraging the family to share concerns, to support one another outside our sessions, and simply to report their progress. There also was a need for me to shepherd the family through the maze of social services, legal processes, charges, dismissal hearings, and court sessions. The communication patterns in the family continued to improve in their openness and Father regained his confidence in his role as family provider and protector. One significant session saw Father supporting Justin in teaching the younger brother how to avoid the inappropriate or undesired advances of someone. Justin told his younger brother of the importance of telling an adult if situations occur that make you feel "weird."

Analysis: It was important for the counselor to adopt the family language, such as the use of the word "weird," to sum up all the emotional and physical reactions that accompany molestation, abuse, or any unwanted contact from another person. To help adjust the *hierarchy* following the abuse, Father was given the assignment to assist Justin in teaching his younger brother about protecting himself. This protective information trickled down the lines of power quite nicely and effectively reorganized the males in the family. The counselor *positively reframed* Father's disengagement as "devotion" to the family.

Case 9
Demonstrating Respect for a Disrespected Mother
Counselor: Scott Hinkle

Greensboro, North Carolina

Lloyd was a 16-year-old sophomore who was having various problems in school, including skipping classes, poor academic performance, and disrespect towards teachers. Following three individual counseling sessions, the counselor consulted with the parents regarding Lloyd's school-related problems. His parents indicated that they also were having problems with his behavior at home.

At the first family session, it was apparent that Mother was very angry with her son and frustrated with her husband's inability to discipline Lloyd. Before the initial session ended, she had even expressed frustration with the counselor. The family agreed to a homework assignment (*directive*) and scheduled another session for two weeks later.

At the second session, Mother was even more angry and frustrated with her son and husband. She had sabotaged the completion of the homework assignment and had made negative remarks about the counseling process. Each attempt by the counselor to allay her anxieties resulted in more negative comments about the counseling profession in general and the counselor in particular. The counselor subsequently withdrew from Mother. This withdrawal only prompted her to berate her family and the counselor more.

It was clear that an effective strategy was needed, quickly. The counselor hypothesized that Mother felt she had been disrespected by the school and especially by the counselor in that none of the school professionals were interested in her theory regarding Lloyd's problems (after all, she was his mother). Rather than challenge her further or retreat from her tirades, both of which would have been easy to do, the counselor implemented a technique similar to "laying down and baring the throat." At the beginning of the next session, Mother was seen alone for approximately ten minutes. The counselor privately apologized for being disrespectful, and that, if he had learned anything in fifteen years of working with children, he knew that "no one knows a son like his mother." Upon hearing this, Mother smiled from ear to ear. Consequentially, she was enlisted as a "co-counselor" and assisted the counselor in positively changing the family.

Analysis: Many counselors may have "fired" this family due to the difficulty of working with the mother. However, the counselor genuinely hypothesized that he and all the other school professionals had not shown this mother the respect she deserved, even though she could be terribly obnoxious. When she was shown respect, her attitude about family counseling changed and the family counseling easily progressed.

Case 10
The Crying Game
Helen Hoggatt Price

Summit, Mississippi
One morning, the father of a second-grade, seven-year-old boy entered my office obviously upset about his son's behavior. He did not hesitate to describe the events that had brought him to seek counseling. The presenting problem was that his son cried every morning upon arriving at school. Father painfully expressed that this behavior had only occurred since

the beginning of the school year six weeks ago. Father added that his son had been elected Class Favorite the previous school year. The student, Jordan, had been in the same school since the age of three, was an "A - B" student, and had no abnormal behavior problems. However, his last grades included four failures. Father expressed his frustration in that he had tried everything from being sensitive to being firm with his son concerning this problem. He stated that both he and Jordan's mother had discussed the problem. Father indicated that his son's behavior was just not like the boy he had always known. No other significant behavioral changes were reported. Jordan gave no explanation for his crying except that he does not want to go to school and that he does not have any friends.

Mother came to the school within the hour to continue the information gathering. She added that Jordan went through a temper-tantrum stage when he was about three- or four-years old and that she felt her son had a low-frustration tolerance. Now, she stated, he tends to hold things in but you can tell when something is bothering him. Before now, Jordan would not cry in front of anyone if he could possibly avoid it.

When questioned about their frustrated reactions as parents, Mother laughed and admitted embarrassingly that she and her husband have thrown things and slammed doors, but do not hit one another (notwithstanding, the same behavior would not be acceptable from their son). Although sharing the same genuine concern, Mother did not seem to display the same emotions as Father. Mother had just finished nursing school (about six weeks ago) and worked from seven a.m. to seven p.m. two days a week and every other weekend. Jordan stays with his paternal grandmother whenever both parents are working. None of Jordan's symptoms are apparent on the weekends or in any other situations or settings. No other significant family changes were reported by Mother.

On consultation with Jordan's teacher, it was found that she had not noticed the crying problem described by the parents. She reported that he had cried in the mornings coming from the car, but she had not seen him crying at any other time. She stated that Jordan is a good student and does not give her any trouble. The teacher felt that his low grades were not historically unusual at the beginning of the school year and that he will most likely improve.

Family Counseling in the Schools:

The faculty member that monitors the car drop-off area did confirm that Jordan cries most mornings. One morning, in the last week, he had to be physically helped out of his father's car. Jordan was observed during recess and found to be without a core group or peers. He would wander around and find something to do, which did not seem to bother him. It was *hypothesized* that problematic elements of the family system were contributing to Jordan's school anxiety.

After an additional session with the family, it was confirmed that Jordan's crying behavior was a result of problematic family interactions. The family system had been instrumental in encouraging and maintaining his problem behavior. Father and Mother had a strained relationship due to the Mother's new, part-time employment. As a part-time nurse, she was making as much as her husband as a full-time fireman who had faithfully been employed for years. This issue had not been openly addressed by the couple, although both were very aware of the differences in income. Instead, it was hypothesized that they could come together and focus on Jordan's problem with separation, and, therefore, not have to feel totally at odds because of the uncomfortableness regarding the differences in their time/pay ratios. The metaphoric purpose of Jordan's separation anxiety was to unite his family, which could have been otherwise separated by the parents' unresolved issue.

Counseling included an agreement between the parents, child, and teacher that the presenting problem was a school problem and would be addressed as such. The faculty member who attended the car drop-off would award Jordan a "happy face" sticker every time Jordan was successful, that is, not crying as he got out of the car and entered school. The teacher would know how he did by Jordan's display of the sticker. Jordan also was assigned "recess buddies" that were to stick together during recess. This opened the door for reestablishing friendships. The teacher sent a note home at the end of each week to report on Jordan's progress.

In the meantime, Jordan's parents were indirectly encouraged to address their unresolved issues in "couples counseling" with the school counselor. It was the first time in their marriage that Mother had surpassed Father's income. During the counseling, the importance of Father's role as a provider for his family was emphasized in many more ways than financially.

The value both of firefighters and of nurses was discussed, and the couple was *metaphorically* identified as team players in the helping professions. A new level of respect for each other was expressed, both as professionals and parents.

Analysis: Jordan's symptoms quickly dissipated as the parents' focus moved from his difficulties to those of the marriage. Family systems counseling restored functional family *homeostasis* and hierarchy among the parents and their child. Reframing was used to change a "suspected" family problem to a "school problem." By doing so, Jordan focused on school and the couple had an opportunity to deal with their relationship. This strategic intervention proved brief and successful for everyone involved.

Family Counseling in the Schools:

Appendix

Suggested Reading List in Family Counseling for School Counselors

This book has cited, for the benefit of counseling professionals in the school, numerous references which examine family counseling. Herein is offered specific readings for school counselors, school psychologists, teachers, or others in the school system wishing to add a family counseling approach to their repertoire of counseling tools. The recommended readings are organized by category. Each resource was included because it contains original works by pioneer practitioners of family counseling, features material felt to be helpful in the actual planning and implementation of family counseling in a school setting, or provides useful information regarding work with students in general. The Reference List for this book is another valuable source of information on family counseling in school settings.

General

Approaches to Family Therapy, by J. C. Hansen & L. L'Abate. 1982. MacMillan.

Brief Strategic Intervention for School Behavior Problems, by E. S. Amatea. 1989. Jossey-Bass.

Change: Principles of Problem Formation and Problem Resolution, by P. Watzlavick, J. Weakland, & R. Fisch. 1978. Norton.

Counseling Families, by D. L. Fenell & B. K. Weinhold. 1989. Love.

Family Counseling in School Settings, by W. M. Walsh & N. J. Giblin. 1988. Charles C. Thomas.

Family Life Cycle: A Framework for Family Therapy, by P. J. Carter & M. Goldrick. 1980. Gardner.

Family Therapy: An Overview (3rd ed.), by A. S. Gurman & D. P. Kniskern. 1991. Brunner/Mazel.

Family Counseling in the Schools:

Family Therapy: Fundamentals of Theory and Practice, by W. A. Griffin. 1993. Brunner/Mazel.

Family Therapy in Clinical Practice, by M. Bowen. 1978. Jason Aronson.

Family Therapy: Major Contributions, by R. J. Green & J. L. Framo. 1981. International Universities Press.

Handbook of Family-School Intervention, by M. J. Fine & C. Carlson (Eds.) 1992. Allyn & Bacon.

Handbook of Family Therapy (Volume I & II), by A. S. Gurman & D. P. Kniskern. 1991. Brunner/Mazel.

Paradoxical Psychotherapy, by G. R. Weeks & L. L'Abate. 1982. Brunner/Mazel.

Problem Solving Therapy, by J. Haley. 1987. Jossey-Bass.

Promoting Change Through Paradoxical Therapy, by G. R. Weeks. 1985. Dow Jones-Irwin.

Steps to an Ecology of Mind, by G. Bateson. 1972. Ballentine.

Strategic family therapy, By C. Madanes. 1981. Jossey Bass.

Systems Psychology in the Schools, by J. M. Plas. 1986. Pergamon.

Systems Theory and Family Therapy, by R. J. Becvar & D. S. Becvar. 1982. University Press of America.

Techniques of Family Therapy, by J. Haley & L. Hoffman. 1967. Basic.

Treating Family of Origin Problems, by R. C. Bedrosian & G. D. Bozicas. 1994. Newbridge.

Understanding Us, by P. J. Carnes. 1981. Interpersonal Communication Programs.

Assessment

Family Assessment: A Guide to Methods and Measures, by H. D. Grotevant & C. I. Carlson. 1989. Guilford.

Family Assessment: Tools for Understanding and Intervention, by A. M. Holman. 1983. Sage.

Handbook of Measurement for Marriage and Family Therapy, by N. Fredman & R. Sherman. 1987. Brunner/Mazel.

Successful Families: Assessment and Interventions, by W. R. Beavers & R. B. Hampson. 1990. W. W. Norton.

Abusive Families

Cry Softly: The Story of Child Abuse, by M. O. Hyde. 1980. Westminster.

Families That Abuse, by A. Cirillo & P. DiBlasio. 1992. Newbridge.

Sex, Love, and Violence, by C. Madanes. 1990. Norton.

Therapeutic Exercises for Victimized and Neglected Girls: Applications for Individual, Family, and Group Psychotherapy, by P. Berman. 1994. Professional Resource Press.

Treating Incest: A Multiple Systems Perspectives, by T. S. Trepper & M. J. Barrett. 1986. Haworth.

Marriage and Divorce

An Introduction to Marital Theory and Therapy, by L. G. Baruth & C. H. Huber. 1984. Waveland.

Cognitive Therapy With Couples, by F. M. Dattilio & C. A Padesky. 1990. Professional Resource Exchange.

Love is Never Enough, by A. T. Beck. 1989. Harper & Row.

Psychotherapy with Children of Divorce, by R. A. Gardner. 1982. Jason Aaronson.

Remarriage and Parenting Today: Research and Theory, by E. M. Hetherington. 1986. Guilford.

Surviving the Break-up: How Children Actually Cope with Divorce, by J. S. Wallerstein & J. B. Kelly. 1980. Basic.

Family Counseling in the Schools:

Substance Abuse

Family Therapy of Drug and Alcohol Abuse, by E. Kaufman & P. Kaufman. 1979. Gardner Press.

The Alcoholic Family, by P. Steinglass. 1987. Basic.

Crisis Intervention

School Crisis Survival Guide: Management Techniques and Materials for Counselors and Administrators, by S. Petersen & R. L. Straub. 1992. The Center for Applied Research in Education.

Turning Points: Treating Families in Transition and Crisis, by F. Pittman. 1987. Norton.

Youth at Risk: A Resource for Counselors, Teachers, and Parents, by D. Capuzzi & D. R. Gross. 1989. American Association for Counseling and Development.

Discipline

Family Roots of School Learning and Behavior Disorders, by R. Friedman. 1973. Charles Thomas.

How to Solve Student Adjustment Problems, by J. P. Smith. 1990. The Center for Applied Research in Education.

How to Talk So Kids Will Listen & Listen So Kids Will Talk, by A. Faber & E. Mazlish. 1980. Avon.

Leaving Home, By J. Haley. 1980. McGraw-Hill.

Journals

American Journal of Family Therapy
Elementary School Guidance and Counseling
The Family Journal
Family Process
Family Therapy Networker
Journal of Counseling and Development
Journal of Family Therapy
Journal of Marriage and Family Counseling
Journal of Psychology in the Schools
Journal of Psychotherapy and the Family

Psychology Review
School Counselor
School Guidance and Counseling
School Psychology Review

References

Adams, C. & Fay, J. (1981). *No more secrets: Protecting your child from sexual assault.* San Luis Obispo, CA: Impact.

Alexander, P. C. (1985). A systems conceptualization of incest. *Family Process, 24,* 79-88.

Aliotti, N. C. (1992). School refusal and family systems intervention. In M. J. Fine & C. Carlson (Eds.), *The handbook of family-school intervention* (pp. 272-287). Needham Heights, MA: Allyn & Bacon.

Amatea, E. S. (1989). *Brief strategic intervention for school behavior problems.* San Francisco: Jossey-Bass.

Amatea, E. S., & Fabrick, F. (1981). Family systems counseling: A positive alternative to traditional counseling. *Elementary School Guidance and Counseling, 15,* 223-236.

Amatea, E. S., & Sherrard, P. A. D. (1991). When students cannot or will not change their behavior: Using brief strategic intervention in the school. *Journal of Counseling and Development, 69,* 341-344.

American Counseling Association. (July, 1993). *The crisis in school counseling: The ACA think tank report.* Alexandria, VA: Author.

Anastopoulos, A. D., Guevremont, D. C., Shelton, T. L., & DuPaul, G. J. (1992). Parenting stress among families of children with attention deficit hyperactivity disorder. *Journal of Abnormal Child Psychology, 20,* 503-520.

Anderson, L. S., III, & Hinkle, J. S. (1994). *An integrated perspective on reality therapy and strategic therapy.* Manuscript submitted for publication.

Andolfi, M. (1978). A structural approach to a family with an encopretic child. *Journal of Marriage and Family Counseling, 4,* 25-29.

Family Counseling in the Schools:

Aponte, H. J. (1976). The family-school interview: An eco- structural approach. *Family Process, 15,* 303-311.

Aponte, H. J., & Van Deusen, J. M. (1981). Structural family therapy. In A. Gurman, & D. Kniskern (Eds.), *Handbook of family therapy* (pp. 310-360). New York: Brunner/Mazel.

Arbour, M., & Bramble, J. (1985). *Characteristics of adolescent substance abuse users attending an intervention program clinic: A pilot study.* Unpublished manuscript. (Available from M. Arbour, 421 Point Road, Little Silver, NJ).

Arnold, J. (1991, April). The revolution in middle school organization. *Momentum,* pp. 20-25.

Asch, R., Price, J., & Hawks, G. (1991). Psychiatric out patients' reactions to summary letters of their consultations. *British Journal of Medical Psychology, 64,* 3-9.

Barker, P. (1992). *Basic family therapy* (3rd. ed.). New York: Oxford.

Barkley, R. B. (1987). *Defiant children: A clinician's manual for parent training.* New York: Guilford.

Barrett, M. J., Sykes, C., & Byrnes, W. (1986). A systemic model for the treatment of intrafamily child sexual abuse. In T. S. Trepper & M. J. Barrett (Eds.), *Treating incest: A multiple systems perspective* (pp. 67-82). New York: Haworth Press.

Bateson, G. (1972). *Steps to an ecology of mind.* New York: Ballentine.

Beal, E. W., & Chertov, L. S. (1992). Family-school intervention: A family systems perspective. In M.J. Fine & C. Carlson (Eds.), *The handbook of family-school intervention* (pp. 288-301). Needham Heights, MA: Allyn & Bacon.

Beavers, R. (1985). *Manual of Beavers-Timberlawn Family Evaluation Scale and Family Style Evaluation.* Dallas: Southwest FamilyInstitute.

Beavers, W. R., Hampson, R., & Hulgus, Y. (1985). Commentary: The Beavers Systems approach to family assessment. *Family Process, 24,* 398-405.

Becvar, R. J., & Becvar, D. S. (1982). *Systems theory and family therapy*. Washington, DC: University Press of America.

Becvar, D. S., & Becvar, R. J. (1993). *Family therapy: A systemic integration* (2nd ed.). Boston: Allyn & Bacon.

Bergman, J. S. (1985). *Fishing for barracuda: Pragmatics of brief systemic therapy*. New York: W. W. Norton.

Berstein, R. M., & Burge, S. K. (1988). A record-keeping format for training systemic therapists. *Family Process, 27*, 339-349.

Bertalanffy, L. von, (1968). *General systems theory: Foundations, development, applications* (rev. ed.). New York: George Braziller.

Birk, L. (1988). Behavioral/psychoanalytic psychotherapy within overlapping social systems: A natural matrix for diagnosis and therapeutic change. *Psychiatric Annals, 18,* 296-308.

Blatt, D. O., & Starr, D. A. (1988). A thriving mini-clinic in a school setting. In W. M. Walsh & N. J. Giblin (Eds.), *Family counseling in school settings*. Springfield, IL: Charles C. Thomas.

Blechman, E. A., Taylor, C. J., & Schrader, S. M. (1981). Family problem solving versus home notes as early intervention with high-risk children. *Journal of Consulting and Clinical Psychology, 49,* 919-926.

Bloch, D. A. (1976). Including the children in family therapy. In P. J. Guerin, Jr. (Ed.), *Family therapy: Theory and practice* (pp. 168-181). New York: Gardner.

Bodin, A. (1991). The interactional view: Family therapy approaches of the Mental Research Institute. In A. S. Gurman & D. P. Kniskern (Eds.), *Handbook of family therapy,* Vol. I (pp. 267-309). New York: Basic Books.

Bohannon, P. (1973). The six stations of divorce. In M. E. Laswell & T. E. Laswell (Eds.), *Love, marriage and family: A developmental approach* (pp. 475-489). Glenview, IL: Scott, Foresman.

Family Counseling in the Schools:

Boniello, M. J. (1986). The family as stage for creating abusive children. *Connections, 1,* 4-5.

Boscolo, L., Cecchin, G., Hoffman, L., & Penn, P. (1987). *Milan systemic family therapy.* New York: Basic Books Inc.

Bowen, M. (1978). *Family therapy in clinical practice.* New York: Jason Aronson.

Braden, J. P., & Sherrard, P. A. D. (1987). Referring families to nonschool agencies: A family systems approach. *School Psychology Review, 16,* 513-518.

Braswell, L., & Bloomquist, M. L. (1991). *Cognitive-behavioral therapy with ADHD children.* New York: Guilford.

Bry, B. H., Conboy, C., & Bisgay, K. (1986). Decreasing adolescent drug use and school failure: Long-term effects of targeted family problem-solving training. *Child and Family Behavior Therapy, 8,* 43-59.

Bry, B. H., & Green, D. M. (1990). Empirical bases for integrating school- and family-based interventions against early adolescent substance abuse. In R. J. McMahon & R. DeV. Peters (Eds.), *Behavior disorders of adolescence* (pp. 81-97). New York: Plenum.

Burgess, T. A., & Hinkle, J. S. (1993). Strategic family therapy of avoidant behavior. *Journal of Mental Health Counseling, 15,* 132-140.

Capra, F. (1982). *The turning point.* New York: Bantam.

Carlson, C. (1992). Models and strategies of family-school assessment and intervention. In M. J. Fine & C. Carlson (Eds.), *The handbook of family-school intervention* (pp. 18-44). Needham Heights, MA: Allyn & Bacon.

Carlson, C. I. (1987). Resolving school problems with structural family therapy. *School Psychology Review, 16,* 457-468.

Carlson, C. I., & Sincavage, J. M. (1987). Family-oriented school psychology practice: Results of a national survey of NASP members. *School Psychology Review, 16,* 519-526.

Carlson, J. (1981). Special column devoted to working with families. *Elementary School Guidance and Counseling, 15,* 279.

Carlson, J., Hinkle, J. S., & Sperry, L. (1993). Using diagnosis and DSM-III-R and IV in marriage and family counseling and therapy: Increasing treatment outcomes without losing heart and soul. *The Family Journal: Counseling and Therapy for Couples and Families, 1,* 308-312.

Carnes, P. J. (1981). *Understanding us.* Minneapolis, MN: Interpersonal Communication Programs.

Carter, E. A., & McGoldrick, M. (Eds.). (1980). *The family life cycle: A framework for family therapy.* New York: Gardner.

Cetron, M. (1985). *Schools of the future.* New York: McGraw-Hill.

Christensen, O., & Marchant, W. (1983). The family counseling process. In O. Christensen & T. Schramski (Eds.), *Adlerian family counseling* (pp. 29-56). Minneapolis, MN: Educational Media.

Cleghorn, J., & Levin, S. (1973). Training therapists by setting learning objectives. *American Journal of Orthopsychiatry, 43,* 439-446.

Conti, A. (1971). A follow-up study of families referred to outside agencies. *Psychology in the Schools, 8,* 338-340.

Coopersmith, E. (1980). The family floor plan: A tool for training-assessment and intervention in family therapy. *Journal of Marital and Family Therapy, 6,* 141-145.

Council for Accreditation of Counseling and Related Educational Programs. (1988). *Accreditation procedures manual and application.* Alexandria, VA: Author.

Cowger, E. L., Hinkle, J. S., DeRidder, L. M., & Erk, R. R. (1991). CACREP community counseling programs: Present status and implications for the future. *Journal of Mental Health Counseling, 13,* 172-186.

Dinkmeyer, D., Jr., & Dinkmeyer, D., Sr. (1991). Adlerian family therapy. In A. Horne & J. Passmore (Eds.), *Family counseling and therapy* (pp. 383-401). Itasca, IL: F. E. Peacock.

Dinkmeyer, D., & McKay, G. (1982). *Systematic training for effective parenting (STEP).* Circle Pines, MN: American Guidance Service.

Family Counseling in the Schools:

Dinkmeyer, D. & McKay, G. (1983). *STEP/Teen*. Circle Pines, MN: American Guidance Service.

Dinkmeyer, D., & McKay, G. (1989). *The parent's handbook (rev. ed.)*. Circle Pines, MN: American Guidance Service.

Dowd, E. T., & Milne, C. R. (1986). Paradoxical interventions in counseling psychology. *The Counseling Psychologist, 14*, 237-282.

Downing, J. & Harrison, T. (1992). Solutions and school counseling. *School Counselor, 39*, 327-332.

Dreikurs, R. (1971). *Social equality: The challenge of today*. Chicago: Henry Regnery.

Duhl, F. S., Kantor, D., & Duhl, B. S. (1973). Learning space and action in family therapy: A primer of sculpting. In D. Bloch (Ed.) *Techniques of family psychotherapy: A primer*. New York: Grune & Stratton.

Eddy, J., Richardson, B. K., & Allberg, W. R. (1982). Strategies for maintaining and increasing counselor's use of time for counseling. *School Counselor, 30*, 122-126.

Elkin, M. (1985). "Plugging the holes in people's souls" - When divorce comes. *Conciliation Courts Review, 23*, v-x.

Feetham, S. L., & Humenick, S. S. (1982). The Feetham family functioning survey. In S. S. Humenick (Ed.), *Analysis of current assessment strategies in the health care of young children and childbearing families* (pp. 259-268). Norwalk, CT: Appleton-Century-Crofts.

Fenell, D. L., & Hovestadt, A. J. (1986). Family therapy as a profession or a professional specialty. *Journal of Psychotherapy and the Family, 1*, 25-40.

Fenell, D. L., & Weinhold, B. K. (1989). *Counseling families*. Denver: Love.

Fine, M. J. (1992). A systems-ecological perspective on home-school intervention. In M. J. Fine & C. Carlson (Eds.), *The handbook of family-school intervention* (pp. 1-17). Needham Heights, MA: Allyn & Bacon.

Fine, M. J., & Carlson, C. (Eds.). (1992). *The handbook of family-school intervention*. Needham Heights, MA: Allyn & Bacon.

Fine, M. J., & Holt, P. (1983). Intervening with school problems: A family systems perspective. *Psychology in the Schools, 20,* 59-66.

Fish, M. C., & Jain, S. (1992). Family-school intervention using a structural model. In M. J. Fine & C. Carlson (Eds.), *The handbook of family-school intervention* (pp. 302-314). Needham Heights, MA: Allyn & Bacon.

Fisher, L., Anderson, A., & Jones, J. (1981). Types of paradoxical interventions and indications/contraindications for use in clinical practice. *Family Process, 20,* 25-35.

Follingstad, D. R. (1988). Marital therapy flow chart. *American Journal of Family Therapy, 16,* 35-45.

Foote, F. H., Szapocznik, J., Kurtines, W. M., Perez-Vidal, A., & Hervis, O. K. (1985). One-person family therapy: A modality of brief strategic family therapy. In R. S. Ashery (Ed.), *Progress in the development of cost-effective treatment for drug abusers* (Research Monograph No. 58, pp. 51-65). Rockville, MD: National Institute on Drug Abuse.

Ford, R. C. (1986). *Family counseling strategies in the schools.* Washington State University. ERIC Document Reproduction Service No. 271 659.

Frankl, V. E. (1975). Paradoxical intention and dereflection. *Psychotherapy: Theory, Research and Practice, 12,* 226-237.

Fredman, N., & Sherman, R. (1987). *Handbook of measurement for marriage and family therapy.* New York: Bruner/Mazel.

Friedman, R. (1973). *Family roots of school learning and behavior disorders.* Springfield, IL: Charles C. Thomas.

Fullmer, D. W., & Bernard, H. W. (1972). *The school counselor-consultant.* New York: Houghton Mifflin.

Gandara, P. (1989, January). 'Those' children are ours: Moving toward community. *NEA Today.* Washington, DC: National Education Association.

Gard, G. C., & Berry, K. K. (1986). Oppositional children: Training tyrants. *Journal of Clinical Child Psychology, 15,* 148-158.

Family Counseling in the Schools:

Gardner, R. A. (1982). *Psychotherapy with children of divorce.* New York: Jason Aaronson.

Gerz, H. O. (1966). Experience with the logotherapeutic technique of paradoxical intention in the treatment of phobic and obsessive-compulsive patients. *American Journal of Psychiatry, 123,* 548-553.

Gerler, E. R., Jr. (1993). Parents, families, and the schools. *Elementary School Guidance and Counseling, 27,* 243.

Gladding, S. T. (1984). Training effective family therapists: Data and hope. *Journal of Counseling and Development, 63,* 103-104.

Gladding, S. T., Burggraf, M., & Fenell, D. L. (1987). Marriage and family counseling in counselor education: National trends and implications. *Journal of Counseling and Development, 66,* 90-95.

Golden, L. (1983). Brief family interventions in a school setting. *Elementary School Guidance and Counseling, 17,* 288-293.

Golden, L. B. (1988). Quick assessment of family functioning. *The school counselor, 35,* 179-184.

Goldenberg, I., & Goldenberg, H. (1988). Family systems and the school counselor. In W. M. Walsh & N. J. Giblin (Eds.), *Family counseling in school settings* (pp. 26-47). Springfield, IL: Charles C. Thomas.

Goldenberg, I., & Goldenberg, H. (1980). *Family therapy: An overview.* Pacific Grove, CA: Brooks/Cole.

Goldenberg, I., & Goldenberg, H. (1985). *Family therapy: An overview* (2nd ed.). Pacific Grove, CA: Brooks/Cole.

Goldenberg, I., & Goldenberg, H. (1991). *Family therapy: Overview* (3rd ed.). Pacific Grove, CA: Brooks/Cole.

Good, T. L., & Brophy, J. E. (1986). School effects. In M. C. Wittrock (Ed.), *The handbook of research on teaching* (3rd ed.) (pp. 570-604). New York: Macmillan.

Goodman, R. W., & Kjonaas, D. (1988). Elementary school family counseling: A pilot project. In W. M. Walsh & N. J. Giblin (Eds.), *Family counseling in school settings* (pp. 113-118). Springfield, IL: Charles C. Thomas.

Green, R. G., & Kolevzon, M. S. (1984). Characteristics of healthy families. *Elementary School Guidance and Counseling, 19*, 9-18.

Griffin, W. A. (1993). *Family therapy: Fundamentals of theory and practice*. New York: Brunner/Mazel.

Gross, H., & Mascari, J. B. (1991). *Survey of families participating in Clifton Mental Health programs*. Unpublished manuscript.

Gurman, A. S., & Kniskern, D. P. (Eds.). (1981). *Handbook of family therapy, Vol. I*. New York: Brunner/Mazel.

Gurman, A. S., & Kniskern, D. P. (Eds.). (1991). *Handbook of family therapy, Vol. II*. New York: Brunner/Mazel.

Haley, J. (1970). Approaches to family therapy. *International Journal of Psychiatry, 9*, 233-242.

Haley, J. (1972). *Strategies of psychotherapy*. New York: Grune & Stratton.

Haley, J. (1973). *Uncommon therapy*. New York: W. W. Norton.

Haley, J. (1976). *Problem solving therapy*. San Francisco: Jossey Bass.

Haley, J. (1980). *Leaving home*. New York: McGraw-Hill.

Haley, J. (1984). *Ordeal therapy*. San Francisco: Jossey Bass.

Haley, J. (1987). *Problem solving therapy* (2nd ed.). San Francisco: Jossey-Bass.

Haley, J., & Hoffman, L. (1967). *Techniques of family therapy*. New York: Basic.

Harari, E. (1990). Diagnosis and family therapy: "Traditional" psychiatry and the concepts of disease and diagnosis. *Australian and New Zealand Journal of Family Therapy, 11*, 160-165.

Hartman, A. (1979). *Finding families: An ecological approach to family assessment in adoption*. Beverly Hills, CA: Sage.

Hechtman, L. (1981). Families and hyperactives. In R. G. Simmons (Ed.), *Research in community and mental health* (pp. 275-292). Greenwich, CT: JAI Press.

Family Counseling in the Schools:

Hetherington, E. M. (1986). Family relations six years after divorce. In *Remarriage and parenting today: Research and theory*. New York: Guilford.

Hinkle, J. S. (1992a). Single-subject research and computer-assisted career guidance: A scientist-practitioner approach to accountability. *Journal of Counseling and Development, 70*, 391-395.

Hinkle, J. S. (1992b, August). *Clinical analysis of today's families: Use of the DSM-III-R*. Paper presented at the Bi-Annual Conference of the International Association of Marriage and Family Counselors, Breckenridge, CO.

Hinkle, J.S. (1993). Training school conselors to do family counseling. *Elementary School Guidance and Counseling, 27*, 252-257.

Hinkle, J. S. (1994). Ecosystems and mental health counseling: Reaction to Becvar and Becvar. *Journal of Mental Health Counseling, 16*, 33-36.

Hinkle, J. S. (1994, April). *Family counseling in the public schools*. Paper presented at the National Convention of the American Counseling Association(ACA), Minneapolis, MN.

Hinkle, J. S., & Peeks, B. (1992, June). *Family counseling in the schools: Past history, current trends, and future directions*. Paper presented at the National Conference of the American School Counselor Association, Albuquerque, NM.

Hobbs, N. (1966). Helping disturbed children: Psychological and ecological strategies. *American Psychologist, 21*, 1105-1115.

Holahan, C. J., & Moos, R. N. (1981). Social support and psychological distress: A longitudinal analysis. *Journal of Abnormal Psychology, 90*, 365-370.

Holman, A.M. (1983). *Family assessment: Tools for understanding & intervention*. Newbury Park, CA: Sage.

Hoopes, M. H. (1987). Multigenerational systems: Basic assumptions. *The American Journal of Family Therapy, 15*, 195-205.

Hyde, M. O. (1980). *Cry softly: The story of child abuse*. Philadelphia, PA: Westminster.

Jackson, D. D. (1977). The myth of normality. In P. Watzlawick & J. Weakland (Eds.), *The interactional view: Studies at the Mental Research Institute, Palo Alto, 1965-1974*. New York: W. W. Norton & Co.

Johnson, K. (1989). *Trauma in the lives of children: Crisis and stress management for counselors and other professionals*. Alameda, CA: HunterHouse.

Kaslow, F. W. (1991). The art and science of family psychology. *American Psychologist, 46*, 621-626.

Kaufman, E., & Kaufman, P. (1979). *Family therapy of drug and alcohol abuse*. New York: Gardner Press.

Kelly, J. B. (1987). *Longer-term adjustment in children of divorce: Converging findings and implications for practice*. Paper presented at the annual meeting of the American Psychological Association, New York.

Kerr, M. E. (1981). Family systems theory and therapy. In A. S. Gurman & D. P. Kniskern (Eds.), *Handbook of family therapy*. New York: Brunner/Mazel.

Kinston, W., Loader, P., & Miller, L. (1985). *Clinical assessment of family health*. London: Hospital for Sick Children, Family Studies Group.

Kog, E., & Vandereycken, W. (1985). Family characteristics of anorexia nervosa and bulimia: A review of the research literature. *Clinical Psychology Review, 5*(2), 159-180.

Kübler-Ross, E. (1983). *On children and death*. New York: McMillan.

Langevin, R. (1983). *Sexual strands: Understanding and treating sexual anomalies in men*. Hillsdale, NJ: Erlbaum.

Larson, N. R., & Maddock, J. W. (1986). Structural and functional variables in incest family systems: Implications for assessment and treatment. In T. S. Trepper & M. J. Barrett (Eds.), *Treating incest: A multiple systems perspective* (pp. 67-82). New York: Haworth Press.

Lewis, K. (1992). Family functioning as perceived by parents of boys with attention deficit disorder. *Issues in Mental Health Nursing, 13*, 369-386.

Family Counseling in the Schools:

Lieberman, R., Minuchin, S., & Baker, L. (1974). An integrated treatment program for anorexia nervosa. *American Journal of Psychiatry, 131*(4), 432-436.

Lorber, R., & Patterson, G. R. (1981). The aggressive child: A concomitant of a coercive system. In J. P. Vincent (Ed.), *Advances in family intervention, assessment and theory: An annual compilation of research* (pp. 47-87). Greenwich, CT: JAI Press.

Lowman, J. C. (1980). Measurement of family affective structure. *Journal of Personality Assessment, 44*, 130-141.

Lusterman, D. D. (1987). The use of psychodiagnostic evaluation in systems therapy. *Psychotherapy, 24*, 511-515.

Madanes, C. (1981). *Strategic family therapy*. San Francisco: Jossey Bass.

Madanes, C. (1984). *Behind the one-way mirror*. San Francisco: Jossey Bass.

Madanes, C. (1990). *Sex, love, and violence*. New York: W. W. Norton.

Madanes, C. (1991). Strategic family therapy. In A. S. Gurman & D. P. Kniskern (Eds.), *Handbook of family therapy* (vol. 2) (pp. 396-416). New York: Brunner/Mazel.

Marshall, V. G., Longwell, L., Goldstein, M. J., & Swanson, J. M. (1990). Family factors associated with aggressive symptomatology in boys with attention deficit hyperactivity disorder: A research note. *Journal of Child Psychology and Psychiatry, 31*, 629-636.

Maynard, P. E., & Olson, D. H. (1987). Circumplex model of family systems: A treatment tool in family counseling. *Journal of Counseling and Development, 65*, 502-504.

McComb, B. (1981a). An interview with Carl Whitaker. *Elementary School Guidance and Counseling, 15*, 195-204, 273-278.

McComb, B. (1981b). Family counseling [Special issue]. *Elementary School Guidance and Counseling, 15*, (3).

McDaniel, S. H. (1981). Treating school problems in family therapy. *Elementary School Guidance and Counseling, 15*, 214-222.

McGoldrick, M., & Gerson, R. (1985). *Genograms in family assessment*. New York: Norton.

McKinnon, L. (1983). Contrasting strategic and Milan therapies. *Family Process, 22*, 425-440.

Meadows, M. E., & Hetrick, H. H. (1982). Roles for counselor education departments in marriage and family counseling: Current status and projections. *Counselor Education and Supervision, 22*, 47-54.

Medler, B. W., Dameron, J. D., Strother, J., & DeNardo, N. B. (1987). Identification and treatment of stepfamily issues for counselors and teachers. *Texas Association for Counseling and Development Journal, 15*, 49-60.

Merrill, M. A., Clark, R. J., Varvil, C. D., Van Sickle, C. A., & McCall, L. J. (1992). Family therapy in the schools: The pragmatics of merging systemic approaches into educational realities. In M. J. Fine & C. Carlson (Eds.), *The handbook of family-school intervention* (pp. 400-413). Needham Heights, MA: Allyn &Bacon.

Milich, R., & Loney, J. (1979). The role of hyperactive and aggressive symptomatology in predicting adolescent outcome among hyperactive children. *Journal of Pediatric Psychology, 4*, 93-112.

Minuchin, S. (1974). *Families and family therapy*. Cambridge, MA: Harvard University Press.

Minuchin, S., & Fishman, H. C. (1981). *Family therapy techniques*. Cambridge, MA: Harvard University Press.

Minuchin, S., Rosman, B., & Baker, L. (1978). *Psychosomatic families*. Cambridge, MA: Harvard University Press.

Mittl, V. F., & Robin, A. (1987). Acceptability of alternative interventions for parent-adolescent conflict. *Behavioral Assessment, 9*, 417-428.

National Board for Certified Counselors. (1993). *A work behavior analysis of professional counselors*. Greensboro, NC: Author

Nevels, R. M., & Marr, J. E. (1985). A supervision approach for teaching structural/strategic therapy in a limited setting. *Journal of Psychology, 119*, 347-353.

Family Counseling in the Schools:

Newby, R. F., Fischer, M. & Roman, M. A. (1991). Parent training for families of children with ADHD. *School Psychology Review*, *20*, 252-265.

Nicoll, W. G. (1984b). School counselors as family counselors: A rationale and training model. *School Counselor*, *10*, 279-284.

Nicoll, W. G. (1992). A family counseling and consultation model for school counselors. *School Counselor*, *39*, 351-361.

O'Brien, J. D. (1992). Children with attention-deficit hyperactivity disorder and their parents. In J. D. O'Brien, D. J. Pilowsky, & O. W. Lewis (Eds.), *Psychotherapies with children and adolescents: Adapting the psychodynamic process* (p. 109-124). Washington, DC: American Psychiatric Association.

O'Callaghan, J. B. (1991, October). Therapists and schools can construct workable partnerships and collaboration. *Family Therapy News*, pp. 7-8.

Office of Technology Assessment, U.S. Congress. (1986). *Children's mental health: Problems and services*. Washington, DC: U.S. Government Printing Office.

O'Hanlon, W. H., & Weiner-Davis, M. (1989). *In search of solutions: A new direction in psychotherapy*. New York: Norton.

Olson, D., Portner, J., & Bell, R. (1977). *Inventory of Parent-Adolescent Conflict*. St. Paul, MN: Family Social Services, University of Minnesota.

Olson, D., & Ryder, R. (1977). *Inventory of Parent-Child Conflict*. St. Paul, MN: Family Social Science, University of Minnesota.

Omer, H. (1990). Enhancing the impact of therapeutic interventions. *American Journal of Psychotherapy*, *44*, 218-231.

Omer, H. (1991). Writing a post-scriptum to a badly ended therapy. *Psychotherapy*, *28*, 484-492.

O'Neil, J. M., Fishman, D. M., & Kinsella, S. M. (1987). Dual-career couples' career transitions and normative dilemmas: A preliminary assessment model. *Counseling Psychologist*, *15*, 50-96.

Overton, J. M., & Hennies, S. E. (1988, February). *A school-based family therapy program: Applications and innovations*. Paper presented at the Second Joint Convention of the South Carolina and North Carolina Associations for Counseling and Development, MyrtleBeach, SC.

Palmo, A. J., Lowry, L. A., Weldon, D. P., & Scioscia, T. M.(1984). Schools and family: Future perspectives for school counselors. *School Counselor*, *39*, 272-284.

Papalia, D. E., & Olds, S. W. (1992). *Human Development* (5th ed). New York: McGraw-Hill.

Papp, P., Silverstein, O., & Carter, E. (1975). Family sculpting in preventive work with "well families." *Family Process*, *12*, 197-212.

Patterson, G. R. (1982). *A social learning approach to family intervention, Vol. 3. Coercive family process*. Eugene, OR: Castalia.

Peeks, B. (1989). Strategies for solving children's problems understood as behavioral metaphor. *Journal of Strategic and Systemic Therapies*, *8*, 22-25.

Peeks, B. (1990). A family approach for treating behaviorally impaired students in the schools. *Oregon Counseling Journal*, *12*, 12-15.

Peeks, B. (1991a, February). Parent-student-school: The problem-solving triad: A training for school professionals. *Communique*, *20*, 27-28.

Peeks, B. (1991b, April). *The divorcing couple's script*. Paper presented at the Annual Convention of the American Association for Counseling and Development, Reno, NV.

Peeks, B. (1992). Protection and social context: Understanding a child's problem behavior. *Elementary School Guidance and Counseling*, *26*, 295-304.

Family Counseling in the Schools:

Peeks, B. (Ed.)(1993a). Parents, families, and the schools [Special issue]. *Elementary School Guidance and Counseling, 27.*

Peeks, B. (1993b). Revolutions in counseling and education: A systems perspective in the schools. *Elementary School Guidance and Counseling, 27,* 245-251.

Petersen, S., & Straub, R. L. (1992). *School crisis survival guide: Management techniques and materials for counselors and administrators.* West Nyack, NY: The Center for Applied Research in Education.

Plas, J. M. (1986). *Systems psychology in the schools.* New York: Pergamon.

Plas, J. M. (1992). The development of systems thinking: A historical perspective. In M. J. Fine & C. Carlson (Eds.), *The handbook of family-school intervention* (pp. 45-56). Needham Heights, MA: Allyn & Bacon.

Pittman, F. (1987). *Turning points: Treating families in transition and crisis.* New York: Norton.

Power, T. J., & Bartholomew, K. L. (1987). Breaking a dysfunctional home-school helping pattern: Systematic intervention through nonclassification. *Techniques: A Journal for Remedial Education and Counseling, 3,* 219-229.

Power, T. J., & Bartholomew, K. L. (1987). Family-school relationship patterns: An ecological assessment. *School Psychology Review, 16,* 498-512.

Prata, G. (1990). *A systemic harpoon into family games: Preventive interventions in therapy.* New York: Brunner/ Mazel.

Remley, T. P., Jr. (1992, September). Counseling specializations. *Guidepost,* p. 4.

Reposa, R. E., & Zuelzer, M. B. (1983). Family therapy with incest. *International Journal of Family Therapy, 5,* 111-126.

Roberts, J. (1984). Antidotes for secrecy: Treating the incestuous family. *Family Therapy Networker, 8,* 49-54.

Rose-Gold, M.S. (1991). Intervention strategies for counseling at-risk adolescents in rural school districts. *The School Counselor*, *39*, 122-126.

Ross, D. A., & Ross, S. A. (1982). *Hyperactivity: Current issues, research, and theory* (2nd ed.). New York: Wiley.

Rotter, J. C. (Ed.). (1984). Families in transition [Special issue]. *Elementary School Guidance and Counseling*, *19*, (1).

Rye, D. R., & Sparks, R. (1991). Planning and management: Keys to a successful K-12 counseling program. *School Counselor*, *38*, 263-267.

Satir, V. (1967). *Conjoint family therapy*. Palo Alto, CA: Science and Behavior Books.

Satir, V. (1972). *Peoplemaking*. Palo Alto, CA: Science and Behavior Books.

School, B., & Cooper, A. (1981). *The IEP Primer and the Individualized Program*. Novato, CA. Academic Therapy Publications.

Seligman, L. (1986). *Diagnosis and treatment planning in counseling*. New York: Human Sciences Press.

Shaefer, C. E., & Millman, H. L. (1981). *How to help children with common problems*. New York: Van Nostrand Reinhold.

Sherman, R., & Fredman, N. (1986). *Handbook of structured techniques in marriage and family therapy*. New York: Brunner/Mazel.

Sherman, R., & Dinkmeyer, D. (1987). *Systems of family therapy: An Adlerian integration*. New York:Brunner/Mazel.

Sherman, R., Oresky, P., & Rountree, Y. (1991). *Solving problems in couples and family therapy: Technique and tactics*. New York: Brunner/Mazel.

Shore, K., & Vieland, C. (1989). And now for something different: The North Mercer Family Consultation Center. *Journal of School Psychology*, *3*, 27-33.

Silver, L. B. (1990). Attention deficit-hyperactivity disorder: Is it a learning disability or a related disorder? *Journal of Learning Disabilities*, *23*, 394-397.

Family Counseling in the Schools:

Smith, J. P. (1990). *How to solve student adjustment problems.* West Nyack, NY: The Center for Applied Research in Education.

Smith, R.L., & Stevens-Smith, P. (1992). *Family Counseling and Therapy: Major Issues and Topics.* Ann Arbor, MI: ERIC Counseling and Personnel Services Clearinghouse.

Sperry, L. (1989). Assessment in marital therapy: A couples-centered biopsychosocial approach. *Journal of Adlerian Theory, 45,* 546-551.

Stanton, M. D. (1981). Strategic approaches to family therapy. In A. Gurman & D. Kniskern (Eds.), *Handbook of Family Therapy* (pp. 361-402). New York: Brunner/Mazel.

Stanton, D. M. & Todd, T. C. (1979). Structural family therapy with drug addicts. In E. Kaufman & P. Kaufman (Eds.), *Family therapy of drug and alcohol abuse.* New York: Gardner.

Stark, K. D., & Brookman, C. S. (1992). Childhood depression: Theory and family-school intervention. In M. J. Fine & C. Carlson (Eds.), *The handbook of family-school intervention* (pp. 247-271). Needham Heights, MA: Allyn & Bacon.

Steinglass, P. (1987). *The alcoholic family.* New York: Basic Books.

Stevens-Smith, P., Hinkle, J. S., & Stahmann, R. F. (1993). A comparison of professional accreditation standards in marriage and family counseling and therapy. *Counselor Education and Supervision, 33,* 116-126.

Stone, G., & Peeks, B. (1986). The use of strategic family therapy in the school setting: A case study. *Journal of Counseling and Development, 65,* 200-203.

Straus, M. A. (1979). Measuring intrafamily conflict and violence: The Conflict Tactics (CT) Scales. *Journal of Marriage and the Family, 41,* 75-85.

Tallmadge, J. M., Paternite, C. E., & Gordon, M. (1989, April). *Hyperactivity and aggression in parent-child interactions: Test of a two-factor theory.* Paper presented at the meeting of the Society for Research in Child Development, Kansas City.

Talmon, M. (1990). *Single-session therapy*. San Francisco: Jossey-Bass.

Thomas, M. B. (1992). *An introduction to marital and family therapy: Counseling toward healthier family systems across the lifespan*. New York: Maxwell McMillan International.

Tindall, J., & Sklare-Lancaster, A. (1981, October). Guidance programs: Is the counselor's role paper- or people-involved? *Nasp Bulletin, 65*, 2-9.

Tracy, T. J. (1983). Single case research: An added tool for counselors and supervisors. *Counselor Education and Supervision, 22*, 185-196.

Tracy, E. M., Green, R. K., & Bremseth, M. D. (1993). Meeting the environmental needs of abused and neglected children: Implications from a statewide survey of supportive services. *Social Work Research and Abstracts, 29*, 21-26.

Turnbull, A. P., & Turnbull, H. R. (1990). *Families, professionals, and exceptionality: A special partnership*. Columbus, OH: Merrill.

Vaillant, G. E. (1984). A debate on DSM-III: The disadvantages of DSM-III outweigh its advantages. *American Journal of Psychiatry, 141*, 542-545.

Visher, E. B., & Visher, J. S. (1979). *Stepfamilies: A guide to working with stepparents and stepchildren*. New York: Brunner/Mazel.

Wallerstein, J. S. (1983). Children of divorce: The psychological tasks of the child. *American Journal of Orthopsychiatry, 53*, 230-243.

Wallerstein, J. S., & Kelly, J. B. (1980). *Surviving the break-up: How children actually cope with divorce*. New York: Basic.

Walsh, W. M., & Giblin, N. J. (Eds.). (1988). *Family counseling in school settings*. Springfield, IL: Charles C. Thomas.

Wass, H., & Cason, L. (1984). *Childhood and death*. Washington, DC: Hemisphere.

Family Counseling in the Schools:

Watzlavick, P., Beavin, J. H., & Jackson, D. D. (1967). *Pragmatics of human communication*. New York: W. W. Norton.

Watzlawick, P., & Weakland, J. (Eds.). (1977). *The interactional view: Studies at the Mental Research Institute, Palo Alto, 1965-1974*. New York: W. W. Norton & Co.

Watzlavick, P., Weakland, J., & Fisch, R. (1974). *Change: Principles of problem formation and problem resolution*. New York: Norton.

Weeks, G. R. (Ed.). (1991). *Promoting change through paradoxical therapy* (rev. ed.). Homewood, IL: Dow Jones-Irwin.

Weeks, G. R., & L'Abate, L. (1979). A compilation of paradoxical methods. *The American Journal of Family Therapy, 7*, 61-76.

Weeks, G. R., & L'Abate, L. (1982). *Paradoxical psychotherapy: Theory and practice with individuals, couples, and families*. New York: Brunner/Mazel.

Weeks, G. R., & Treat, S. (1992). *Couples in treatment: Techniques and approaches for effective practice*. New York: Brunner/Mazel.

Wells, M. E., & Hinkle, J. S. (1990). Elimination of childhood encopresis: A family systems approach. *Journal of Mental Health Counseling, 12*, 520-526.

West, J. D., Hosie, T. W., & Zarski, J. J. (1987). Family dynamics and substance abuse: A preliminary study. *Journal of Counseling and Development, 65*, 487-490.

West J. D., & Zarski, J. J. (1983). The counselor's use of the paradoxical procedure in family therapy. *Personnel and Guidance Journal, 62*, 34-37.

Whiteside, R. G. (1993). Making a referral for family therapy: The school counselor's role. *Elementary School Guidance and Counseling, 27*, 273-279.

Wilcoxin, A. A. (1986). Family-counseling practices: Suggested reading guide for school counselors. *School Counselor, 33*, 272-278.

Wilcoxin, S. A., & Comas, R. E. (1987). Contemporary trends in family counseling: What do they mean for the school counselor? *School Counselor, 34,* 219-225.

Williams, J. B. W., Spitzer, R. L., & Skodol, A. E. (1985). DSM-III in residency training: Results of a national survey. *American Journal of Psychiatry, 142,* 755-758.

Williams, J. B. W., Spitzer, R. L., & Skodol, A. E. (1986). DSM-III in the training of psychiatric residents and medical students: A national survey. *Journal of Psychiatric Education, 10,* 75-86.

Woody, R. H., & Woody, J. K. (1994). The fourth revolution: Family systems in the schools. *The Family Journal: Counseling and Therapy for Couples and Families, 2,* 19-26.

Worden, M. (1981). Classroom behavior as a function of the family system. *School Counselor, 28,* 178-188.